Futures Research
New Directions

Contributors

Futures Research
New Directions

Edited by

Harold A. Linstone
Portland State University

W. H. Clive Simmonds
National Research Council of Canada

1977

Addison-Wesley Publishing Company
Advanced Book Program
Reading, Massachusetts

London·Amsterdam·Don Mills, Ontario·Sydney·Tokyo

Futures Research: New Directions

The cover design was inspired by the representation of scenario as paths or branches used by Russell Rhyne. His schematic is detailed in the article "Technological Forecasting Within Alternative Whole Futures Projections" (*Technological Forecasting and Social Change,* Vol. 6, No. 2 [1974], American Elsevier Publishing Co., New York, pp. 133-162).

The endpapers depict a woodcut map from the March 1518 edition of Sir Thomas More's "Utopia" showing the Island of Utopia. (Reproduced by permission of the Trustees of The Pierpont Morgan Library.)

Library of Congress Cataloging in Publication Data
Main entry under title:

Futures research.

Includes bibliographical references and index.
1.   Forecasting—Methodology—Addresses, essays, lectures. I. Linstone, Harold A.   II. Simmonds, Walter Henry Clive, 1917—
CB158.F875   001.4′33   77-14233
ISBN 0-201-04096-4

ABCDEFGHIJ-HA-7987

Contents

Biographical Data

THE EDITORS

Harold A. Linstone   holds B.S. and M.A. degrees from the City College of New York and Columbia University, respectively. He received his doctorate in Mathematics from the University of Southern California in 1954. He has been a member of the Rand Corporation, a Senior Scientist at Hughes Aircraft Company, and Associate Director of Corporate Development Planning at Lockheed Aircraft Corporation. From 1965 to 1970, he was also Adjunct Professor of Industrial and Systems Engineering at the University of Southern California. There he introduced courses in "Technological Forecasting" and "Planning Alternative Futures." The latter won USC's Dart Award for Innovation in Teaching in 1970. He has presented numerous seminars on Technological Forecasting and Long-Range Planning in the United States and Europe. In recent years he has also been a consultant to Stanford Research Institute and to various industrial and governmental organizations. In 1970 he became Professor of Systems Science at Portland State University, directing its new interdisciplinary Ph.D. program in this field. Currently he holds the title of University Professor and heads the PSU Futures Research Institute. He is co-editor of the books, *The Delphi Method* and *Technological Substitution,* as well as Senior Editor of the international journal, *Technological Forecasting and Social Change* (now in its eleventh volume).

W. H. Clive Simmonds   received his B.Sc. and M.A. degrees in 1940 and 1943 in the Natural Sciences (Chemistry) from the University of Oxford, has been a member of the Institution of Chemical Engineers since 1945 and a Chartered Engineer in the U.K. since 1966, and received his B.A. degree from Sir George Williams University, Montreal, in Sociology in 1971. He has been a member of Lever Brothers and Unilever Ltd., Dominion Tar and Chemical Company, and Canadian Industries Ltd. in the areas of research, development, planning and forecasting studies. He established a postgraduate course in chemical engineering in the University of Durham, U.K., from 1947 to 1952. In 1964 he was on loan to the Theme Group of the Canadian World Exhibition, EXPO 67. Since 1970, he has been with the Industrial Programs Office, National Research Council of Canada. He is a founder member of the Canadian Association for the Club of Rome, an Associate Editor of the international journal, *Technological Forecasting and Social Change,* a member of the New York Academy of Sciences and of the Society for General Systems Research. He has taken part in numerous courses on technological forecasting and in futures studies with a wide variety of organizations.

THE CONTRIBUTORS

Göran Bäckstrand

is associated with the Swedish Secretariat for Future Studies established in 1973. Previously he was desk officer for problems on the human environment at the Ministry for Foreign Affairs where he also worked with other issues within the framework of science and technology. After university (BL) he held a one-year scholarship in France and graduated from the European Institute of Business Administration in Fontainebleau.

Richard Bellman

is Professor of Mathematics, Electrical Engineering, and Medicine at the University of Southern California. He has published more than 550 research papers and thirty books, and has served as the editor of several book series. He is the recipient of the 1976 John von Neumann Award of TIMS and ORSA, and has honorary doctoral degrees from universities in three countries.

Marvin J. Cetron

is the President and founder of Forecasting International, a pioneer in all aspects of technological forecasting, technology assessment and R&D planning. He has lectured extensively throughout the world, and has served as expert consultant to U.S. Government agencies, foreign governments and industry, in these and related areas. Two of his nine books were awarded the Armed Forces Management Literary Award.

C. West Churchman   is Professor of Business Administration, University of California, Berkeley. He was one of the founding fathers of operations research in America. His chief field of interest is the philosophy of planning.

Audrey Clayton   has been associated with applications of advanced technology since 1949, earning her M.Sc. in mathematical logic while working with A. M. Turing on the first experimental computer at Manchester University in England. Her recent studies have focused upon methods of forecasting technological changes in information dissemination, and the wider application of such methods to non-technological areas.

Willis W. Harman   is Associate Director of the Center for the Study of Social Policy at Stanford Research Institute, and Professor of Engineering-Economic Systems at Stanford University. He has extensive experience in policy analysis, social forecasting, technology assessment, and analysis of major societal problems.

C. S. Holling   received his undergraduate training at the University of Toronto (1952) and his Ph.D. at the University of British Columbia (1957). He worked for some years in the laboratories of the Department of the Environment, Government of Canada, emphasizing research on mathematical and experimental analysis of ecological processes. Since then he has been, at various times, Professor and Director of the Institute of Animal Resource Ecology, U.B.C., and Director, Ecology Project, International Institute for Applied Systems Analysis, Vienna. During this latter period his emphasis has been on theoretical and applied aspects of ecological systems and ecological policy. The goal has been to blend concepts of stability theory and ecology with modeling and policy analytic techniques.

Peter M. S. Jones   is Director of the Programmes Analysis Unit in the United Kingdom, a unit sponsored jointly by the Department of Industry and the UKAEA to assist with problems of resource allocation. He is currently also acting as Head of Economics and Programmes Branch of the UKAEA.

Ritva Kaje   is an architect-planner with an "interdisciplinary" doctorate who considers herself a social systems designer, management consultant, and writer. She has served as Associate Editor of the journal, *Technological Forecasting and Social Change,* and led innovative Systems Approach Workshops in the United States and in Europe.

Denis J. Loveridge   is Joint Manager of the Business Futures Unit, Group R & D, Pilkington Brothers Limited. He has experience in the chemical, engineering and fuel industries and has been concerned with systems and futures work since 1962. He has a bachelor's degree and is a Chartered Engineer and Fellow of the Institute of Fuel.

John McHale   is Director of the Center for Integrative Studies, College of Social Sciences, University of Houston. His futures work ranges from global resources analyses to the social and cultural implications of change.

Mick McLean   is associated with the Science Policy Research Unit, University of Sussex. After researching into the methodological basis for the mathematical modeling of social and economic systems for several years, he is currently working on the future social and economic consequences of technical change in the electronics industry.

Donald N. Michael   is a Professor of Planning and Public Policy, Professor of Psychology and a Program Director at the University of Michigan. He is concerned with the social psychological prerequisites for making planning into a social learning process rather than one of social engineering.

Ian I. Mitroff   is a Visiting Professor at The Wharton School of the Univeristy of Pennsylvania on leave from the University of Pittsburgh. He is concerned with the psychology of science, particularly as it pertains to long range planning.

Wladimir M. Sachs   is a senior investigator at Center for Prospective Studies, Fundacion Javier Barros Sierra, Mexico City. He was a researcher in the Busch Center, Wharton School, University of Pennsylvania. He holds a Ph.D. in Social Systems Science from the University of Pennsylvania and a

Diploma of Advanced Studies in Mathematics from the University of Paris-South.

Devendra Sahal has been associated with Portland State University as Visiting Professor of Systems Science. He holds a Doctor of Technology degree in Industrial Engineering from Helsinki University of Technology. He has written numerous papers in the areas of Industrial Engineering, Technological Forecasting, and General Systems Theory. He is co-editor of the recent book, *Technological Substitution.*

Peter Schwartz is a policy analyst at the Center for the Study of Social Policy at Stanford Research Institute. He has experience in futures research and methodology development. He was leader of the future problems assessment project that is discussed in the last chapter.

Henryk Skolimowski received his Ph.D. in Philosophy from Oxford University. He is presently Professor of Philosophy in the Department of Humanities of the University of Michigan. His field is the philosophy of science and the philosophy of technology. Since 1972 he has been Coordinator of Science, Technology, and Future Societies Faculty Seminars at the University of Michigan.

Peter Teige is a research analyst with the Center for the Study of Social Policy at Stanford Research Institute. He is currently completing his M.S. degree in Cybernetic Systems.

Geoffrey Vickers is a U.K.-based independent writer and lecturer on the application of systems theory to the understanding and control of human, political, economic and socio-cultural systems. Sir Geoffrey has wide experience as a corporation lawyer and public administrator and is currently president of the Society for General Systems Research.

Heinz Von Foerster is Professor Emeritus of Biophysics and Physiology and of Electrical Engineering at the University of Illinois in Urbana. He lives now in California.

Preface

Futures research is changing and moving in new directions. In the era of economic growth, the formulation of problems could often be taken for granted and the main task lay in forecasting, using one or more of the forecasting methodologies. Today all this has changed. Questions in the past were mainly *know-how:* how to grow; questions confronting government, industry, and organizations as well as the general public are now more likely to be *know-why:* why grow? Thus there is a widespread need in all of our institutions for more guidance as to what it is that we should be doing, how to pose the "right" questions. For example, it is no longer just a matter of forecasting the ways in which we can go on producing and consuming energy and enlarging the economy at historic rates. Now, we first must decide whether we should consume energy at the present rate or not, and, if not, what rate of energy consumption we should plan for? These are the very different kinds of futures questions which demand attention today and clearly require new approaches.

The book itself arose from the independent actions of two men on each side of the North American continent. One of the editors, Clive Simmonds, tired of reading "mechanical" forecasts with their tacit assumptions, wrote a paper entitled *The Nature of Futures Problems.* This he sent to Harold Linstone, editor of the journal *Technological Forecasting and Social Change,* and to members of the invisible college of researchers tied together through this journal. Did they react in the same way? And, if so, would they present their point of view in the form of a short paper? The result is the series of commentaries in this book: Part II dealing with shifting foundations, Part IV questioning the methodology, and Part V concerning recent experience.

Meanwhile, on the other side of the continent, Harold Linstone had become equally uneasy about the state-of-the-systems approach in dealing with the complex behavioral-social-technological issues faced by planners. He organized a lecture series at Portland State University entitled *Managing Complexity.* The setting and the title were different, but the message was similar. No longer are we just dealing with methodological issues but with challenges to long-accepted paradigms. Asking the right questions must precede the computation of detailed answers. Contributors to this volume discuss the problem of complexity (and how to handle it) and two examples of the curious behavior of complex systems from the fields of biology and ecology.

However, both sets of writers agree in emphasizing our growing awareness of the influence of the personality, experience, and character of those doing futures work, those requesting futures work, and the organizational and institutional environment in the selection of issues chosen for study. The heart of the matter is the perceptual change in the research worker himself. First, and foremost, futures research *is* the formulation of the questions. Given the questions, we can define and structure the problems, produce insights and gain the understanding to make plans. But unless the first step is executed with care, the rest is nonsense — even that sixth consecutive numeral which the computer prints out and someone may believe.

The interest in this book derives, therefore, not from a logical assembly of linear, sequential, causal chains of thought between different people, but from the fact that some twenty-three well-known workers in this field have arrived at very similar conclusions from different interests and starting points, and differing experiences, in a variety of countries. They agree that we must move beyond the objective, analytic, reductionist, number-oriented, optimizing, and fail-safe approach to futures problems and learn to think with equal fluency in more subjective, synthesizing, holistic, qualitative, option-increasing, and safe-fail ways. The reader can select his author and watch how he or she develops this change in viewpoint, in different fields, and for problems of different levels of complexity. But whatever the reader chooses to do, the conclusion awaits: we are embarking on new paths; we stand at the beginning of a most exciting era in futures research. The options are open, the needs for wider ranging thought and for new concepts are clear, and in the face of current and expected difficulties, more people are willing to listen than before. For futures research the time has come to turn in new directions!

The editors would like to take this opportunity to express their deep gratitude to the contributors and to Ann Corrigan, Kathy Pesta, and Ruth Miller, whose dedication in transcribing, typing, and indexing made their task much easier.

HAROLD A. LINSTONE
W. H. CLIVE SIMMONDS

Futures Research
New Directions

I. Prologue

I. 1. Confessions of a Forecaster

HAROLD A. LINSTONE

> I have, alas, studied philosophy,
> Jurisprudence and medicine, too,
> And, worst of all, theology
> With keen endeavor, through and through—
> And here I am, for all my lore,
> The wretched fool I was before.
> Called Master of Arts, and Doctor to boot,
> For ten years almost I confute
> And up and down, wherever it goes,
> I drag my students by the nose—
> And see that for all our science and art
> We can know nothing.

> *Faust,* Part I
> Goethe

In my graduate studies in mathematics I was dazzled by the elegance of subjects such as the Theory of Complex Variables and Topology. Subsequently, the ability to optimize solutions to problems of search, inventory, and product mix for maximum effectiveness or profit convinced me of the power of quantitative mathematical tools to "solve problems." Operations and systems analysis were the keys. In the aerospace industry they were the basis for the design of incredibly complex hardware, and the RAND Corporation mastered strategic nuclear weapon planning through convincing mathematical modeling. The development of linear and dynamic programming as well as game theory at RAND were fascinating by-products.

The first cracks in this edifice became visible in the early 1960's, but there were warning rumbles even earlier. The problems solvable by game theory had a strangely surrealistic tinge. One example suffices:

> Suppose that a pair of Blue bombers is on a mission; one carries the bomb and the other carries equipment for radar jamming, bomb-damage assessment, or what-have-you. These bombers fly in such a way that Bomber 1 derives considerably more protection from the guns of Bomber 2 than Bomber 2 derives from those of Bomber 1. There is some concern lest isolated attacks by one-pass Red fighters shoot down the bomb carrier, and the survival of the bomb carrier transcends in importance all other considerations. The problem is: Should Bomber 1 or Bomber 2 be the bomb carrier, and which bomber should a Red fighter attack?[1]

---

[1] J. D. Williams, *The Compleat Strategyst,* The RAND Corporation, 1954, p. 47.

Futures Research: New Directions, Harold A. Linstone and W. H. Clive Simmonds (eds.)

ISBN 0-201-04096-4

3

By 1960 Tom Schelling had started to illuminate the cracks in game theory:

> There is no way that an analyst can reproduce the whole decision process either introspectively or by an axiomatic method . . . an analyst can deduce the decisions of a single rational mind if he knows the criteria that govern the decision; but he cannot infer by purely formal analysis what can pass between two centers of consciousness.[2]

Meanwhile, systems analysts blithely built mathematical models to measure the cost-effectiveness of alternative conventional weapons and operations — including those in Vietnam. And they were not the only entranced group.

The triumphs of science and technology virtually gave modern man a new religion. Objectivity, reductionism, quantification, and optimality were its canons. Starting with astronomy and calculus, success led to success as Western society was galvanized by science and technology into industrialization and unprecedented material prosperity. It swept along the social sciences — quantification appeared necessary to be "with it" in psychology, economics, and sociology. The ability to obtain funding from the scientific establishment was a powerful incentive for conversion to the fold.

The pinnacle of optimism seemed to be at hand in 1967 when Max Ways wrote in *Fortune's* survey, "The Road to 1977":

> "The further advance of this new style [systems analysis] is the most significant prediction that can be made about the next ten years. By 1977 this new way of dealing with the future will be recognized at home and abroad as a salient American characteristic."[3]

Was it naïve optimism or was it intellectual arrogance?

Deeper immersion slowly engendered some doubts in my mind. Why was long-range planning not effective? Why did model complexity seem to be related inversely to its usefulness? Why was there so much failure in applying those tools which had been eminently successful in strictly technological systems analysis to societal systems? My frustration grew as I spent more time in forecasting and planning activities in industry as well as developing a graduate Systems Science program in academe. Most forecasting reports were not really used by corporate decision-makers, and much of the standard curriculum of courses seemed unsatis-

---

[2]T. C. Schelling, *The Strategy of Conflict,* Harvard University Press, Cambridge, Massachusetts, 1960, p. 163.

[3]M. Ways, "The Road to 1977," *Fortune,* January 1967, p. 4.

ISBN 0-201-04096-4

factory — a compendium of methodologies propagating the science-technology paradigms. I began to empathize with Faust's first words in Goethe's epic version (quoted on p. 3), even if I could not bring myself to his subsequent inference.[4]

These concerns were obviously not unique, and critics — both incisive, e.g., Ida Hoos, and shrill, e.g., W. I. Thompson[5] — launched their fusillades against the systems approach in planning with some effect.

My own first reaction to the dilemma was to focus on an explanation for the ineffectiveness of long-range planning. I saw as the most obvious reason the pervasive tendency to discount the future.[6] We apply a psychological discount rate to our perception of future problems and opportunities the same way a businessman applies a discount rate to future income. A dollar received in 1987 is not worth nearly as much as a dollar received next year *even without any inflation* (since the money received early can be reinvested to earn more). Figure 1 illustrates the discounting phenomenon in the case of world population using data in Meadows' *The Limits to Growth.*[7] An oil shortage thirty years from now is not perceived nearly as serious a crisis as the same shortage occurring in six months. We look at the future as if through the wrong end of a telescope. The most dangerous consequence is that we thereby reduce the options of future generations — a true moral issue.

I even suggested some counteractions: (1) bringing the future crisis closer by creation of imminent minicrises, (2) conversion of time-distant, physically close problems to physically distant but near-term problems (e.g., future societal issues in

---

[4]Continuation of verse on page 3:

. . . .

No dog would want to live longer this way!
Hence I have yielded to magic to see
Whether the spirit's mouth and might
Would bring some mysteries to light,
That I need not with work and woe
Go on to say what I don't know;
That I might see what secret force
Hides in the world and rules its course,
Envisage the creative blazes
Instead of rummaging in phrases.

Faust, Part I
Goethe

[5]Ida R. Hoos, *Systems Analysis in Public Policy: A Critique,* University of California Press, Berkeley, California, 1972.

W. I. Thompson, *Evil and World Order,* Harper & Row, New York, 1976. (Systems Science/Management is the "evil.")

[6]H. Linstone, "On Discounting the Future," *Technological Forecasting and Social Change,* Vol. 4, 1973, p. 335.

[7]D. Meadows, D. Meadows, and J. Randers, *The Limits to Growth,* Universe Books, New York, 1972.

ISBN 0-201-04096-4

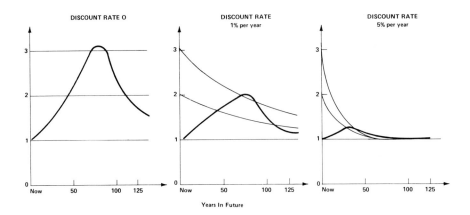

Fig. 1. The discounting phenomenon in the case of world population, based on Meadows' Standard Run (*The Limits to Growth*, Universe Books, New York, 1972, p. 124, Fig. 35). (1970 = 1.)

Country A are current issues in Country B[8]), as well as (3) future-oriented education to extend the individual's planning horizon.

However, I also found two justifications for discounting. One of these ironically came through application of a systems method — decision or relevance trees.[9] A modification permits their use as a problem-solution concept tree. Consider the concern with chronic unemployment as a future major societal "problem" area in the United States. There are clearly many possible responses or "solutions." Examples: reduction in the available labor force (early retirement, more education time, cut in immigration, etc.) and increased labor demand (large-scale national projects, volunteer activity programs, incentives to growth and consumption, etc.). However, each "solution" creates new problems. Early retirement means a longer period of feeling unneeded in the society; with simultaneously improving health through the medical conquest of diseases, the "retirement" period will approach a duration in the life span equal to the work period. Economic growth obviously exacerbates the projected resource shortages until the energy problem is resolved.

[8]M. J. Cetron and A. Clayton, "Investigating Potential Value Changes" (Part V of this volume).

[9]In the context of the project described by Teige, Schwartz, and Harman (Part V of this volume).

ISBN 0-201-04096-4

I can, of course, envision solution concepts for these problems as well. In a similar vein, I find that reforms to solve today's governmental abuses create new dilemmas: curbing an imperial presidency can create an imperial bureaucracy.[10] It becomes evident that I have a never-ending problem-solution sequence, an analogue to a divergent infinite series in mathematics. The tree branches into the heavens! Only application of a discount rate makes the problematique tractable. In effect, it makes a divergent series convergent. The question is the magnitude of the rate in the varying situations. It is, in this context, not surprising that formally undiscounted forecasts such as those sponsored by the Club of Rome have been considerably discounted de facto by politicians and the public. I further begin to recognize that the words "problem" and "solution" (at least the possibility thereof) are a priori connected. If I cannot conceive of a solution, I have a "condition" rather than a "problem." Further, it is hazardous to talk about "right" and "wrong" problems or solutions:

1. The oft-denied, but unavoidable, subjectivity means that the "rightness" of a problem or a solution is a function of the formulator, the time, the organizational setting, and other environmental factors (as McHale and Mitroff observe[11]).
2. I usually do not "solve" a problem at all.

Since I cannot avoid creating new problems by the "solution," I would be more accurate in saying that I am *shifting* problems. In the process I, as an optimist, expect to perceive a gain, a sense of achievement and improvement, a forward motion.

The second reason for discounting is the state of the art of forecasting and planning. The edifice of rationality erected by the paradigms of the technological era may look invincible to those trained ("brainwashed") in the orthodox school of science. From other perspectives it appears to be something of a mirage. The paradigms of the scientific heritage not only provide the basis for continuing technological advances, but also lead the unwary into traps: the search for a "best" solution to a "problem," the drive for quantification and for "the most satisfactory" model. As Kenneth Boulding has observed, "The name of the devil is suboptimization." And Heinz Von Foerster in his First Law proclaims:

> The more profound the problem that is ignored, the greater are the chances for fame and success.[12]

---

[10]I. Kristol, "Post-Watergate Morality," *New York Times Magazine,* Nov. 14, 1976, p. 35.

[11]J. McHale, "Future Problems, or Problems in Future Studies?" and I. I. Mitroff, "On the Error of the Third Kind" (Part II of this collection).

[12]H. Von Foerster, "Responsibilities of Competence," *Journal of Cybernetics,* Vol. 2, No. 2, 1972, p. 1.

ISBN 0-201-04096-4

If the system cannot be solved, it is compartmented and each subsystem is analyzed and optimized. The result is a series of beautiful (and publishable) subsystem solutions which often constitute a very poor solution to the total system.

> In our economy each subunit tries to externalize costs from its own balance sheet in order to show "profits." These costs get pushed around the system until they can be forced into some other group's balance sheet, or hidden in environmental degradation or pushed forward onto future generations.[13]

The federal deficit fuels inflation, and each generation has to run faster to stay in place on the resulting treadmill. The problem is exacerbated by fractionated organizational arrangements — departments in universities, single-purpose agencies in governments, etc.

If a model is unsatisfactory, the proposed cure involves the introduction of more variables, alteration of the relationships, and development of a more comprehensive version. And model complexity is confused with holism. Analysis of a system in terms of many elements and interactions does not constitute a holistic view of the system.[14] The familiar reductionist analytic processes are inherently unsuited to this task. Actually, combinatorial topology forms a far more appropriate mathematical basis for this purpose than calculus or linear algebra.

Christopher Alexander writes with the eyes of an architect:

> For physical forms, we know no general symbolic way of generating new alternatives — or rather, those alternatives which we can generate by varying the existing types do not exhibit the radically new organization that solutions to new design problems demand.[15]

He leads us to the concept of misfit variable, recognizing that one object in a holistic approach is not to optimize or maximize, but to minimize disharmony or discordance in a complex system.

We can learn much about synthesis and holism from artists. Style — in music, painting, and design — provides rich illustrations. It is no coincidence that the most effective scenarios are produced today by artists and not by technologists. The desirable blend of scientist and artist in one person, embodied by H. G. Wells in forecasting, is a rarity indeed.

Perhaps the most important lesson I have learned is the need to consider *simultaneously* multiple models and *Weltanschauungen,* even if they appear to be contradictory.[16] Let me emphasize that I do not mean multiple mathematical models

---

[13]H. Henderson, "Constraints Affecting the Future of the Packaging Industry," *Human Resource Management,* Vol. 16, No. 1, Spring 1977, p. 10.

[14]D. Sahal, "Conception of Futures in a Systems Framework" (Part IV of this collection).

[15]C. Alexander, *Notes on the Synthesis of Form,* Harvard University Press, Cambridge, Massachusetts, 1964, p. 74.

[16]Cf. C. W. Churchman (Part III of this volume), and M. McLean (Part IV).

ISBN 0-201-04096-4

(although they may prove useful) but refer to a much larger domain. One enlightening example of multiple models is contained in the study of the Cuban missile crisis by Allison.[17] He uses the following:

- *The rational actor model,* viewing the problem with the eyes of the systems analyst (e.g., the nation as a unitary actor, alternative solutions, objective criteria for evaluation, selection of the best alternative).
- *The organizational process model,* seeing the problem in terms of relevant organizations, their standard operating procedures, repertoires, and programs.
- *The bureaucratic politics model,* looking at the problem through the eyes of individuals, Chiefs and Indians, each with his own interests, bias, and style, in a bargaining situation.

We perceive a correspondence:

  rational actor model – quasi-technological system focus
  organizational process model – social system focus
  bureaucratic politics model – behavioral system focus

The inadequacy of the traditional rational actor model becomes evident when we see how much insight is gained by adding the other perspectives. We thus recognize that traditional systems approaches usually commit two sins: (1) the assumption that human beings (including scientists) are objective,[18] and (2) excessive reliance on one modeling approach.[19] The rationality assumption is fundamental in game theory and other optimization methods; the single-mindedness of modelers is evident in their output – they rarely use more than one model. I would venture a subjective reason: like the sculptor Pygmalion, they fall in love with the model they have created. Legend tells us that Pygmalion begged the goddess Aphrodite to give the statue life and married his creation when the goddess complied. How many analysts wish their models would become reality!

Another example of multiple perspectives is found in the work of C. West Churchman. He discusses five inquiring systems:[20]

- Lockean: Agreement on observations or data – i.e., empirical.
- Leibnizian: Formal model providing theoretical explanation.
- Kantian: Theoretical model and empirical data complement each other and are inseparable.

---

[17]G. Allison, *The Essence of Decision,* Little, Brown & Co., Boston, Massachusetts, 1971. For a summary of his models, see pp. 137-138 of this book.

[18]Cf. I. I. Mitroff, *The Subjective Side of Science,* Elsevier, New York, 1974.

[19]Psychologists may see a relationship to Western cultures' espousal of monotheism and monogamy.

[20]C. W. Churchman, *The Design of Inquiring Systems,* Basic Books, New York, 1971.

ISBN 0-201-04096-4

- Hegelian: Dialectic confrontation between opposing models or plans leading to resolution.
- Singerian:. Pragmatic meta-inquiring system including application of all other inquiring systems as needed.

Again, there is a richness here which has completely escaped most forecasting and planning efforts.[21] Clearly the emphasis of forecasters has been on the first (Lockean) inquiring system, which leads directly to trend extrapolation — by far the most popular forecasting tool. Churchman (Part III) emphasizes the importance of concurrently maintaining two specific conflicting *Weltanschauungen:* the individual and the total system. How well has futures research managed to do this?

Using Jung's psychological type classification we begin to recognize the significant differences among individuals in their thinking about time — clearly a vital aspect in their approach to futures research.[22] It is interesting to note that a study of drug users by a team of psychologists revealed similar categories:[23]

Jung Type	Time Orientation	Approach to Futures	Drug User Type
Sensation	Present	Discounting	Psychedelic
Feeling	Past	Exploratory (trend extrapolation)	Alcoholic
Intuition	Future	Normative (utopian, goal setter)	Addict (narcotic)
Thinking	Past-present-future	Cybernetic (feedback between exploratory and normative)	Normal

The most widely used forecasting method, trend extrapolation, is not only past-oriented but, more specifically, "recent-past"-oriented. In other words, the forecasters themselves apply a considerable discount rate — to the past, if not to the future. They base their forecasts on recent history and ignore the more distant past. Their ahistoricity is reflected in the rare use of historical analogy — in spite of the fact that history provides very insightful "models" of complex sociotechnological systems.[24] The modern practitioner of technology assessment would also

---

[21]G. Majone writes: "Uncritical acceptance of the 'scientific method' as the model which systems analysts should strive to imitate only generates disillusionment when it is realized that the conclusions of analysis suffer from the same limitations as science without sharing its strengths" ("Pitfalls of Analysis and the Analysis of Pitfalls," International Institute for Applied Systems Analysis, Laxenburg, Austria, p. 19).

[22]*Psychology Today,* December 1972, pp. 76-84.

[23]H. Yaker, H. Osmond, and F. Cheek, *The Future of Time,* Doubleday & Co., New York, 1971, p. 340.

[24]The value of this direction of inquiry is shown by Lynn White, Jr., in "Technology Assessment from the Stance of a Medieval Historian," *Technological Forecasting and Social Change,* Vol. 6, 1974, p. 359.

ISBN 0-201-04096-4

be surprised to learn that Giuseppe Ceredi's 1567 book on his proposed mechanical irrigation scheme included a technology assessment: an analysis of economic feasibility, implications to public health, land utilization, navigable streams, and the effect on the poor of a competitive export advantage.[25]

Another perspective on models is voiced by Ritva Kaje: no attempt is usually made to balance the masculine and feminine — the Yang and Yin — in forecasting approaches.[26] This concern is related to one that we have never overcome in systems work — the overwhelming stress on *analysis* at the expense of holism and synthesis.

And Wladimir Sachs argues that modeling separates form from content, that modeling is inherently deductive: a model is created about the perceived "reality," and analysis leads to conclusions *about the model*.[27] But a human or societal

---

[25]S. Drake, "An Agricultural Economist of the Late Renaissance," in B. S. Hall and D. C. West (eds.), *On Pre-Modern Technology and Science,* Center for Medieval and Renaissance Studies, University of California, Los Angeles, 1976.

[26]R. Kaje, "Bringing the Feminine into Forecasting" (Part II of this collection).

[27]W. Sachs, "Some Thoughts on the Mathematical Method and Futures Problems" (Part IV of this collection). Alfred North Whitehead terms the mistaking of the abstract for the real the Fallacy of Misplaced Concreteness. The situation may be schematically represented as follows:

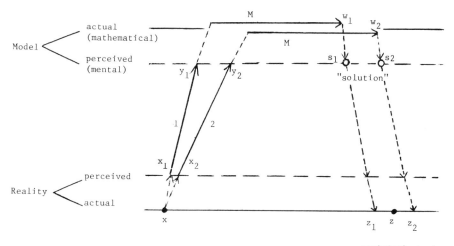

empirical check

Observer "1" perceives the reality x as x_1, "2" perceives it as x_2. "1" perceives the model M as y_1, "2" sees it as y_2. The model M is exercised and the output w_1 and w_2 is misread by "1" and "2" as s_1 and s_2, respectively. Either is taken as solution to the perceived problem, to be further misinterpreted (z_1, z_2) as the real world behavior z.

ISBN 0-201-04096-4

system is inductive — consider the development of goals, for example[28] — and thus the basic tool kit of science simply cannot suffice. Taking a still different perspective, we observe that science is commonly described as searching for "truth." However, societal planning (including technology assessment[29]) exhibits aspects of a judicial process. The aim of an adversary proceeding is to arrive at a resolution of conflict. Historically it replaces the fight and feud. As every lawyer knows, key elements are nonrational ("the outcome depends on the judge's digestion"). Similarly, the course of the future depends on nonrational occurrences (e.g., the assassination of a leader). It is affected by events and factors that can hardly be anticipated and included a priori in *any* model. "Realities" are created by human beings, individually or collectively, and change constantly. This process indeed represents the essence of a self-organizing, self-referential, or evolutionary system.[30]

Substance often precedes structure, just as money was used before economics was invented. The structuring process of system dynamics does not create new societal concepts — it attempts to explain and extrapolate the current ones, and it can design sterile mechanistic technocracies.[31] Even in the design of buildings there is clearly a difference between technical and humanistic design. The Parthenon, long a symbol of symmetric perfection, was actually built for the human eye, not the calculating brain. Departures from uniformity were intentional, yet

> deliberately casual and designedly unsystematic, having been taken at random for a purely aesthetic purpose, in order to temper lifeless mathematical rigidity with those minute irregularities which distinguish the living organism from its abstract generic pattern.[32]

Humanism, animism, mystique, spirituality — seeds that trigger new societies — are not the stuff of structural modeling.

Thus, we have ample indication that the state of the art of futures research justifies a high discount rate on the part of the user. It has exhibited an imbalance, painting the future in single colors, those handed down to us by the dominant paradigm preservers.

If confession is good for the soul, it may also be good for the future of futures research. Indeed, this collection of papers revives my battered optimism.

---

[28]M. Maruyama, "Toward Human Futuristics," *Co-Existence,* Vol. 9, 1972, p. 101.

[29]G. Majone states, "Technology assessment is policy science," but policy science is a self-contradictory term. Policy is not in the domain of science.

[30]See H. Von Foerster in Part III and D. Sahal in Part IV of this volume.

[31]W. I. Thompson, *op. cit.*

[32]R. Carpenter, *The Architects of the Parthenon,* Pelican Books, Middlesex, England, 1970, p. 14.

ISBN 0-201-04096-4

I. 2. The Nature of Futures Problems

W. H. CLIVE SIMMONDS

This paper starts from the simple proposition that in 1975, when it was first being written, we did not seem to possess a satisfactory statement of futures problems, but that we did have a number of promising leads. It also looked as if the futures movement were suffering from an over-identification of futures research and futures studies with methodologies; in my mind it was also clear that a very weak link in the futures chain was the last: the communication of the results to those who had requested them with a resulting lack of impact.

Thus, it seemed that the time was appropriate for a more disciplined statement of what futures work could, and could not, achieve. The first step in this direction was, therefore, to establish the nature of problems which, by definition, deal with events that have not yet happened. How do such problems differ from conventional problems? Given the differences, what can we do about them? It is the purpose of this paper to attempt this in the light of recent developments in several related areas.

Characterizing Problems

The simplest way to start is to look at the characteristics of problems themselves, starting with the ability to define and structure them. The degree of definability and structuring in turn affect the probability relationships, the requirements for measurement, the ways to communicate the results, and the relation of client to researcher.

Problems can be classed as aptly-perceived or inaptly-perceived; they can be precisely-structured or imprecisely-structured; or they can simply remain unstructured, as shown in Fig. 1.

The pluses refer to precision in definition and structuring, the minuses to imprecision or lack of definition or structure.[1]

The probability relationships, measurability and communicability of results can now be set out in relation to the degree of definition and structuring of the problem, as shown in Fig. 2.

Thus typical pure science or classical statistical problems can be aptly-defined, precisely-structured; the probability relationships are explicit; the measurements can be assessed by any competent observer; and the results can be communicated through the printed word since the assumptions are normally established and agreed

---

[1]Sir Geoffrey Vickers and Denis Loveridge pointed out the need to avoid the use of the adverbs well- and ill- in connection with definition and structure, in view of their connotations. I have accordingly adopted their terminology and approach.

Futures Research: New Directions, Harold A. Linstone and W. H. Clive Simmonds (eds.)

ISBN 0-201-04096-4

between the researcher and his peers. This is the tremendous strength of the scientific method and of its paradigms.

A typical futures problem is almost exactly the inverse or opposite of normal science. The problem cannot usually be aptly-defined, nor precisely-structured; the probabilities of success and failure do not add to unity on any basis; the measurements may or may not be accepted; and since there is not normally general agreement on the basic assumptions, communication requires the establishment of a basis and agreed language between the researcher and the client.

How many workers with scientific and technical backgrounds recognize the extent of the difference between the conventional kinds of problem with which they began their careers and the nature of futures problems?

PROBLEMS		STRUCTURING	
		PRECISE	IMPRECISE OR UNSTRUCTURED
DEFINABILITY	Aptly Perceived	+ +	+ −
	Inaptly Perceived	− +	− −

Fig. 1. The Definition and Structuring of Problems

PROBLEM TYPE	++	+−/−+	−−
Probability Relationships	$p + q = 1$	---$p' + q' \neq 1$---	
Measurability[2]	$h\nu$	---$V(S) = P.E.V.$---	
Communicability	→ 100%	< 100%	≪ 100%

Fig. 2. The Probability Relationships, Measurability and Communicability of Results

---

[2]The uncertainty principle sets a limit on physical measurement. The second relation is taken from R. L. Ackoff and F. E. Emery, *On Purposeful Systems,* Aldine, N. Y., 1972. It refers to the efficiency E of a particular means C for obtaining objective O of value V.

ISBN 0-201-04096-4

The Definability and Structuring of Futures Problems

In business and industry many problems are daily converted into aptly-perceived and more or less precisely-structured form through agreement among the parties concerned that we are dealing with this kind, and not that kind, of problem. In this way an illusion of greater certainty is, and can be, maintained. This in turn creates an on-going, self-propagating chain of people who maintain this approach by means of appropriate values, beliefs, rewards, and myths.[3] So long as results are reasonably satisfactory or can be explained in terms of unexpected events, this system persists.

However, unexpected events may force a reevaluation of policies. At this point the differences between different people's perceptions of their problems become evident. What is cataclysmic to one may appear trivial to another, with many shades of opinion in between. Hasan Ozbekhan's concept of planning deals with this by establishing the logical future for the organization (that future which it would anticipate, given its past plus known or expected changes in its environment). But he also notes the existence of interventions. These unexpected, unpredicted and unpredictable events may be sufficiently powerful to force the organization to change course,[4] and are the element which gives the future its chief characteristic, its unknowability.

Fortunately, the problem of *definability* has been clarified by the work of Mitroff and Turoff.[5] Using the mathematics of the Ackoff school,[2] they have shown that there are third and fourth sources of statistical error arising from the inability to define futures problems precisely. The well-known first and second sources of statistical error (rejecting the null hypothesis when true — E_I; accepting the null hypothesis when false — E_{II}) assume that the problem has been 'correctly' defined, which is only possible for precisely-structured problems. For imprecisely or unstructured problems this is exactly what is in doubt, and Mitroff and Turoff demonstrate the finite possibility of solving the wrong problem — E_{III} and E_{IV}. Thus the crucial element in all futures work is:

have you posed the 'right' question(s)?[6]

But how does one pose a futures question? What seems to be involved is set out diagrammatically in Fig. 3 as an iterative process for both an individual and an

---

[3]See M. J. Mulkay, "Conformity and Innovation in Science," *Sociological Rev. Monograph,* Vol. 18, 5-23 (1972) for a review of such mechanisms in the field of natural science; also "Problem Areas and Research Networks in Science," *Sociology,* Vol. 9, No. 2, 187-203 (1975).

[4]H. Ozbekhan, "The Emerging Methodology of Planning," *Fields within Fields,* No. 10, Winter, pp. 63-80 (1973-4).

[5]I. I. Mitroff and M. Turoff, "On Measuring the Conceptual Errors in Large Scale Social Experiments: The Future as Decision", *Technological Forecasting and Social Change,* Vol. 6, pp. 389-402 (1974).

[6]Herman Kahn, "On Thermonuclear War," Princeton University Press, 1960.

ISBN 0-201-04096-4

organization. The first step consists in projecting one's perception of the future in relation to some need, want, mission, responsibility, etc., which may be done by rational or intuitive methods or both.[7] Then from the projected future the perceiver extracts what appear to him to be the relevant problems. In doing so, he begins to define them. The definition of the perceived problems does not mean necessarily that he can easily solve them, and so the perceiver goes round the cycle again, this time to find a structure which can be used to solve the problems which he perceives, thinks, are relevant. Finally, and only after this sort of mental process, can the situation be set out in the kind of conventional dispassionate terms used in management decision-making.

The interesting thing about this is the level of subjective input. Perception of the future is highly colored by one's experience, the accidents of birth, inheritance and education, the social and cultural impress, the organization's experience, recent events, and one's own predilections. It is anything but objective! Organizationally individual characteristics can be offset by appropriate conferencing,[8] but this may not overcome organizational proclivities.

Figure 3 helps reveal why organizations in apparently the same business can see the world quite differently and hence pose different "right" questions. It is only recently that we are becoming more willing to recognize publicly the degree to which the researcher, the planner, the decision-maker, and the manager are themselves involved subjectively, humanly, and emotionally, in what the current mythology terms objective decisions, rationally defined, and dispassionately arrived at.[9]

Figure 3 indicates how one arrives at questions about the future. But how does one determine what the "right" question is, and when does one do this? X months or years after a decision has been taken, it may be possible to say that the decision was "right"; but (X+Y) years later this may no longer be true. The manufacturers of buggy whips were "right" for years, but X proved to be a finite number and their business largely faded away. Railroad companies held similar beliefs and in our own time many aerospace companies. One of the most obvious examples is the cyclical reevaluation of merit (or variation in taste) in literature, music, and art. The history of putting a man on the moon may follow a similar course.

The reason for this is that, in futures problems, we are dealing with a multiple, feed-forward, feed-back system, as shown schematically in Fig. 4.[10]

The process envisaged in Fig. 3 allows an organization to agree on what it

[7]Ritva Kaje, "Bringing the Feminine into Forecasting," (Part II of this volume).

[8]M. Turoff, "Human Communication via Data Networks", *Ekistics 211,* June, 337-341 (1973); S. R. Hiltz and M. Turoff, "Potential Impacts of Computer Conferencing upon Managerial and Organizational Styles," 1976, Computerized Conferencing and Communications Center, New Jersey Institute of Technology.

[9]Erich Jantsch has addressed himself to this subject in *Technological Planning and Social Futures,* Cassell/ABS, London, 1972.

[10]Stafford Beer, *The Brain of the Firm,* Allen, The Penguin Press, London, 1972; Jay Forrester, *Principles of Systems,* Wright-Allen, 1968.

ISBN 0-201-04096-4

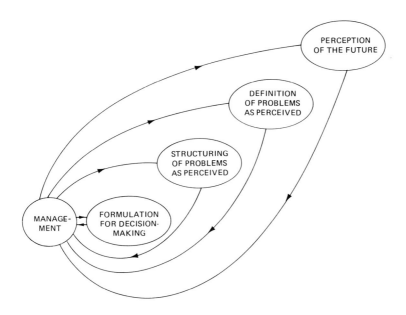

Fig. 3. Steps in Perceiving, Defining, and Structuring Future Situations Prior to the Decision Stage

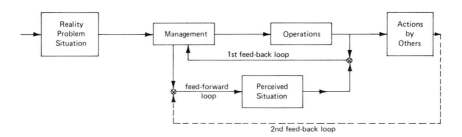

Fig. 4. Schematic Feed-Forward, Feed-Back Loop Situation

ISBN 0-201-04096-4

believes to be the more likely futures. Given this agreement, it can determine the "right" questions to be posed and make its decisions in terms of them. To find out whether it has defined its possible futures correctly and hence made the "best" decisions, it must set up feed-back loops to monitor the results of its feed-forward thinking, in terms of its own actions (whether carried out properly or not) and of their effects on the intended customers, clients, or beneficiaries.

The feedback of information on results may modify or confirm management's perception of the situation, and we have an on-going, but not necessarily repetitive system. However, such systems will oscillate or hunt unless suitably damped.

Management is thus constantly faced with the need to strike the balance between too tight a control and reduced sensitivity in its feed-forward, feed-back decision/ monitoring loops, which filters out vital pieces of information, or too lax a control which can give rise to oscillations and ultimately collapse. In real life, management also has the problems of cross-interaction between different loops (different activities). Thus, it is not sufficient just to recognize that one can choose and solve the wrong problem. We are in fact constantly making our choices on the basis of what the psychologists term a *gestalt*, or whole view of the situation. This is peculiar to ourselves, or, with adequate planning, to the organization or unit, may change with time and experience, and may or may not be agreed to by others.[11]

Thus, the perception of a business by those in charge plays a critical role in determining what problems are considered "right" and therefore which decisions are actually taken.[12] The significance of this will be referred to later on.

These remarks make it clear that the probability relationships in futures work are likely to differ significantly from those in conventional science.

Probability Relationships

One of the characteristics of normal science is that, for any event A, the probability of the complementary event "not-A" is 1 minus the probability of A.[13] This statement represents what we mean by a fully defined situation; and a problem becomes precisely-structured as and when the limits placed on it enable such a probability statement to be made in reference to it.

In futures work this is exactly what is not true. The situation is no longer completely definable. We are therefore confronted by probabilities which cannot be completely stated. It may still be helpful to define such probabilities while admitting that some elements have been left out. But if so, the two probabilities must be calculated separately, i.e.:

$$p' + q' \neq 1.$$

Additionally, even though the probabilities, p' and q', are dimensionless ratios, they do not necessarily contain the same elements. In industrial and business situations, for example, the criteria for success may well be technical, financial, and marketing; but the criteria for failure in such projects have turned out subsequently to depend on *totally different* things, for example, noise effects (the SST), safety (nuclear reactors), aesthetics (power line location), wild-life and nature preservation (the San Francisco Bay area), eco-destruction (upper atmosphere effects); or such projects may simply afford the opportunity for the venting

[11]See for example, R. D. Gastil, "A General Framework for Social Science," *Policy Sciences,* Vol. 3, No. 4, 385-403 (1972); E. Jantsch, "Forecasting and the Systems Approach: A Critical Survey," *ibid,* 475-498.
[12]W. H. C. Simmonds, "Towards an Analytical Industry Classification," *Technological Forecasting and Social Change,* Vol. 4, 375-385 (1973).
[13]For example, W. L. Hays, *Statistics,* Holt, Rinehart, N. Y.,1963.

ISBN 0-201-04096-4

of alienation and frustration against "impersonal institutions" (anti-fluoridation campaigns, environmental movements, earth-preservation projects).

For imprecisely or unstructured problems such as those in the social sciences and futures, the probabilities for success and for failure therefore must always be calculated separately since the success and failure modes usually differ. Only when the problem is converted into a precisely-structured one by making appropriate assumptions can the two kinds of probability come together and become the same, with the same elements in both p and q.

This is profoundly important for governments to understand. The "success" of political progress is frequently predicated in terms of short-term cost-benefits, while subsequent events have revealed their "failures" in the form of unintended consequences in other areas with high human, social, and environmental costs.[14]

Measurability

The implications for measurement can be looked at in two stages.

The first stage is the Heisenberg-Schrödinger uncertainty principle which states that the act of measurement affects the system measured even though the entities in it remain unchanged.

The second stage deals with the situation, now recognized to be general, in which the act of measurement affects not only the system but the measurer and the measured. The days of the detached, objective, observer are over.[9] There are three aspects here. The first concerns the self-fulfilling/self-defeating nature of forecasts.[15] The second deals with holism and self-referential systems and is discussed by D. Sahal in this book.[16]

The third aspect is less well-known but is important since it sets limits to knowledge and the ability to find out. Laplace held that the future of the whole universe should be calculable, if given its state at one instant.[17] This condition is exactly what cannot be met in either the physical world or the human and social world.

T. P. Wilson has clarified this situation in the field of social psychology by comparing the normative and interpretive paradigms regarding the interaction of two or more actors.[18] In the normative paradigm, actors are assumed to share a

---

[14]M. Gibbons and R. Voyer, *A Technology Assessment System,* Science Council of Canada Background Study, No. 30, Ottawa, March, 1974.

[15]J. Martino, *Technological Forecasting for Decision-making,* Elsevier, N. Y., 1972; see also R. L. Henshel, "Effects of Disciplinary Prestige on Predication Accuracy," *Futures,* Vol. 7, No. 2, 92-106 (1975).

[16]D. Sahal, "Conception of Futures in a Systems Framework," (Part IV of this volume).

[17]Ross Ashby, *Design for a Brain,* Chapman & Hall, London, 2nd ed., p. 28 (1960). For a current discussion of these points see M. Skolimowski, "Epistemological Aspects of Technology Assessment" (Part IV of this volume).

[18]T. P. Wilson, "Conceptions of Interaction and Forms of Sociological Explanation," *Amer. Soc. Rev.,* Vol. 35, No. 4, 697-710 (1970); R. E. Stokes and J. P. Hewitt, "Aligning Actions," *Amer. Soc. Rev.,* Vol. 41, 838-849 (1976).

ISBN 0-201-04096-4

system of culturally-established symbols and their meanings, including language and gestures. They interact in terms of their dispositions and role expectations, role conflict, conformity and deviance, and sanctioning or reinforcement processes. For stability in any exchange, the actors must refer to the shared system of meanings of the group within which the interaction takes place. If they do not do this, there is no way *for an observer* to decide whether two behaviors, performed by different actors or the same actor at different times, are repetitions of the same action or represent totally different actions. The normative paradigm therefore implies that each actor always knows what role the other is taking. Given this, an objective description of the interaction can be made, provided that the observer has learnt the culture of the group he is observing.

The interpretive analysis rests precisely on the point that *alter* can never really know what role *ego* is taking at any point in the interaction, and must constantly search for verbal and non-verbal clues to see if he has changed his role. Consequently, the perceived purpose and meaning in the other's actions are always provisional and subject to revision in the light of subsequent events in the course of the interaction. The *role-expectation* approach assumes that the roles are known and continue to be known to both parties throughout the interaction; the *role-taking* approach rests on the well-known fact that we never know what is going on in somebody else's mind, and can only infer this from the clues which they give us, from our own experience, and from the general cultural background and situation. Uncertainty is therefore inherent in human interactions, and interest shifts from the act of measurement to the process of measurement and its influence.[19]

It is apparent from the above brief presentation that much of the current discussion in the social sciences concerning their basic paradigms is closely related to this discussion of the nature of futures problems, since both deal with imprecisely or unstructured problems.[20] Moreover both fields involve expectations, which raises the issue of the kinds of mathematics which are appropriate.[21]

The difficulty in defining the "right" problems discussed above makes it clear that conventional, value-free, mathematics is not likely to be fully adequate in the analysis and synthesis of imprecisely-structured problems and situations. Since we cannot describe futures problems without reference to a gestalt or whole view of the situation as seen by someone or some group, we are in the position of imposing our value-structure in the act of choice of problem. "This" is more important than "that"; therefore, we will look at "this." Subsequent events may or may not

---

[19]See the discussion of measurements in the field of fertility given by L. L. Bumpass and E. D. Driver in reviews of A. V. Cicourel's book, "Theory and Method in a Study of Argentine Fertility," John Wiley, New York (1974) in *Contemporary Sociology*, Vol. 4, No. 5, 474-481 (1975).

[20]See, for example, G. Ritzer, "Sociology: A Multiple Paradigm Science," *The American Sociologist*, Vol. 10 (August), 156-167 (1975); P. M. Blau (ed.), *Approaches to the Study of Social Structure*, The Free Press, New York 1975.

[21]Wladimir Sachs, "Some Thoughts on the Mathematical Method and Futures Problems," (Part IV of this volume).

ISBN 0-201-04096-4

justify the choice, or we may manipulate them to try to justify our choices; but we cannot make a value-free choice in regard to futures problems. We could choose them at random, or accept other people's appreciation of the situation,[22] or we may simply extend the present and dodge the issue that way. Since human institutions display the phenomenon of inertia and resistance to change,[23] this is usually felt to be reasonable for short time periods.

Fortunately, the school of Ackoff, Churchman, Emery, and Trist has struggled with this problem for some thirty years and produced a mathematics for purposeful systems.[3] Mitroff and Turoff used this mathematics to establish the third source of statistical error, E_{III} — solving the wrong problem.

James Coleman has developed a somewhat different approach.[24] He notes that this kind of action theory "provides an economy that allows it to make predictions with a less extensive data base than is true for causal theories." We shall pick up this point in connection with behavior patterns and their value for futures work.

The approaches of René Thom and E. C. Zeeman promise new insights as does the work on self-referential systems.[16] Significant new developments appear likely here and are needed.

Communicability

After we have defined what we believe to be the "right" problem or group of problems, and made measurements with due regard to the uncertainty principles involved, we still face the problem of communicating the results to our colleagues or to those who have commissioned the studies. It appears to be a universal experience in futures work that this, the last step in the chain, is systematically and regularly underestimated! The reasons are not far to seek. The boss naturally assumes that his higher position in the organization implies better judgment on his part[25] and greater ability to achieve[26] than is possessed by those working for him. On what grounds then can someone junior proffer advice which recommends that his boss do something different from what he originally intended, in regard to events which have not yet happened?

(i) THE "FUTUROR" AND HIS CREDIBILITY

The "futuror" (futurist, forecaster, planner) must establish his credibility

[22]Geoffrey Vickers, *The Art of Judgment: A Study of Policy Making,* Methuen, London, 1965.

[23]Donald N. Michael, *Planning to Learn and Learning to Plan,* Jossey-Bass, San Francisco (1973); E. Trist, "Resistance to Innovation — Human and Organizational," Innovation Canada, Proceedings of the Fourth Seminar, 1974, Innovation Canada, 533 Arbor Road, Mississauga, Ontario.

[24]James Coleman, *The Mathematics of Collective Action,* Aldine, New York 1973.

[25]W. H. C. Simmonds, "How to Make Sure You Have a Future," *Innovation Twelve,* 36-43 (1970).

[26]W. F. Christopher, "The Achieving Enterprise," *Amer. Manag. Assoc.,* New York 1974.

ISBN 0-201-04096-4

opposite management or his client in areas where they can judge him, i.e. in terms of their current problems. This is where the hard work comes in, since this kind of credibility can only be gained and maintained by a better, deeper insight into these problems than the current "wisdom." However, once such credibility has been established, management has a basis on which to refer future problems to the "futurors."

A major element in credibility is clearly the ability to discern what turn out later to be the "right" questions in, for most organizations, the short-term. Given agreement on what constitute the "right" questions, numerical forecasts can be generated and tested on the basis of varying assumptions. This is best left to those who normally provide such data. It is easy to be out by several hundred percent numerically, but only by 100% (right or wrong) in the choice of questions to be asked!

(ii) THE "FUTUREE"

Credibility cannot be established without a relation-interaction between the "futuror" and the "futuree," his client. We noted that assumptions regarding imprecisely or unstructured problems cannot be simply explicated. Thus, the possibilities for misunderstandings in setting up a futures study, during the study, and in the reporting of the study, are real and serious. They must be circumvented by ensuring that management or the client is involved in, and made part of, the study, — from its conception, definition of scope, conduct, and right through to the final report and recommendations. The client must set limits to the scope; he should contribute certain information appropriate to his position; he must never be allowed to disengage under excuses of pressures of work; he should review progress and suggest improvements; his advice concerning recommendations and conclusions is crucial if he is going to implement them. At no point under these conditions can he disown the study, nor is he likely to do so if he has contributed to it.[27]

Thus "futurors" must "thread" futures studies into an organization so that the studies become the organization's. In addition, each level of management involved in these studies must "hook on" to the next level and to adjacent areas of management to ensure the upward momentum of the study and its results, *if these are to have any real impact on events*. The saddest sight in the futures world is the report lying unused on a shelf, whether incomplete, unedited, or beautifully bound. The last step in the futures chain is the hardest, to convince someone else that one's findings are valid, useful, and worth acting on.

(iii) THE CHARACTERISTICS OF "FUTURORS" AND "FUTUREES"

Since values and beliefs enter into the choice of futures problems, the personal philosophies of the "futuror" and his "futuree" and their interrelationships become important. Mitroff and Turoff have set these out as Leibnizian, Lockean, Kantian,

---

[27]D. J. Loveridge, "Values and Futures," (Part II of this volume).

ISBN 0-201-04096-4

Hegelian, and Singerian in terms of inquiring systems, and applied this thinking to specific cases.[28]

Harold Linstone has noted that the differences between "futuror" and "futuree" can also be expressed as a difference in discount rates. He has already noted the pervasive tendency to discount the future, a fact largely ignored by the Club of Rome's modellers.[29]   What seems important here is that there is a *differential* discount rate between the "futuror" and the "futuree," and that this offers a way of treating this difference as noise introduced into a communication process, i.e. a potential link between futures work and communication/information theory.   In practice, line managers have a three months' time frame (one business quarter), presidents one year, politicians one election, all of which are extremely short in real terms; even a five-year planning time frame implies a discount rate approaching 50%.   The only realistic long-term discounter appears to be a girl assessing a proposal of marriage.   Her "yes" is based on something close to a 5% discount rate, longer, one guesses, than that of her erstwhile future husband!

This raises the questions: do different "philosophers" have different discount rates? How do the different philosophical attitudes interact in hierarchical organizations (is this the origin of Professor Parkinson's famous yes-no alternation in hierarchies)?   Can communication theory be extended along these lines to take account of differences in the characteristics of human receivers and senders?

Linstone has made a start in this direction with his paradigm of futurists as discounters, extrapolators, goal-setters, or cyberneticists (p. 10).   Can we go further?

(iv) CONSTRAINTS AND CHOICE

There appears to be a continuing confusion between constraints and choice. Thus predictions of G.N.P., G.N.P./capita, total population, population by age group, regional distributions, etc., are in effect constraints. As Kahn and Wiener pointed out,[30] India's per capita G.N.P. cannot equal that of Japan overnight. These constraints can be compared in baseball language, to the physical size of a ball park, the height and distance of the left-field fence, the distance between bases. But note that they tell us nothing about who is at bat or who is pitching. Thus, the evaluation of the probable G.N.P., population, does not tell us what human beings, groups, and institutions will decide to do, wisely or less wisely, under those circumstances.[31] Such choices are made in terms of the perception of the situation by

---

[28]I. I. Mitroff and M. Turoff, "Technological Forecasting and Assessment: Science and/or Mythology," *Technological Forecasting and Social Change,* Vol. 5, No. 2, 113-134 (1973); "A Case Study of Assessment Applied to the 'Cashless Society' Concept," *ibid.,* Vol. 7, No. 3, 317-325 (1975). See also I. I. Mitroff, "On the Error of the Third Kind," (Part II of this volume).

[29]H. Linstone, Review of the Mesarovic-Pestel Club of Rome II Report, *Technological Forecasting and Social Change,* Vol. 7, No. 4, 331-4 (1975); also "On Discounting the Future," *ibid.,* Vol. 4, No. 4, 335-8 (1973); "Confessions of a Forecaster," (Part I of this volume).

[30]H. Kahn and A. Wiener, *The Year 2000,* Macmillan, N. Y., 1967.

[31]One of the most serious developments in recent times has been the decision of groups to go "over the edge," as in Northern Ireland, Cyprus, Lebanon, and potentially, in Africa.

ISBN 0-201-04096-4

the decision-makers. Our perceptions of what is significant or important change
with time. A good example of this was the change over a decade in the U.S.
perspective on the Viet Nam war. The hardest part of forecasting is therefore:
how will I (or management) see (perceive) the world in five . . . . ten years' time?
One of the valid criticisms of some forecasting methods is that this is not included
or explicated. The key weakness in Delphi always has been that certain questions
were *not* asked; they did not seem important when the study was started. Later
we know better! The analysis of what causes us to change our perceptions of the
world in which we live is therefore one of the most important elements in forecasting.

(v) THE RESULTS

Before communicating, futures results should be evaluated, as Martino has
pointed out, for need, underlying cause, relevance, and reliability.[32] These checks
reduce the likelihood of an elementary error or omission from slipping through
by a systematic interrogation of the work and results. Martino has given an excellent description of this; there is no need to repeat it further.

The above shows that the successful forecaster, long-range planner, or futures
worker not only must be creative, technically competent, understand economic and
financial implications, and be able to withstand cognitive dissonance for longer than
usual periods of time, but he must also possess diplomatic skills. There is no appeal
in this kind of work to this or next year's profit, growth, market share, successful
research or design. The results may not show for three, five, or even ten years, but
they still may be decisive in terms of corporate, organizational, or departmental
success. In one industrial company with some 10,000 total employees, a careful
analysis of all the managerial and professional people suggested that only about
2-3% of them had this kind of combination of technical and personal skills. Therefore wise management makes good use of such people.

(vi) THE OTHER PARTIES INVOLVED

In their Science Council of Canada study on technology assessment (T.A.),
Gibbons and Voyer noted that T.A. was worth little unless it took into account
the social consequences of technological change (the T.A. system); and that there
was always a minimum of three social groups involved; the protagonists, the
antagonists, and the group indirectly affected (normally negatively); and that all
three groups should be involved in any T.A.[33]

The Swedish analysis of possible futures also supports strongly the need for the

---

[32]J. P. Martino, "Evaluating Forecast Validity," in J. Bright and M. E. F. Schoeman (eds.),
A Guide to Practical Technological Forecasting, Prentice-Hall, N.Y., pages 27-52 (1973).

[33]M. Gibbons and R. Voyer, "A Technology Assessment System: A Case Study of East
Coast Offshore Petroleum Exploration," Science Council of Canada Background Study, No. 30,
Ottawa, 1974.

ISBN 0-201-04096-4

public to be involved in its own future.[34]   In practice, the problem is to separate
the discussion of alternative futures from the necessarily confidential matter of
deciding between alternative futures, whether governmental, business, or institutional. It is too easy at present to equate open discussion with loss of confiden-
tiality; on the other hand, an informed public can more readily support longer term
decisions in its own interests. The public has minimum interest in politicians
fighting zero sum games (the lowest social gain situation) simply to not lose their
power, when the higher level games which individual human beings normally play,
could give higher social gains plus an equal or better chance of retaining power.[35]

Summing-Up

Where does this bring us? It appears that forecasting and futures work is at a
point of change.[36]   Jonas Salk terms this the shift from Epoch A dominated by
Ego and short-term survival considerations to Epoch B in which both Being and
Ego co-exist and a balance is continuously being struck between short-term and
long-term survival.[37]   John Platt calls these watershed events of which he has
given many instances.[38]   Bertrand de Jouvenel notes "that the vision of progress
given us by the economists is in monetary terms and strictly monetary." He
reasons for a future based on an economics of the whole, in which resources (le
sous-sol) are accorded value.[39]   The President of France, M. V. Giscard d'Estaing,
argues publicly for conscious change.[40]

In dealing with situations which contain both subjective and objective components, many of the conventional methodologies display weaknesses. Coleman
pointed out that adaptive theories are better suited to complex problems than
causal theories.[24]   Nowhere is this clearer than in the use of behavior patterns.

[34]Royal Ministry for Foreign Affairs, "To Choose A Future," Stockholm, Sweden, 1974.
See also Göran Bäckstrand, "The Public and the Future," (Part V of this volume).
[35]N. Howard, "Paradoxes of Rationality: Games, Metagames and Political Behavior,"
M. I. T. Press, 1971.
[36]J. McHale, "Futures Problems or Problems in Futures Studies," (Part II of this volume).
[37]Jonas Salk, *The Survival of the Wisest,* Harper & Row, N. Y., 1973.
[38]John Platt, "The Greatest Jump in Evolution", *Ekistics,* Vol. 207, Feb., 57-58 (1973);
"Science for Human Survival," *The Science Teacher,* Vol. 40, No. 1, Jan. (1973).
[39]Bertrand de Jouvenel, *La Civilisation de Puissance,* Fayard, Paris, 1976.
[40]V. Giscard d'Estaing, *Démocratie française,* Fayard, Paris, 1976 (American edition,
French Democracy, translated and with a Preface by Vincent Cronin, Doubleday, New York,
1977).

ISBN 0-201-04096-4

This writer has demonstrated elsewhere that the high technology industries have followed an on-going behavior pattern for the past 25-30 years.[41] An operational classification of industry can be developed on this basis.[42] The method can be extended forward to predict changes in industrial behavior patterns.[43]

Behavior pattern analysis differs from systems dynamics and modelling in that it includes the human actors as separate elements in the system. Companies are run by people who carry a picture or perception of what the company is and what it is trying to achieve.[44] They impose this *gestalt* or viewpoint on to the purely technical, economic or financial aspects of any situation. The resulting decisions may be wise or less wise, but they include the ambitions of the people involved, the friendships and the personality clashes, the power struggles and the ups and downs of real life. This broader, adaptive framework permits directions of change to be detected and their implications anticipated. The more complex, the more fluid, the situation – the greater the power, the greater the insight, of this kind of approach.

Summing up, by identifying the nature of futures problems, it becomes clearer what futures work can and cannot do.[45] We can identify the strengths and weaknesses of different methodologies on a more rational basis, and will be better able to choose methodologies in relation to problems. Such methodologies however, must be able to cope with wider inputs than before.[46] The position of people working in this field and what they can and cannot be expected to do is clearer, and the expectations of clients for futures work can become more realistic.

The chapters which follow reveal the advantages to be gained from this wider view of the nature of futures problems.

[41]W. H. C. Simmonds, "The Analysis of Industrial Behavior and its Use in Forecasting," *Technological Forecasting and Social Change,* Vol. 3, 205-224 (1972); reprinted in J. Bright and M. E. F. Schoeman (eds.), *Guide to Practical Technological Forecasting,* Prentice-Hall, N. Y., 1973, 215-237. "L'analyse des configurations du comportement industriel comme technique de prévision," *L'Actualité économique,* Vol. 51, No. 2, avril-juin, 289-321 (1975).

[42]W. H. C. Simmonds, "Patterns of Industry Behavior and What They Tell Us", *Chem. Tech.,* July, 416-420 (1975); Proceedings of the C.M.R.A.-C.C.D.A. Conference, St. Louis, Nov., 1973, 72-80.

[43]W. H. C. Simmonds, "Industrial Behavior Patterns for Planners", *Futures,* Vol. 7, No. 4, 284-292 (1975); "Planning and R&D in a Turbulent Environment," *Research Management,* Nov., 17-21 (1975); "Forces for Change in the Chemical Industry," *Chemistry in Canada,* Vol. 27, No. 10, 27-31 (1975); Forces for Change in the Metallurgical Industry," *C. I. M. Bulletin,* March, 1976, and the Journal for Metals, Jan., 1976; "Forces for Change," *Innovation Canada,* 1975; *Journal of the International Society for Technology Assessment,* December, 43-48 (1975).

[44]cf. page 18.

[45]M. McLean, "Getting the Problem Right – A Role for Structural Modelling", (Part IV of this volume).

[46]See Geoffrey Vickers, "The Future of Culture," (Part II of this volume).

ISBN 0-201-04096-4

II. Shifting Foundations

II. 1. Introduction

HAROLD A. LINSTONE

All systems are false; that is to say, all systems are and cannot help but be merely images, different ways of imagining or representing the world, which is only the starting point of these representations. All systems begin with reality, which is amorphous, and go on from there. The more perfect, complete, believable, convincing, logical, and coherent a system is, the more unreal and artificial it is. All systems, therefore, are fundamentally artificial and far removed from reality.

Present Past, Past Present
E. Ionesco (1971)

In 1763 an anonymous future-oriented book appeared in England: *The Reign of King George VI – 1900-1925.* It forecast international political realignments such as a Franco-Russian alliance threatening England and a Pax Britannica in Europe. In the area of technology it envisioned improvements such as a series of canals to carry cargo between English towns. Yet in 1763 James Watt was working on the Newcomen steam engine, and the Montgolfier manned balloon flight was only twenty years away. In other words, the Western world was on the brink of the Industrial Revolution. Today we see in this anonymous work a fatal present-oriented culture-bound bias. It is not a weakness confined to forecasters – we observe it in historians as well. Mommsen's *History of Rome* was an image seen through the filter of nineteenth-century Germany.

Extrapolation of current trends is still the habit of most organizational planners today. Allison, in fact, sees it as an inherent characteristic in his "organizational process" model (Part IV, Introduction, Table 1). Values, institutions, and regulations are seen through today's lenses. And in this Part, McHale, Vickers, and Mitroff insist that our perception of "problems" is anchored in today's values and institutional settings. We "see" them in terms of present (or recent) categories, organizations, and cultures. Further complicating matters is the fact that each individual sees through his own personal lenses, forming his own subjective perception. Thus the definition and identification of future problems itself becomes a major problem – perhaps the most difficult one, as Simmonds points out (Part I).

A typical consequence of this situation is Coates' Fallacy of the Argument from Incompetence: If we do not know how to solve a problem today, there is no solution.[1] This is a primary reason for a systematic bias in forecasting – undue pessimism for the long range, undue optimism for the short range. In the former case we see no solution and thus assume that there will be no solution; in the

---

[1] J. Coates, "Antiintellectualism and Other Plagues on Managing the Future," *Technological Forecasting and Social Change,* Vol. 4, 1973, p. 250.

Futures Research: New Directions, Harold A. Linstone and W. H. Clive Simmonds (eds.)

ISBN 0-201-04096-4

latter we recognize the solution today and cannot see any obstacles to achieving it. On this basis we have consistently underestimated the problems in implementing "known" solutions in desalination,[2] United States supersonic transport aircraft, and breeder reactors.[3]   On the other hand, impenetrable limits to growth in the long term are seen in water, energy, materials, etc., based on today's gaps in knowledge.

One could also apply a corollary of Coates' Fallacy to societal forecasting: If we cannot envision new societal concepts, assume that the present will persist or be replaced by a nostalgic return to the (idealized) past.

The question is whether there are ways to alleviate such distortions consciously. Mitroff, Loveridge, and Kaje see achievement of a balance between polarities in human behavior as a key to improvement in future problem perception. As Mitroff points out, a "wrong" problem may result from a wrong methodology which results from a wrong problem formulator/solver. He suggests the use of Jung's psychological typology, and the reader may find it interesting to compare this with Linstone's categorization of futures thinking in Part I (p. 10). Loveridge and Kaje illuminate the individual's behavioral patterns using biological concepts — left-right brain halves and masculine/feminine, respectively (Table 1). It is very clear that there is presently a gross imbalance which impairs futures study. Right-brain-half activities seem to be in short supply almost everywhere. One of the aims of this book is to encourage a conscious effort to achieve a better balance on the part of individuals in a team, something which could have a reverberating effect on group values and norms, and then on policy and strategy formulation.

Vickers relates social/cultural to biological rates of change. In particular, he asks whether human beings are biologically fit to accept the cultural revolution he believes is now needed in consequence of the technological revolution which has already engulfed modern societies. The same question has been raised in connection with reduction of discount rates.   The focus on the present was clearly

Table 1

The Dichotomy

Left-Brain Hemisphere	Right-Brain Hemisphere
Sequential thinking	Spatial thinking
Reductionist	Holistic
Analytic	Synthetic
Well-structured problems	Ill-structured problems
Problem solvers	Problem formulators
Sensation (Jung)	Intuition (Jung)
Perceptual, external experience	Conceptual, internal experience

[2]T. Gordon and O. Helmer, "Report on a Long-Range Forecasting Study," Report No. P-2982, The RAND Corporation, Santa Monica, California, September 1964.
[3]E. Jantsch, "Technology Forecasting in Perspective," Organisation for Economic Co-operation and Development, Paris, 1967, p. 106.

ISBN 0-201-04096-4

essential to biological survival in early human history. First came the struggle for
self-survival, then the care of, and concern with, offspring. How future-sensitive
can human beings become?

In this connection we should evoke the work of John C. Calhoun.[4] His experiments with colonies of mice imply that excessive populations and interactions
produce behavioral pathology — e.g., loss of the ability to cope. The result is
reversal of the population growth and demise of the society. Will rapid technological change ultimately lead to similar incapacity in complex social behavior patterns
and to breakdowns? Herman Kahn insists that such deduction from mice to men
is unfounded, but hardly provides more than an intuitive rejoinder.[5]

One psychological problem never adequately addressed is the trap of prediction.
Most laymen and even some technologists assume that forecasting and futures
studies are synonymous with prediction. In the case of laymen this confusion is
understandable. Most people dislike uncertainty. As children we were told fairy-
tales and they always had a precise ending ("the prince and princess lived happily
ever after"). They were not probabilistic and we did not find them to have alternative endings (e.g. 50% chance of living happily ever after, 30% chance of breaking
up, and 20% of living unhappily together). Most people would rather hear a precise
prediction or future story even if they recognize its likelihood of correctness is
virtually zero, than a series of alternatives, "if-then" forecasts, or probabilistic
analyses of the future. Wrong certainties seem more satisfying than correct uncertainties, a human trait already well understood by ancient prophets. Uncertainty tends to paralyze decision-making[6] and, in Hamlet's words, "makes us rather
bear those ills we have than fly to others that we know not of". It gives us another
excuse to discount the (uncertain) future and focus on the (more certain) present.

McHale and Vickers recognize a need for fundamental changes in paradigms
which are usually not questioned in futures research, while Mitroff, Loveridge,
and Kaje point to the human (behavioral/biological) inadequacy of the typical individual or group forecast.

These difficulties are not as abstract as they may seem to some readers. The
recent Stanford Research Institute study for the White House Office of Science and
Technology Policy wrestled with them in its attempt to determine critical future
problems (see Teige, Schwartz, and Harman in Part V). Their article may serve as
a crude gauge to determine the gulf between the state of the art and the desiderata
in futures research.

A menu of fundamental societal options is sampled in the final section of the
book (Part VI, Epilogue).

---

[4]John C. Calhoun, R$_x$EVOLUTION, Tribalism, and the Cheshire Cat: Three Paths from
Now," *Technological Forecasting and Social Change,* Vol. 4, 1973, pp. 263-282.

[5]H. Kahn, *The Next Two Hundred Years,* Morrow, New York, 1976, p. 32. However, see
also John C. Calhoun, "From Mice to Men," *Transactions and Studies of the College of
Physicians of Philadelphia,* Ser. 4, Vol. 41, No. 2, October 1973, pp. 92-118.

[6]Note that Allison's organizational process model has "avoidance of uncertainty" as an
organizing concept (p. 137).

ISBN 0-201-04096-4

II. 2. Future Problems or Problems in Future Studies?

JOHN McHALE

It is possible that some of the more critical aspects of emerging problems do not lie inexorably "in the future" but rather depend on present perceptions. This bias is inherent in any attempt to explore the future, but some of the unexamined premises upon which various future states are projected may indeed be problem-oriented by their very nature. This problem syndrome may, in some cases, be indicative of a deep-lying conservatism and unease regarding change. By projecting elements of present problems in this way, we can overdetermine the future and foreclose possibilities for action in the present.

Two salient points of weakness in future studies may, therefore, be suggested:

- The tendency to forecast future options and constraints on the basis of under-lying structural certainties and regularities, derived from past or present conditions, or from assumed absolutes, which are held to be relatively constant in the long-term future.
- The difficulties inherent in projecting and evaluating future changes while undergoing strong shifts in the major paradigms that organize the conceptual framework through which we make judgments regarding problems and their definition.

Some of the certainties and regularities carried forward in future projections range from assumptions regarding the functions and continuing centrality of major social institutions to the fixity of resource capacities and technologies and to those that impute universality to locally preferred values and norms.

In evaluating future problems, the structures and interrelationships of present institutions can certainly be called into question, not only in relation to their future roles but in terms of their present dysfunction. Many of our current problems — reified as occurring in the environment, in energy supply, in technology, or in the urbs — are really crises in the institutional arrangements governing these sectors. Critical attention to reorganizing such arrangements in the shorter term might solve problems more effectively than misplaced emphasis on the end impacts of their means in the longer-term future. Institutional assessment may need to come before technology assessment.

In longer-range terms, we might also ask more searching questions regarding the roles and functions of our currently central institutional forms as the major goal-setting and legitimizing agencies in society. How far, and in what proportion, will they continue to function in such ways? Agriculture until recently was an institutional sector in the United States whose attitudes and folkways colored many of

Futures Research: New Directions, Harold A. Linstone and W. H. Clive Simmonds (eds.)

ISBN 0-201-04096-4

the core values and attitudes which permeated the society. Earlier, central roles were accorded to such institutions as organized religion and hereditary aristocracies whose influences are now less central, and in some cases peripheral, as value-setting agencies in present societies. We might also speculate, in this regard, that where past societies have tended to be dominated by one calculus or measure for social or cultural worth, such measures could be more diversified in the future. Where previously, for example, military prowess, or more recently the economic calculus, was the dominant measure for evaluating individual and collective activities, we could envisage social orders in which the esthetic calculus became paramount or coequal to other measures. In a period preoccupied with the centrality of economic, political, and military power, it may be more difficult to project a society in which the striving for such power is avoided, gauged as a demonstration of gross insecurity, or where its single-minded pursuit is regarded as an eccentric abnormality.

The projection of future changes in the social order tends to be focused more on the disruption of traditional forms than on their transformation, and on the disorder and shocks which threaten established ways of life. There is an underlying anxiety and uncertainty which reflects Durkheim's question of a century ago: "When the old social order based on kinship and the tribe breaks down, what will be the elements from which the new order will be built up?"

Even given that some anxieties and uncertainties may be justified, our future-oriented answers to this kind of question are still almost exclusively focused on the range of alternatives which derive more from a mythical past than possible futures.

The models of social action upon which we operate tend to constrain future thinking within restricted and historically conditioned experience which may no longer be valid. There is a lingering set of unquestioned assumptions about the alienation, anomie, and routinization of modern society which expresses itself in many future images of stressless and well-ordered states of simple living, high thinking, and tranquility. Were it only nostalgia, it would not be too important, but more often than not, the alternatives to present and future problems are viewed in the return to previous forms of collective security, folk solidarity, and "organic" social bonds. In the projected need for order as construed, the group, the collectivity, or the great society is assumed as the saving entity through which the individual may escape the perils of anomie and alienation. Dissonance and undue diversity are to be reduced by the resumption of new conformities and frugalities imposed by the imperatives for future survival.

Apart from the uncritical acceptance of this kind of problem-oriented value indictment of modern society, there are few attempts to explore what the content and texture of social and cultural experience might be in different ranges of time and change.

The treatment of individual futures is also overconstrained by implicit assumptions regarding the invariance of human nature. There is a generalized use of concepts like dehumanization and depersonalization which imply some ultimately fixed sense of the human which various social contexts repress or distort. While we

ISBN 0-201-04096-4

may normatively frame our expectation of human behavior and the norms that should regulate it in terms of "the better" or "the good," it is necessary to recall Vickers' statement:

> Men, institutions and societies learn to want as well as how to get, what to be as well as what to do; and the two forms of adaption are closely connected. Since our ideas of regulation were formed in relation to norms which are deemed to be given, they need to be reconsidered in relation to norms which change with the effort made to pursue them.[1]

Many of our problem-oriented views of the nature of human nature over-determine and rigidify the sense of being human — not as being in continuing change but as a set of givens which restrict change. As another commentator has noted:

> The various universal models that we are offered . . . tend to be celebrations of an image of the human with which we feel most comfortable . . . to really accept the idea of a protean (diversely plural) society is also to accept the idea of protean people. Both are inseparable aspects of the same process . . . Our models of scenarios of the future must incorporate the human as a variable in the multiple sense in which that term is used.[2]

The need for closer attention to the role of underlying assumptions and structural viewpoints in problem-oriented futures work is also closely involved with the idea of paradigm change. Kuhn, in his work *The Structure of Scientific Revolutions,* describes the paradigm as the set of basic assumptions, conceptual framework, and accepted techniques which constitute a particular "world view" and thereby define and circumscribe the traditional set of beliefs and ways of exploring specific topics and fields. The prevailing paradigm supplies the criteria for identifying those problems that will be commonly worked upon and legitimizes their exploration. At a lower level of explanation, this also functions as part of those selective personal screens and latent assumptions which may not only bias our viewpoints but also preselect and identify what may or may not constitute a problem.

Many of our problems, particularly those social problems and pathologies that are often the target of future solutions may therefore be time- and culture-bound. As our paradigms change, some of the problems may also change or may no longer be regarded as problems. Many social problems — of deviance, of the breakdown of norms, of "social pathology" — are of this order; they are identified and classified as problems in one period but not necessarily in another. Many critical physical problems of energy supply, technological development, and environmental impingements are obviously time-bound and closely dependent on specific social and

---

[1] Sir Geoffrey Vickers, "The Sociology of Management," Chapman & Hall, London, 1967.

[2] William Simon, *Reflections in the Relationship between the Individuals and Society, Human Futures,* IPC Press, London, 1974, pp. 144, 146.

ISBN 0-201-04096-4

economic modes which may also be in the process of change.

The problem syndrome itself evidenced in much futures work may, indeed, be the expression of a critical period of major paradigm change when much that was familiar and relatively fixed is now in question.

Although we cannot discuss at length here what the emerging new paradigm(s) might constitute, the widespread preoccupation with the longer-term future may be a part of the pronounced change in world view now ongoing. Certainly a new awareness of change, and of the longer range and increased scale of the consequences of human action, seems part of a larger shift in human consciousness and conceptuality. There is a perceptible change in the governing set of ideas and attitudes which begins to alter interpersonal actions with the planetary habitat. It is both a temporal and a spatial shift. There is a considerable time dissonance and discontinuity which arises in part from technologies that have abruptly compressed our time and space relationships. There are a series of ongoing changes in conceptuality and experience which are both inwardly oriented, from the unraveling of the micro-life code at the molecular level to the intense re-evaluation of human purposes; and outwardly oriented, from the successful maintenance of human life beyond the earth's atmosphere and under its oceans, to the distant monitoring of other worlds and galaxies.

The pervasive qualities and complexities involved in this magnitude of paradigm change have already affected many of our perceptions, values, and attitudes and considerably modified our conceptual frameworks. There may be some time lag before their more widespread effects become evident in collective social processes and policies. Inevitably, they will influence our identification, definition, and assessment of problems in ways that are difficult to prefigure.

Given this premise of change, it becomes even more important to re-examine and reconceptualize those past and present assumptions which constitute the basis for our prevision of problems. It is not that many problems will go away or be minimized, but rather that the basis for their assessment and degrees of priority is changed and, even more important, that their locus for social action in the present may be considerably altered.

Were futures studies merely an academic exercise, many of the concerns expressed above would be interesting but not of pressing urgency. The more recent emergence of, and emphasis on, policy-oriented futures work and its support and purported use for large-scale decision-making gives them a much graver import. The implications of many of our present social, economic, and technical activities seem to enforce careful projection of their long-term effects and consequences ever further into the future. Many of our social and environmental problems appear to require the projected commitment of relatively enormous investments of human and physical energies over longer and longer time spans.

Some of the directions for the solution of currently perceived problems not only demand high risk and investment in the present but lay the major burden of the resolution of these problems as a charge on future generations. One critical area is

ISBN 0-201-04096-4

the use of current nuclear energy techniques in which the secure storage of radio-active wastes may require more than a century of strict safeguarding; recently, for example, a United States utility applied for rate increases to cover entombment of its nuclear plant some thirty years from now and its guarding for another hundred.

When such projected problem solutions are linked to large-scale social, economic, and technological planning and translated into binding political legislation and physical action, the overall connotations become more questionable. In the commitment of present resources to ever longer-range goals and purposes, we may need to give more careful consideration to amortizing the future in terms of what may be wholly temporal constraints, or economically preferred problem solutions. We need also to ask whether we can justify the sacrifice of present time and human resources to the more speculative exigencies of the future — and conversely how, in our preoccupation with solving problems within current frames of reference, we can protect the future from untoward erosion by our present actions and concerns.

One strong latent assumption which colors evaluation of work in these areas is that future inquiry, by its label, tends to be accepted as "progressive" and "open-ended." On closer attention, much may be found to be problematic in itself — as singularly past-oriented and conservative. A specific field weakness is the lack of any interval future-critical function whereby substantive assessment and judgment of ideas and work could be conducted in ongoing fashion.

ISBN 0-201-04096-4

II. 3. The Future of Culture

GEOFFREY VICKERS

The Role of Culture

By far the biggest question mark that hangs over the future is in my view the question of culture.

I use the word in its anthropologic sense to include all a society's habitual ways of perceiving itself and its situation, as well as its habitual ways of acting and expressing itself. It thus includes both its formal institutions and its shared concerns and standards of expectation, especially its standards of what each should expect from others and from himself. This body of concerns and expectations and habitual ways of appreciating its situation (whether they are institutionalized or not) are what enables a society of any kind to hang together "sufficiently." By "sufficiently" I mean sufficiently to interact as a whole with its surround to the minimal extent needed for its own survival. This in turn implies that changes in that surround and in its demands on the society will not require changes in shared standards and expectations greater than the society can achieve in the time available.

Virtually every scenario of the future assumes radical changes in relations both between political societies and within them. No scenario that I have read has examined the limitations which restrict the rate at which cultural change can move or the results of overstepping those limitations. There is, of course, a general awareness that "authoritarian" regimes tend to arise in societies that cannot change their cultures as fast as their situation requires. But a far more precise analysis is needed and is possible. Within the scope of this paper I can only indicate what it could and should include.

Theories of social cohesion have varied greatly in the importance which they have given to coercive authority; and actual societies vary greatly in the degree of coercive authority which they use to sustain themselves. But even where this is most in evidence, its legitimacy and effectiveness depend also on what I have described as its shared concerns and expectations and its habitual ways of appreciating its situation. (Indeed, authoritarian governments spend much effort in trying to create and sustain the concerns and expectations on which they need to rely.) The formal and informal aspects of culture are intimately related, and for the purpose of this paper I need not distinguish between the two. I include both formal and informal controls in the concept of culture, as anthropologists do when they explore both the institutions of a society and the accepted standards and assumptions on which these rest.

A society's institutions may be regarded as god-given or as devised by severed ancestors, the society's most precious heritage. They may be accepted as inescap-

Futures Research: New Directions, Harold A. Linstone and W. H. Clive Simmonds (eds.)

ISBN 0-201-04096-4

able or unalterable, even though often unwelcome, as men accept the climate. They may even be regarded as impositions by an alien ruler, equally inescapable though even more unwelcome. They may also be regarded as evolving, with or without the initiative of their members, and in this case they may be viewed with anything from complacency to the fervor of reform or revolution. In a large society all these attitudes may coexist in varying degrees in different subcultures. But whatever they may be, they are part of what I mean by the culture.

Similarly, the members of these societies may do what the culture requires (in so far as they do) from prudent calculation of the alternatives or from habit, reinforced, if questioned, by fear of the unknown effects of departing from it or from inward allegiance, because the individual has come to accept its demands and to expect compliance from himself, as part of his self-image and his realization of himself. These alternatives also do not exclude each other. They can coexist in many admixtures in different subcultures and even in individuals (for even the individual, unique in genetic inheritance and in experience, is a subculture of one). These differences may be crucially important in determining the coherence of a society and its capacity to accommodate cultural change. But they are in no way inconsistent with the concept of culture as I am using it.

Thus regarded, there is a genuine analogy between culture in society and the genetic code in the biological development of an individual organism. The genetic code is by no means a rigid linear program. It is sensitive to context. Organisms repair themselves, and compensate for injury by transferring functions. Transplanted parts may develop the functions which their new contexts require them to fulfill. Yet this flexibility is at the service of an inflexible ideal of biological order. The code defines how the whole ought to function. The specialisms and variations of particular parts are in the service of that built-in ideal of order.

Even that overall uniformity must be qualified when we use the scale of evolutionary time. Many mutations must have survived for countless generations before it could have become apparent what new ideal of biological order was latent in the early changes which would ultimately produce, for example, the airborne life of the swift. The only "mutations" which we may be sure were never adaptive were those that involved cancerous proliferation rather than ordered growth. Biology knows more varieties of order than the societies of men have ever produced. But biological, like social, development reveals the difference between all the varieties of sustainable order and the formless disorder of mere proliferation.

The History of Culture

Analogies are never complete. If culture be regarded as a society's encoded directions for reproducing and sustaining its form, its differences from biological coding will strike the modern eye far more than its similarities. Its mechanisms for transmission, besides being totally different in character, are far less strong. Its capacity for change is far greater. It even admits some scope for self-designed change — or at least it encourages in modern men an insuperable urge to behave as

ISBN 0-201-04096-4

if this were so.

The contrast is less sharp when we consider primitive societies. Through all but the last 1% or 2% of our existence as a species, men have subsisted in loose associations of families, of which some examples (such as the Australian aborigines) still survive. Such groups demonstrated by their survival that they had found a way to win their support from their environment, even where (as with the Eskimos) their regular yearly pattern included huge seasonal variations. Their own numbers and technology were not sufficient to change the milieu. Except — a big exception — when they collided with another human group seeking to destroy or replace them or to share their resources, the relation between the society and its milieu could remain unchanged for centuries.

Internal relations tended to be equally stable. Technological change was too slow to disturb them. Social changes were opposed by the prestige as well as the inertia of tried and trusted custom, often supported by mythological and religious sanctions. Moreover, the experience of life was so similar and so widely shared by every member of the tribe that its culture invited no thought of deviance.

Social order, in these simple societies, looked and felt — and *was* — more like biological order than is easily conceivable today. It was a datum to which individuals adapted, as their society had adapted to its milieu.

When the first great civilizations made possible the accumulation of wealth, the concentration of power, and the division of function, the cultural pattern became more complex, but powerful forces existed to keep all its elements within a single cultural framework. The rich, the powerful, and the skilled acquired special status which they often exploited. But the framework of positions with complementary rights and duties, which constituted society, was accepted by most people at most times as the way things were, inescapable if not beyond criticism, and in any case an order far better than disorder.

Contemporary Western Culture

I have traced elsewhere the steps by which in the West the concepts of social order as evolving and as designed invaded the older concept of order as given; and I have suggested that all three concepts have their place and find their limitations within the concept of systemic order. I have also observed that all Western societies for the last two hundred years (an epoch which I regard as abruptly ending now) have exaggerated the scope for design open to their societies in the social no less than the technological field, and at the same time have fallen further short than they might have done of what might have been their more modest objectives. I have attributed this to their lack of understanding of systemic limitations. This understanding is now dawning austerely and rapidly in the technological field. It is far less in evidence and far more needed in the cultural field.

In the technological field it is becoming accepted that no one can change state A into state B without affecting countless other states which may be of equal or greater importance to others or even to himself. Sometimes such projects fail even by their own criteria. State B when achieved does not realize the hopes that were attached to it. Such, I understand, is the common judgment on the St. Lawrence Seaway. Sometimes, although the benefits of state B come up to expectations, its hidden costs set far greater and more insoluble problems than those which were solved by attaining it. This will, I think, prove true of the multiplication of atomic energy plants with its ancillary production of plutonium and its growing mass of radioactive waste. But these fears seldom inhibit the project.

It is even harder, and as yet far less familiar, to count the costs, benefits, and limitations of cultural change. Consider, for example, the cultural changes involved in developing ideas of distributive justice.

Western countries today are obsessed by problems of distributive justice, both internationally and intranationally.

Intranationally, they have learned to redistribute 40% to 50% of their national product among their citizens, either by the unconditional transfer of income or by the provision of common services which necessarily benefit users in shares quite unrelated to their share in the cost of providing them. But they have not yet learned to understand, still less to deal with, the cultural repercussions of this change.

Internationally only the Scandanavian countries have achieved anything like the standard of unrequited transfer (under 1%) established by the United Nations. And the use, even of what is so transferred, is restricted by the cultures, as well as the political competence, of most receiving nations. Here again it is useful to reflect what *cultural* changes in both giving and receiving nations would be needed to make any kind of unrequited redistribution of resources possible internationally on a significant scale.

It is easy to state the answer in general terms. In all the examples cited, effective action would require a huge widening in the boundary between "I" and "not-I," and between "now" and "not yet," in the cultural consciousness of all whose support is significant in the making and changing of policy. More exactly, it would require a much livelier realization of the multiple systems of which each of us is in fact a part and a great extension of the time horizon within which we can attach reality to the future course of those systems.

It would also require a hugely increased acceptance by all concerned of the constraints which the new policies will involve — constraints which may be felt as constraints of obligation arising either from a new and accepted view of the situation or from a greatly increased acceptance of obedience to those in seats of power — or both.

A more interdependent world must obviously be a world of much greater constraint or much greater conflict or both — greater constraint in so far as individuals accept the demands of interdependence; greater conflict in so far as they do not. Western culture is peculiarly unfitted for such a change because it has been nourished for two centuries on the myth that more interdependence means more freedom to the individual to do as he pleases. The opposite is manifestly the truth. But the illusion had some historical justification.

ISBN 0-201-04096-4

So long as rights and duties were distributed with huge disparity and economic potential was greatly underdeveloped, societies that were developing economically could also develop socially and politically, in such a way that for the many freedom and interdependence did indeed increase together. Opinions may differ on the question of whether this process has wholly come to an end, but I can imagine no logical ground for withholding assent to the proposition that greater factual interdependence can be sustained only by accepting greater mutual responsibilities, and that every increase in equality will spread the burden of constraint and responsibility more evenly and more widely.

Central to the culture of every tribe ever explored by an anthropologist are its answers to two questions: "Who is my neighbor?" and "What is my duty to him?" The wider the definition of "neighbor" the greater — and usually also the more conflicting — becomes the load of "duties," even if the duties do not themselves increase in variety. And of course they do increase in variety, as well as in volume. Even within a single Western country, local governments today perform a host of functions designed to discharge collective duties to a host of disadvantaged "neighbors" which a century ago were no business of government and largely beyond the scope of any individual. Their achievements are beyond the dreams of our grandfathers; but they have not generated a marked sense of duty done, either in the doers or in the recipients. Escalating expectations constantly outstrip performance and now have to come to terms with falling resources. The whole concept of "service delivery" may be coming to the end of its useful life (as others beside Ivan Illich have suggested). Yet today's acceptance of responsibility and its measure of realization both fall short of the minimum needed to maintain any kind of order in the world which is already with us, internationally and in many cases intranationally.

It is possible, of course, to question whether a species biologically endowed and evolved as ours is capable of sustaining any kind of social order on its crowded planet. It is possible, but it is not useful. We have to do the best we can. The situation admits of at least three responses, all of which are abundantly in evidence now. I have space only to mention them. The first two, though in part contradictory, can, I believe, become complementary to some extent — and need to do so, if we are to minimize the threat from the third.

Uncoupling

One response to such a world would be predictable even if evidence for it were not proliferating around us daily. This is the response of *uncoupling*. We cannot avoid the demands of an increasingly interdependent world, but we should minimize them when and where we can. Neither Sweden nor Britain, for example, is an isolated country. But Sweden has far greater scope to go its own way because it is economically independent. Its standard of living, higher than Britain's, reflects the value of what it produces. Britain, by contrast, has come to rely on a standard of living so much higher than its real earnings that it is sustained only by the

ISBN 0-201-04096-4

astonishing readiness of foreigners to lend it money, thus increasing its disequilib-
rium by every step taken to support it. "The stability of the internal milieu is the
condition of free and independent life." So wrote the French biologist Claude
Bernard at the beginning of the nineteenth century. He was describing the progress
made by those species (commonly called "warm-blooded") that have learned how
to maintain an internal blood temperature constant within a few degrees while the
temperature of the air about them ranges over anything up to a hundred degrees.
Few statements, true in their own context, have been capable of so many true
applications to fields far outside their own. Every political state today is concerned
as never before with the stability of its "milieu intérieur." Many are torn by
demand for devolution or fission, devised to create smaller systems more capable
of maintaining their own stability even at a lower level of economic prosperity.
Such demands may be cogent and timely. None should be dismissed as contrary
to the tide of contemporary history. On the contrary, they are its most revealing
manifestation.

They are none the less ambivalent. Are they recursions to a size more capable of
the coherence needed today by political systems — needed no less for effective
international cooperation than for internal stability? Or are they symptoms of a
decay of culture for which they offer no logical stopping point — that decay which
in the name of self-determination at one level and self-actualization at another
demands the dissolution even of those cultural bonds that give coherence to the
individual (that "subculture of one") and produce the alienation of the divided
self? Even when they achieve the coherence at which they aim, it is sometimes at
the cost of impoverishing external relations and often at the cost of internal perse-
cution of all who, by reason of race, creed, or color, do not fit the stereotype of
the in-group. It is nonetheless a development potent for good as well as ill.

Shared and Complementary Cultures

Cultures are not coextensive with national or linguistic frontiers, and it is regarded by some as a hopeful sign that so many people today participate in cultural
systems with very different boundaries. The scientist shares an international
culture with other scientists which may focus his loyalties more sharply than his
political or linguistic culture. The ancient cultural bond of language is becoming
more widespread, though it may be weakening in consequence. Both the English-
speaking and (still more) the French-speaking worlds today include African peoples
whose cultural roots are far removed from those of the peoples whose language
they speak. Much has been made of the "barrier of a common tongue"; and every
Englishman and American who visits the other's country often is likely to discover,
with time, more, rather than less, cultural differences between them. But the
common speech at least makes the discovery easier.

A variety of cultures may share common elements from a common heritage,
such as that shared by the ultimate successors to the Roman Empire. Equally, they
may develop common elements through the impact of common situations as may

ISBN 0-201-04096-4

conceivably occur in the European Economic Community. Even debates in the constituent bodies of the United Nations (such as the long-drawn debate on the meaning of "aggression") help to reveal differences of cultural evaluation, even if they do not make them narrower. A common world culture seems to me to be neither a possible nor a desirable dream; but we can at least hope for a world in which diverse cultures share more elements than they now do — especially the acceptance of common *constraints* — and understand far better the differences between those elements that are not shared.

Cultural Vacuum

By far the greatest danger that threatens the cultural future seems to me to be an increasing cultural vacuum.

A culture seldom prescribes either comprehensively or consistently all the attitudes, standards, and assumptions of people living together in a society. Where its voice is weak or silent, there is more scope for individual artistry — and individual cluelessness — in the shaping of individual and social life. In most Western countries the area left unstructured by culture has greatly widened in recent decades. Family relations, work relations, and civic relations lack the relatively firm structure of norms which shaped them a few decades ago. To some extent these have been replaced by a wider and deeper understanding and acceptance of principles governing the playing of more fluid roles with greater sensitivity to context, the felt need to understand the individual person and situation without premature stereotyping. This is a cultural change with promise as well as danger. To some extent, on the other hand, it sanctions a claim to freedom from any cultural restraint in "doing one's own thing," and a corresponding cultural injunction on others to "mind their own business."

The second represents what I am describing as a cultural vacuum. It can be viewed either as a breakdown or as a distortion of culture. I have already argued that an increasingly interdependent world is a world which can afford an ever-smaller area where each individual is free to go his way indifferent to his neighbors. It is significant and sinister that in our age the plea "none of my business" is so often heard. (Men can be kicked to death in public places without exciting in by-standers a sense that it is "their business" to do something about it). Freedom to do one's own thing need not necessarily breed this indifference. But the two seem currently to be growing together.

Conclusion

I conclude that the world's future depends not so much on economic or political revolutions, and still less on technological revolutions, as on a cultural revolution on a scale which has never yet been attempted or imagined, but which it is our duty to attempt even though we may be biologically unfit to achieve it sufficiently in the time available. It is an educational task — or rather it would be if we gave educa-

ISBN 0-201-04096-4

tion more adequate meaning, designing every aspect of life so that we can learn its lessons instead of being shielded against them. It is difficult, formidable, and inspiring. I have no idea of how my own or other countries, Western or otherwise, will rise to its demands, but I feel at least one certainty about it.

It should not be — as it usually now is — forgotten, ignored, or brushed under the carpet.*

*Editor's Note: It is significant that the futures-oriented industrialist Aurelio Peccei, founder of the Club of Rome, has independently come to a similarly drastic conclusion:

"There cannot be any salvation, unless people themselves change their values, mores, and behavior for the better. The real problem of the human species . . . is that it has not been able culturally to keep pace with, and thus fully adjust to, the changed realities which it itself has brought about . . . It is only by developing adequately human quality and capacities all over the world that our material civilization can be transformed . . . This is the human revolution, which is more urgent than anything else if we are to control the other revolutions of our time . . ."

("The Human Quality," Pergamon Press, Oxford, 1977, p. xi.)

ISBN 0-201-04096-4

II. 4. On the Error of the Third Kind

Toward a Generalized Methodology for Future Studies

IAN I. MITROFF

The Fundamental Problems of TF: Finding and Solving the Right Problem

We are at a turning point, if not a crisis point, in the present course of future studies. We have before us a clear choice of either facing up to the "fundamental" problem underlying technological forecasting (TF) or of continuing to ignore it. In the opinion of this author, the fundamental problem of TF is *not* that of building bigger and better forecasting devices (technologies) to predict future trends or events with greater accuracy. The goal of accuracy presupposes that we already know what the appropriate questions are that we should be addressing to the future. The (at times) seemingly obsessive concern with accuracy presupposes that the fundamental problem lies with securing the answers to already known or pre-existent questions. I believe that just the opposite is the case. The problem lies with the questions themselves, not with the answers. If a comprehensive and generalized methodology for TF is ever to be realized, then it is my belief that it basically has to do with the discovery of a process for learning how to pose and to ask the right questions. In an even more basic sense, it has to do with learning how to recognize, formulate, solve, and finally implement the "correct" solution to the "right" problem.[1,2]

On the Elements of a Holistic Theory of Problem Finding and Problem Solving

We have no reason to expect that a generalized and comprehensive methodology for TF in particular and for problem finding in general will either be simple in its constitution or easy in its attainment. Indeed, I believe that more and more of us are beginning to suspect that one of the major reasons why such a methodology has been so long and hard in coming is that it fundamentally cuts across the most diverse and disparate of academic disciplines and research traditions. To paraphrase an appropriate aphorism of Russell L. Ackoff,[3] the problems of the real world are not organized in the same way that the problems of the academic disciplines are. Real-world problems are neither identical with nor do they map neatly on to the problems of the separate academic disciplines.

---

[1] I. I. Mitroff and T. R. Featheringham, "On Systemic Problem Solving and the Error of the Third Kind," *Behavioral Science,* Vol. 19, November 1974, pp. 383-393.

[2] I. I. Mitroff and M. Turoff, "On Measuring the Conceptual Errors in Large Scale Social Experiments: The Future as Decision," *Technological Forecasting and Social Change,* Vol. 6, 1974, pp. 389-402.

[3] R. L. Ackoff, "Toward an Idealized University," *Management Science,* Vol. 15, 1970, pp. B-121-B-131.

Futures Research: New Directions, Harold A. Linstone and W. H. Clive Simmonds (eds.)

ISBN 0-201-04096-4

Real-world problems are systemic and holistic in their nature.[4,5] This means that they can neither be simply nor be easily broken down to fit the modes of representation and analysis of any of the separate disciplines without an essential aspect of the problem being lost or distorted. Real-world problems are all-too-"messy"[4] combinations of elements taken from all the disciplines currently known, if indeed they are not something "vitally more" beyond the current disciplines. Indeed, that vital "something more" always seems to get lost when we treat important problems as if they were merely (or, what amounts to the same thing, essentially) "economic," "political," "psychological," "philosophical," "technical," etc.[5]

Can we find a way then of treating problems so that we can satisfy two equally important and yet at the same time strongly competing (if not opposing) demands? The first demand is that of breaking a problem down into constituent parts or components so that we can then proceed to analyze it. Indeed, this first demand has become so natural and so prevalent that to break a problem down has become virtually synonymous with the notion of analysis. The second demand embodies the notion of putting the parts back together again. It is, however, much more than this. It not only means putting the parts back together again; it also means recognizing that the original "parts" have no natural existence, let alone meaning, independently of the original "whole" of which they are a part. Most of all it means approaching a problem in a spirit that attempts to preserve, as much as is humanly possible, the essential wholeness of the problem.[4,5]

It would be presumptuous in the extreme to claim to have found such a methodology. What I would like to do instead is to share some of the work that my close colleagues and I have been engaged in which we hope is leading toward such a methodology — i.e., a methodology for forming real-world problems. The confines of a limited paper unfortunately prevent me from talking about anything more than the following four elements of the methodology. It should thus be strictly understood that there are many more elements than the following. Limitations also prevent me from talking about the elements in any detail. The elements are:

- A typology of fundamentally different kinds of problems.
- A typology of fundamentally different kinds of problems solvers or problem modelers.
- A typology of fundamentally different kinds of methodologies for modeling problems.
- A decision mechanism or adjudicating procedure based on the concept of E_{III}, the error of the third kind, for choosing which problem to solve as proposed by a particular modeling methodology, as in turn proposed by a particular problem solver.

---

[4]R. L. Ackoff, *Redesigning the Future,* John Wiley & Sons, New York, 1975.

[5]C. W. Churchman, *The Design of Inquiring Systems,* Basic Books, New York, 1971.

ISBN 0-201-04096-4

In short, the contention is that anything pretending to be a comprehensive methodology for TF must at an absolute minimum deal with the following: problems, solvers, methodologies, and a decision mechanism. Not only has the field of TF in general lost sight of this "fact," but particular forecasting techniques have been especially derelict. What one technique treats in excruciating detail, another blandly takes for granted. For example, although I personally regard the Delphi technique[6] as an important advance worthy of continued investigation, use, and development, it is in my terms only one example of a rather special and limited class of methodologies for modeling future problems.[7] In its original and classic formulation, Delphi says little about the kinds of problems and problem solvers for which it is most appropriate. As a result, it presupposes, without its knowing it, a particular class of problems and problem solvers. Whatever the ultimate merits of such techniques, the time is long overdue to make explicit the philosophical and methodological presuppositions upon which the field of TF rests.[7]

Different Problems for Different Problem Solvers

Table 1 represents a very brief summary of some of the major dimensions that my colleagues and I[8] have found useful for categorizing a wide variety of problems. Since the typology directly follows from an application of Jungian personality theory applied to problem solving (as described in a previous article[8]), the table is also a direct representation of different personality types — i.e., of how different types of problem solvers look at the world. We have found as a general rule that different personality types not only prefer to work on fundamentally different kinds of problems but also that, when given the opportunity to mold a common problem from scratch, they formulate the very same problem in very different terms. For example, we have found that Jung's[9] Sensing-Thinking types not only prefer to work on operational-technical problems but, even stronger, to cast all problems into the mold of an operational-technical format. This style of problem forming and problem solving is governed by the search for *an* optional or best solution *within* the tight constraints of a *single, well-defined,* and *precise* formulation of the problem or paradigm. Above all, this style values consistency, logic, precision, technology, and an impersonal, dispassionate approach as *the* approach to *all* problems.

In a similar vein, Jung's Sensing-Feeling types tend to prefer operational-social

---

[6]H. A. Linstone and M. Turoff, *The Delphi Method: Techniques and Applications,* Addison-Wesley, Reading, Massachusetts, 1975.

[7]I. I. Mitroff and M. Turoff, "Technological Forecasting and Assessment: Science and/or Mythology?" *Technological Forecasting and Social Change,* Vol. 5, 1973, pp. 113-134.

[8]I. I. Mitroff and R. Kilmann, "On Evaluating Scientific Research: The Contribution of the Psychology of Science," *Technological Forecasting and Social Change,* Vol. 8, 1975, pp. 163-174.

[9]C. G. Jung, *Psychological Types,* Routledge & Kegan Paul, London, 1923.

ISBN 0-201-04096-4

Table 1
A Typology of Problems

		Type of Structure and Time Decision	
		Operational – Current	Strategic – Future
Type of Content and Subject Matter	Technical, Technological, Scientific	**Operational – Technical** Search for an optimal or best technical solution within a single-problem format within the constraints of given technology; short-time horizon; adherence to the critical standards of a single discipline; continual imposition of fixed structure on the phenomenon underlying the problem; the problem is *judged* to be essentially operational and technical in character.	**Strategic – Technical** Search for alternative solutions within multiple-problem formats outside the constraints of current technology and thinking; long-time horizon; adherence to the critical standards of no one single discipline; continual perturbing of the imposition of fixed structure on the phenomenon underlying the problem; the problem is *judged* to be essentially strategic and technical in character.
	Social, Moral, Political	**Operational – Social** Search for an optimal or best social solution within a single-problem format within the constraints of given societal institutions and customs; short-time horizon; adherence to the critical standards of a single discipline, continual imposition of fixed structure on the phenomenon underlying the problem; the problem is *judged* to be essentially operational and social in character.	**Strategic – Social** Search for alternative solutions within multiple-problem formats outside the constraints of current social institutions, thinking, and customs; long-time horizon; adherence to the critical standards of no one single discipline; continual perturbing of the imposition of fixed structure on the phenomenon underlying the problem; the problem is *judged* to be essentially strategic and social in character.

ISBN 0-201-04096-4

problems. With the major exception of his concern for people, feelings, and values, this approach tends to be the same as the Sensing-Thinking type's. There is the same emphasis on consistency and precision, on working within a single well-understood and widely accepted formulation of the problem or research paradigm. The main difference is that, where the Sensing-Thinking type musters consistency and precision in favor of a technical or logical approach to the problem, the Sensing-Feeling type musters these same virtues in favor of a personal or moral approach to the problem. Whereas Thinking types tend to see and hence to stress the technical features of problems, Feeling types tend to see and hence to stress the people, the personal, the moral, and the value features of problems.

Jung's Intuition-Thinking and Intuition-Feeling types prefer, respectively, to work on strategic-technical and strategic-social approaches to problem solving. The emphasis in both cases is on a broad, global approach to problems. It is not on exploring a problem in depth from *within* the confines of a single point of view or paradigm, but rather it is on examining how a problem looks and changes in character as we shift *between* paradigms and points of view.

To summarize briefly, operational problem solvers are strongly oriented to perceiving and to formulating all problems as well-structured problems.[8,10] In the extreme, this means that something is a problem if and only if it possesses a precise and unambiguous solution *within* a single and tight formulation of the problem. Problems or issues that are perceived of as ambiguous or subject to sharply conflicting opinions tend (again, in the extreme) to be rejected as problems that can be subjected to scientific analysis. Strategic problem solvers, on the other hand, tend to perceive and to formulate all problems as ill-structured. In the extreme, this means that something is a problem if and only if it changes drastically in character as we move *between* different formulations of the problem. In short, operational problem solvers are "within-schema" *solvers,* whereas strategic problem solvers are "between-schema" *formulators* or problem *finders.* Operational problem solvers stress the "solving" side of the inquiry process, whereas strategic problem solvers stress the "finding" side.

It was with the preceding distinctions in mind that Ralph Kilmann, Murray Turoff, Tom Featheringham, and I[1,2,8] formulated the concept of E_{III}, the Error of the Third Kind – i.e., the "probability of solving the 'wrong' problem when one should have solved the 'right' problem." At this point, without going into the technical details as to how one might possibly compute a value for E_{III} in a particular instance,[1,2] the important thing is that the concept of E_{III} leads one to raise the following basic questions: *How* does one decide in a specific case whether something is an operational-technical problem versus, say, a strategic-behavioral problem? *Who* should do the deciding; under *which* circumstances? If problems are a direct reflection of the particular type who defines them, to which type does one turn in order to define the "right" problem? And, lastly, what can the term

---

[10]I. I. Mitroff, *The Subjective Side of Science: A Philosophical Inquiry into the Psychology of the Apollo Moon Scientists,* Elsevier, Amsterdam, 1974.

ISBN 0-201-04096-4

"right" possibly mean in such a process?

Without pretending that there are necessarily definitive "answers" to these questions, the first thing to note is that an assessment of the type-three error can be made only at the strategic level of problem solving. That is, even if one gives up the notion that there is some absolute "right" or "wrong" formulation of a problem, the computation of E_{III} demands that we compare at least two diverse formulations of the same problem. In this minimal sense, a strategic attitude toward problem solving is absolutely necessary. This does not mean, however, that the operational attitudes are unnecessary. In making an assessment of E_{III}, all four approaches to problem solving are absolutely necessary.

In any particular problem, it is not a case of one of the four approaches being right, and the others thereby being wrong. Rather, it is a case of relative emphasis. Real-world problems are complicated mixtures of all four perspectives. Instead of problems being *either* well-structured *or* ill-structured, all problems have their well-structured and their ill-structured aspects. Examining a problem from all four perspectives not only allows one to engage in an explicit comparative analysis as to the underlying nature of the problem, but also allows one to make a determination with regard to the relative degree of structure of the problem.

Most important of all, we have found that examining a problem from four very different perspectives allows for integrated synthetic perspectives to emerge.[8] Further, we have also found that these integrated perspectives are not only more likely to emerge in the first place but to be accepted in the second place *if* they are first preceded by the four pure problem-solving perspectives in Table 1. That is, we have found that problem solvers not only need to be made consciously aware of their own perspective (e.g., how deeply ingrained in it they are, how much they take it for granted, how they overlook and depreciate other perspectives, etc.) but that they need to be made aware of other perspectives and to be given explicit training in those other perspectives. To this end, we have evolved a program for training problem solvers to appreciate other perspectives.[8] The nature of the program is such that it not only works in the laboratory but it also works in the field — i.e., in real organizations facing all-too-real practical problems. We have applied the program to such diverse problems as strategic planning for a large government bureau and having business executives examine the issue of corporate bribery from a dialectical perspective.[11,12]

This leads us directly to a discussion of the important issue of who should dictate a choice of the problem. The answer quite properly is, "all the types." None of the types ought to be excluded from the decision process. The failure to include all the types in any important situation means that in all likelihood vital

---

[11]I. I. Mitroff, R. Kilmann, D. Smethers, and R. Buchholz, "Corporate Bribes: Their Necessity, Desirability and Usefulness — A Dialectical Policy Analysis," *California Management Review*, 1978.

[12]R. O. Mason, "A Dialectical Approach to Strategic Planning," *Management Science*, Vol. 15, 1969, pp. B-403-B-414.

ISBN 0-201-04096-4

aspects of the problem will be overlooked.

Instead of asking the question *who* should choose, the question *how* the choice should be made may actually be more important. If anything, our preliminary work suggests that the choice of a problem, its formulation, its solution, and its final implementation ought to be made by decision makers who are appreciative of all four perspectives. This does not require that a problem solver give up his or her preferred style with all its subsequent strengths. What it does require is that they be prepared to broaden their perspectives so that they can compensate for their weaknesses – in effect, their blind spots.

The Error of the Third Kind and Beyond

It would be a serious mistake to regard the preceding discussion as a mere qualitative prelude to the "real essence" of E_{III} – i.e., as a quantitative concept. Although the quantitative development of E_{III} is important, if only for the reason that it lends needed precision and structure to the concept, it cannot be over-emphasized that E_{III} not only originated out of a basic qualitative notion but that the qualitative notion still remains of paramount importance. While the quantitative notion is helpful for clarifying and expanding on the initial qualitative notion, the quantitative expression remains lifeless (an abstract formalism) if its fundamental qualitative underpinnings are lost sight of.

Consider the matter as follows: E_{III} is defined as "the probability of solving the 'wrong' problem when one should have solved the 'right' problem."[1,2] In previous papers, my colleagues and I have shown that E_{III} can be computed by considering the probability (P) of the difference between the relative expected values $[V(S)]$ of different formulations of the same problem. That is, we commit one form of a type-three error if we say the relative expected values of the two problem formulations are the same, $V(S_1) = V(S_2)$, when in fact they are not – i.e., when in fact $V(S_1) \neq V(S_2)$. We commit another form of E_{III} if we say $V(S_1) \neq V(S_2)$, when in fact $V(S_1) = V(S_2)$. The fundamental importance of the qualitative underpinnings of E_{III} becomes apparent as soon as we examine the nature of $V(S_1)$ or $V(S_2)$.

The term $V(S)$ is defined as $\sum\limits_{i}^{n} \sum\limits_{j}^{m} P_i E_{ij} V_j$, where P_i represents the probability with which a decision-maker (dm) chooses a course of action (C_i) by which to obtain an objective O_j of value V_j to dm. E_{ij} represents the probability of obtaining O_j by means of C_i – i.e., $E_{ij} = P(O_j/C_i)$. The crucial point is that $V(S)$, and hence both $V(S_1)$ and $V(S_2)$, depend on *how many* potential courses of action (or solutions) and *which ones* (i.e., their character) a dm "perceives" *within* a particular formulation of a problem $[V(S_1)$ or $V(S_2)]$ as well as *between* varying formulations of the same problem. In many senses, the quantitative treatment of E_{III} is only an explicit "tagging" or scoring system for keeping track of how a dm orders his qualitative views.

None of this is meant to underestimate the importance of quantitative analyses.

ISBN 0-201-04096-4

Indeed, as someone who struggled long and hard to find an appropriate quantitative treatment of E_{III}, I think I can personally testify to the personal satisfaction and gains that are derived from quantitative analysis. The point is, however: When will we realize that quantitative tools are only as good as the qualitative concepts underlying them? When will we appreciate that quantity and quality are only opposite sides of the same coin and that neither is complete without the other? In short, will we ever come to realize that a comprehensive methodology for TF will never be forthcoming until we learn how to develop equally both its qualitative and its quantitative aspects?

The most general error is not just that of solving the wrong problem but that of solving the wrong problem at the wrong time in the wrong organization or institutional context by the wrong person. There are more errors between heaven and TF than we have even begun to dream of.

ISBN 0-201-04096-4

II. 5. Values and Futures

DENIS J. LOVERIDGE

The most singular and deepest themes in the history of the Universe and Mankind to which all the rest are subordinate, are those in which there is a conflict between Belief and Unbelief, and all epochs wherein Belief prevails under what form it will, are splendid, heart-elevating and fruitful. All epochs on the contrary, where Unbelief, in what form soever, maintains its sorry victory, should they even for a moment glitter with a sham splendour, vanish from the eyes of Prosperity, because no one chooses to burden himself with a study of the unfruitful.

Goethe

It's a Funny Thing. This growing thing — we talk about growing up but as soon as we grow up we grow old, we grow fat, or we grow thin. The common factor in growing is that we consciously or unconsciously, and whether we like it or not, are changing all the time. To be alive is to be in a process of change.

That is true not only of the physical body but of ideas and convictions, character and personality. Obviously there are continuing areas of conviction and certainty but even these change in expression and in depth of assurance.

Colin Cooper

Introduction

The role of the individual, and the way he or she relates to the lack of structure, which typifies futures problems, is vital to futures thinking and to creating possible futures. The relationship the futures researcher develops toward unstructured problems tends to be highly individual and poses acute demands on communication. This paper sets out to explore some of these features of relating and communicating, which lead to the formulation of policy and action.

Purpose of Futures Research

No one has yet offered a satisfying definition of futures research, which leaves it a concept of infinite variety with a basic intent — to influence the future of whatever is being considered.

Futures thinking, or futures research as it is presently and more respectably called, has suffered much disbelief, no small amount of ridicule, and an inordinate amount of misunderstanding in what it (and the researcher) tries to do. Futures research seeks to raise, in the present, believable, interrelated issues that may occur in the future; these set present possibilities for development in a wider context, and

Futures Research: New Directions, Harold A. Linstone and W. H. Clive Simmonds (eds.)

ISBN 0-201-04096-4

longer time frame, than usual. The emphasis is on the interconnectedness of events
and the synthesis of information into forces for change, which can give rise to a
spectrum of possible futures. Historicism then forms a single, special case of the
holistic mode of inquiry (closely aligned to Churchman's Singerian mode of
inquiry[1]) which futures research requires. In this sense futures research is concerned with the derivation of what "ought" to be in human affairs and should not
be confused with what "can" and "will" happen, which are the realms of strategic
and tactical planning.

Futures research can be conducted only from a base of what is known and
events that are judged to be possible but highly uncertain. By synthesizing this
information into more, or less, likely conjunctions of events, at some points in the
future, a spectrum of conjectures about the future can be created. However
imaginative these conjectures may be, or however comprehensive the methodology,
futures research cannot forecast events that depend on the completely unknown or
the unimaginable.[2]

A corollary of synthesizing future possibilities from unbounded conjecture is
that the full set of outcomes remains unknown and the certainty that any single
outcome will occur is low. In probabilistic terms this implies that the sum of the
probabilities for a set of outcomes cannot reach one.[3] Since there is no way of
formally structuring these problems, they may be termed "unstructured."

However, working with unstructured problems ultimately requires the delinea-
tion of a boundary, outside of which events are considered too weakly related to
have any effect in the context of the inquiry. Boundary setting is a highly
individual, philosophical, and psychological process. While the researcher may
repeatedly widen (or narrow) the boundaries as more is learned concerning the
unstructured problem, he must at some point agree on a boundary with his client.
The difficulty of doing so should not be underestimated.

By its nature and purpose, futures research constitutes the forward-looking part
of a continuum of thought, starting with the past and moving through the present
into the future. The criticism often made that futures research is pure speculation
(much of it arises through confusing prediction and forecasting) does not stand up
well when it is realized that history, which is questioned far less than it should be,
is the record of perception, observation, and judgment of scholars either at the time
of, or sometimes very much later than, the events themselves. Human perception,
observation, and judgment are not noted for their infallibility. Since perception,
observation, and judgment are common to both historical and futures research,

---

[1]C. West Churchman, *The Design of Inquiring Systems; Basic Concepts of Systems and Organizations,* Basic Books, New York, 1971.

[2]At this point it is necessary to distinguish, as the dictionary does, between *prediction,* which implies exactitude in the time, nature, and magnitude of future events, and *forecasting,* which deals in uncertainty, conjecture, and a spectrum of possibilities. Futures research recongizes only the latter.

[3]W. H. C. Simmonds, "The Nature of Futures Problems," paper presented to Science Policy Research Unit, University of Sussex, 1975 (Part I of this volume).

ISBN 0-201-04096-4

those who place so much emphasis on history as a precedent for the future might do well to inquire into the real nature of history. However, history has its living image in the cultures of the present time, represented by the behavior of individuals and groups in the present. In this sense history gives each generation an inheritance of behavior which, to some degree, determines that generation's ability to perceive future possibilities. Perceiving future possibilities is a widely distributed ability, but the futures researcher has a special responsibility for seeing that the process is well understood in its relationship to the choices society may make from a spectrum of possibilities — what "ought" to be in human affairs, as the cornerstone of viable policy making and of action.

A Concept of Behavior Related to Futures Research

The present discussion comments on the relationship between behavior and the nature of future problems.

A relatively simple model can be used to develop a behavioral relationship between the futures researcher and the unstructured problems he deals with; it embodies values, norms, information, and genetic inheritance, a set that spans the individual from his psychological to his physiological development and, in communication, from the metaphysical to the physical. Each of the three terms values, norms, and information has its own semantic characteristics of evaluation, potency, and activity;[4] each of these same three terms has also been at the heart of debates stemming from rival behavioral theories. What, then, would be acceptable meanings of these terms for the futures researcher? In the set of terms values, norms, information, and genetic inheritance, only the latter stands out as having unequivocal meaning; however, the set as a whole should indicate, not so much that the researcher has "free will," but how the researcher will learn to perceive unstructured problems and to conjecture future possibilities, through processes of environmental learning and thought, where a synthesis of many streams occurs with a Gestalt outcome.

For the futures researcher values may be considered as general, but explicit, and norms as specific and tacit standards in the human world of relating.[5] An individual's value set is characterized more by an absence of doubt, revealed by questioning concerning fundamentals such as freedom or order, independence or interdependence, and so on, than by stated belief. A value set is not immutable or mutually exclusive, is time-dependent, and may be in a highly dynamic state. Norms are clearly dynamic and, though tacit, they are used in advertising, pressure group actions, and other forms of interpersonal relating, to seek to modify or reinforce existing norms; in this sense the process is one of conditioning through mutual persuasions. The relationship between values and norms is highly dynamic,

---

[4]C. E. Osgood, "Probing Subjective Culture. Part 1: Cross-Linguistic Tool-Making," *Journal of Communication,* Winter 1974, pp. 21-35.

[5]Sir Geoffrey Vickers, *Making Institutions Work,* Associated Business Programmes Ltd., London, and Halsted Press, New York, 1973.

ISBN 0-201-04096-4

and it is often difficult to distinguish between the two.

Every individual carries around much acquired information which is not, at any particular time, related to values and norms directly. Characteristically this information is physical and often numerical, such as the numbering system of a housing estate, octane ratings for petrol and the telephone numbering system. Values and norms can quickly work on such information when, for example, a value of communication (or noncommunication) is created, followed by the norm (expectation) of a telephone system, allied to the value of freedom, which yields the norm of choice to have (or not to have) a telephone. Up to that point telephone numbering is unused information; then having a telephone number rapidly becomes a norm once the choice of having a telephone has been created.

Finally there is genetic inheritance, which governs the physiology of the individual, including the size of the brain, sex, hormone balance, and other physical states of functioning, which influence the capacity for thought and experience.

The crude expression of an individual's behavior pattern, as entirely related to external experience, is insufficient to explain thinking about either the past or the future or of their expression in language; none of these can be experienced externally. Perception of the present, which is an historical inheritance, and of future possibilities, depends on achieving a mismatch between internal and external experience; without this, the present and the future are simply continuations of an uncertain past. The root of the mismatch lies in internal experience (commonly imagination); the more unbounded this is, the greater the mismatch and more widely are problems and possibilities perceived. This may be a simple truism perhaps, but one which has been under great attack from the rational-logical culture of recent years, typified perhaps by "rational economic man."

The reason for proposing a behavior pattern based on values, norms, information, and genetic inheritance now becomes clear. The researcher's perception of an "unstructured" problem will depend on what his current behavior pattern accepts, modifies, and rejects of the external environment, and how that same set can be stripped away in imagining new values and new norms which allow the creation of future possibilities. Once these new values/norms have been created within the individual, they become "current." They may remain unsatisfied for a long period of time, causing a feeling of dissatisfaction or crisis for the individual, because he has already adopted the new values/norms. As Tolstoy's Platon Karatayev says in *War and Peace,* ". . . thinking man is not a happy man"; he must live for long periods of his life with unsatisfied values/norms.

Brain Modes and Futures

Two brain modes seem to be involved in relationships between the researcher and unstructured problems; these are a sequential, analytical mode and a holistic, picture-creating mode. The brain is composed of two halves, joined by a nerve mass called the corpus callosum. The right half is now known to be concerned mainly with spatial tasks and works holistically: the left half is concerned mainly with

ISBN 0-201-04096-4

sequential tasks such as speech and arithmetic. The two halves are not completely independent in their mode of function, and there is some limited interchange-ability. Information flows freely between the two halves via the corpus callosum.[6]

Thinking about the future requires another, and peculiar, ability of the brain, that of working within its own space-time domains. It is this ability that is used to contract many years of future events into a current thought pattern. In this context three space-time domains may be defined: conceptual, perceptual, and physical.[7] The conceptual space-time domain is primarily that of spatial, holistic thinking; it has no existence whatsoever except to the individual, and it goes out of existence when he stops thinking in that mode. It would seem to be associated largely with the right half of the brain. The perceptual space-time domain is associated with the experiencing and perception of the external environment, ordering objects in their arrangement and closing the feedback loop in such sequential tasks as writing and speech, and is largely associated with the left half of the brain. Perceptual space-time, too, is private to the individual. The physical space-time domain is that of the external world and is public, though it still allows for many different ways of measuring time.

Perception and Value/Norm Changes

An interpretation of perception of events in physical space-time (external environment) takes place via perceptual space-time and constitutes a mapping, in a linear sequence (perceptual time being one-dimensional), of incoming information onto an existing pattern of values, norms, and information; this produces the partial mismatch referred to earlier. The mismatch either is happily disregarded, because at the (physical) time sufficient of the value/norm set is satisfied; or it is manifested as dissatisfaction which will require for its alleviation either a modifi-cation of the individual's value/norm set or intervention in physical space-time to modify the environment. Value/norm changes of this kind result from an increase in information in an individual due to external experience. This is likely to be as-sociated with the left half of the brain since it is perceptual space-time dominated. As an aside, it is clear, from the physical time dependence of an individual's behavior pattern, which includes physiological states through genetic inheritance in addition to values, norms, and information, that identical perception of repeat events in the external environment is likely to be the exception rather than the rule.

The creation of new values and norms from internal experience is equally important and seems to proceed through information synthesis occurring, perhaps, through meditation or reflection. Information synthesis requires the running together of streams of information in such a way that the outcome, if one is generated, is a Gestalt picture in which new values and norms are embedded. To

---

[6]R. E. Ornstein, *The Psychology of Consciousness,* Viking Press, New York, 1973.

[7]Sir James Jeans, "Physics and Psychology," Cambridge University Press, Cambridge, 1943.

ISBN 0-201-04096-4

work with such pictures requires the researcher to trust in the unknown.[8] The process is essentially holistic and associated with conceptual space-time; it is likely to be dominated by the right half of the brain.

The two processes just outlined, by which value/norm changes are thought to occur, form discontinuities in an individual's mental processes. The shift from one mental model to another may be describable, in due time, through catastrophe theory,[9] incorporating, through its time dependency, the dynamics of value/norm changes, which are at present highly uncertain. However, once the discontinuities have occurred, the new values and norms are absorbed into the individual's set, which then becomes "current," giving the individual a new paradigm of perception.

Group Phenomena

Up to now it is the individual who has dominated the discussion, since only individuals can have values and norms. However, there are group phenomena which are profoundly important in organizations and (seem to) arise from the coincidence of behavior patterns of individuals. It is this coincidence of values and norms of individuals which gives rise to the so-called group values/norms. In everyday experience an individual's paradigm of perception identifies issues where his values/norms, irrespective of information and genetic inheritance, coincide with those of other individuals sufficiently for coalitions to be formed (Fig. 1). The temporary formation of a group results from this "issue coincidence" of values/norms and imparts to that group an apparent behavior pattern. The reality of this issue coincidence is seen in the use, by an individual, of language and symbols to convey sufficient of his values, norms, and information concerning an issue to cause confidence in, or coincidence with, those of others. The myth of issue coincidence lies in the extent to which, by the same means, the individual conceals the many values/norms that other individuals would reject if they were obvious or were beyond their normal experience. The very process of aggregation by these means results in the group's being formed around a subset of any one individual member's value/norm set. As a result, the individual can agree to actions based on mythical group values/norms, while simultaneously disowning the group set, thus freeing himself from "responsibility" for the outcomes of group actions.

The creation of a group through issue coincidence axiomatically means that other groups can readily form around individuals whose behavior patterns have coincided differently. The resulting conflict is endemic to human relating, but seems on most occasions to stop short of self or mutual destruction through the ultimate altruistic working of the value of life. The altruistic norm seems to have much to do with the strength of the coalitions formed between individuals, relates

[8]E. M. Matchett, "Tuning the Human Instrument," *Theoria to Theory*, Vol. 9, 1975, pp. 243-258.
[9]Rene Thom, *Structural Stability and Morphogenesis*, Addison-Wesley, Reading, Massachusetts, 1975.

ISBN 0-201-04096-4

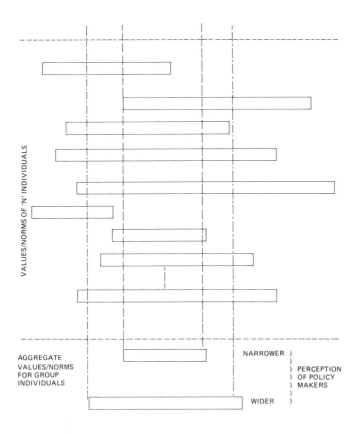

Fig. 1. Aggregation of values/norms.

to self-interest, and is far from uniform through the group. The process of conflict resolution then depends on detaching those who form the weakest coalitions — that is, those whose self-interest becomes threatened most quickly through remaining in the group. Catastrophe theory, through the butterfly catastrophe, promises to describe this process well; detachment of the weakest coalitions initiates the growth of the mid-plane with the ultimate dissolution of the catastrophe cusp. Bearing in mind the right/left brain activity and its possible relation to value/norm changes, it is not uncommon to find, particularly in management situations, coalitions formed between those who are dominantly holistic (right-half) thinkers or those who are dominantly sequential (left-half) thinkers. The conflict in these circumstances is very great, since it is based on a polarization of behavior patterns which requires considerable communication skill if the polarization is to be overcome.

ISBN 0-201-04096-4

Kinds of Error

The role of a person's behavioral pattern in perceiving unstructured problems is profound. Because such perception is value-laden, futures research is concerned with four kinds of error: those of the first and second kinds associated with the null hypothesis; errors of the third kind associated with solving the "wrong" problem (see Mitroff's article in this volume, also Mitroff and Turoff[10]); and errors of a "fourth" kind associated with asking questions to reveal an unstructured problem, as the "rightness" or "wrongness" of the questions is indeterminate in any absolute sense. It is for this reason that the probabilities of the outcomes do not sum to unity in an unbounded futures problem and that in Singerian inquiry truth is pragmatic and time-dependent.

Errors of the third kind lie in communication between individuals. It was conjectured earlier that perception and communication require an interaction between the left and right halves of the brain. For an individual to express conceptual space-time thought, essentially a right-half, holistic activity, the only tools he has are language and symbols, which are essentially sequential and therefore left-half-associated. It seems that some form of internal transformation must occur to allow the content of conceptual thinking to be expressed, via perceptual space-time, in physical space-time, where it can be perceived by the recipient. Through symbols the difficulty of this transformation is often apparent to the recipient, causing a heightening or diminution of awareness. If the conceptual thought contains ideas for which the recipient has no paradigm of perception (the source of the meta-language problem), then there will be no possibility of meaningful communication, and an error of the third kind is a certainty. The extent to which the error can be mitigated will depend on the joint skills of the researcher and his client in evolving a mutually understood paradigm of perception, for the time being, of the unstructured problem.

To evolve such paradigms the individuals must accept or create, in conceptual space-time, values and norms allowing syntheses of information in ways that may be beyond their experience in physical space-time. Many of these futures would be rejected in physical space-time by the current behavioral pattern, but by permitting temporary modifications to values, norms, and information, all futures beyond normal experience can be retained, and it is paramount that they are. The expression of these futures in physical space-time, via the medium of language and the process of internal transformation conjectured about earlier, is a major accomplishment if errors of the third kind are to be avoided.

Influencing Future Developments

Among all the activities that influence future developments, where does futures

---

[10]I. I. Mitroff and M. Turoff, "On Measuring the Conceptual Errors in Large-Scale Social Experiments: The Future as Adhesion," *Technological Forecasting and Social Change*, Vol. 6, No. 4, 1974, pp. 389-402.

ISBN 0-201-04096-4

research stand? Futures research seeks to identify forces for change (which stem from changed behavioral patterns among a few and later spread) and the interaction between them. Subsequently synthesis of possible futures and their consequences, through conceptual thinking, creates understanding of the uncertainties, crises, and possibilities that will attend these futures. The selection of options for human development from this spectrum of possible futures requires the conscious formulation of policy, which sets out the framework within which an organization will work in developing its future: policy then sets the "ought" of an organization's intentions. Strategy — the art of choosing the instruments to implement policy and of planning and directing their use to achieve policy ends — and tactics — the management of the resources needed to achieve the strategy — must follow.

Futures research is then associated with the making of policy and strategy, while its exploratory role defines it as complementary to, not a substitute for, and conducted at a broader level than, formal strategic planning. A proposed hierarchical relationship, due to Erich Jantsch,[11] between behavioral patterns and policy, strategy, and tactics, is shown in Fig. 2.

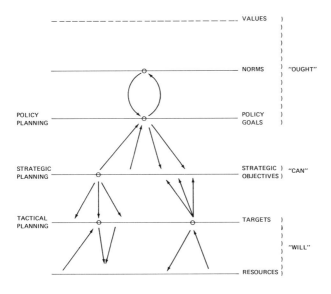

Fig. 2. Value/norm hierarchy.

[11]E. Jantsch, "Social Responsibility and Its Effect on Technological Innovations: Roles for World Corporations," University of Sussex/University of Stirling Seminar, September 1974.

ISBN 0-201-04096-4

A policy has as its underlying theme changes in relating which, when drawn together in a framework, create a spectrum of strategic choices, which require the use of some or all of the policy instruments for their attainment. Within the framework the strategic choices change as time moves on, so that the strategic time-frame is essentially shorter than the policy time-frame. The changes in relating may be between individuals, between individuals and organizations, between individuals and nations, between organizations, and so on, though where groups are concerned the changes in relating are essentially between individuals at the group leader level. The changes in relating are both internal and external phenomena, and it seems that policy making is in the end about how a balance "ought" to be effected between the changing internal values/norms in an organization and the changing external norms for that organization. An organization or an individual is at heart an inquiring system, constantly seeking to understand what its (his) external environment is and what that environment expects of it (him): then, by a process of internal and external mutual persuasion, the organization (or the individual) tries to shape a framework for its (his) purposeful connection with the external environment. The framework of relational changes, and the opportunities for these, embody a perception (dependent on behavioral pattern) of the external and internal environments, which the organization believes will allow it to remain a viable system in the future, although there can be no certainty of this: the nature of the perception needed is shown below.

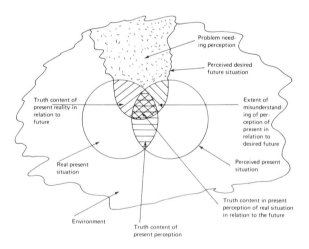

If the "truth content in present perception of real situation in relation to the future" is absent — that is if the real present and the perceived present do not intersect — there can be no related truth in an organization's perception of the future for itself, since it does not understand its present situation. Such an organ-

ISBN 0-201-04096-4

ization is unlikely to remain viable, except through external intervention. One of the major tasks for futures research seems to be to help to establish future values and norms and to understand how these may be learned more rapidly than ever before. The need is for values/norms that de-emphasize competition and emphasize cooperation and harmony with, rather than dominion over, nature.

Personal Philosophy in Use

However desirable futures thinking may be, it is, for many and good reasons, subjected to criticism and to scepticism. For this reason alone the futures researcher needs to have his work rooted in a personal philosophy, which he or she has consciously searched out. By developing a personal philosophy, the futures researcher establishes a personal reference point toward unstructured problems, allowing a conscious choice between the methodological/technique-oriented approach, or thinking things out differently. At this reference point a balance has to be struck between objective and subjective influences, as, although interpretations enter into both influences, the subjective is highly dependent on cultural effects. The role of behavior, as described earlier, is important to the development of all these influences. The researcher's philosophy must not be immutable, but the rate of change must not be so fast that his or her philosophy appears ephemeral. In Colin Cooper's words, "to be alive is to be in the process of change," but the rate of change needs to be such that the researcher retains credibility and sanity.

In Pilkington those concerned with futures research have developed their own individual philosophies, and each is quite different, allowing some measure of "fit" to the work in hand. In some instances the holistic, picture-creating mode has been the appropriate form of inquiry, opening new ways of thinking. In other instances the technique-oriented philosophy, introducing structured discussion, has been more suitable. The personal "fit" of the researcher then becomes highly important, since the individual's behavior pattern may make him or her more (or less) appropriate to the client and/or the unstructured problem. In the turbulence surrounding the study of unstructured problems, the researcher needs the support of a well-developed personal philosophy. So often this turns criticism into a growth in knowledge and understanding rather than the reverse, enabling the researcher to fulfil the special responsibility outlined earlier — namely, to see that the process of perceiving possible futures and their relationship to policy making is well understood.

Epilogue

A forecast represents the forecaster's beliefs about conjunctions of events in the future and will be strongly influenced by his behavioral pattern. The idea of a value/norm-free forecast is absurd. Predicting the future, with spurious numerical accuracy, based on no imaginable future conjunctions of human events, has much to answer for in the world today, a responsibility equally shared by those who have

ISBN 0-201-04096-4

been prepared to formulate policies on these predictions. Let us hope that that age is passing and that a new age of human development embracing uncertainty, conjecture, and spectra of possibilities is beginning.

Thinking about the future is entirely legitimate and necessary to Man's continued survival, perhaps never more so than now. Only the time scale is open to argument, and there is little to suggest that thinking "thirty years" ahead is much more dubious than thinking about next week. "Trusting in the unknown" is a very real concept. It is the hope of mitigating some of these unknowns that drives futures thinking, creating some conscious choices concerning what the present generation may do legitimately in relation to the inheritance left to the next. Any reader with an infant family is helping now to shape their world, a world they can expect to live in until 2050 A.D. Do we now have the right not to think in that time scale? Perhaps since World War II and the advent of nuclear weapons, interest in the future of a culture has declined, particularly in the "Western" styles, in favor of immediate affluence and the belief that present cultures are immutable and therefore require no maintenance or conscious development in which all take part. Nothing could be further from the truth, and the demise of a neglected culture is only a matter of time.

Signals of cultural change now abound; these stretch from the obvious of political accessibility to resources, including food, water, and energy, to the not-so-obvious of enzyme chemistry, genetic modification, and other changes in knowledge in biochemistry. Similarly, the obviousness of population change overarches the less-obvious effects in crime, divorce, and abortion, and in many matters relating to economic activity; these, too, reflect in the subtleties of language. George Orwell's canvas of 1984 was painted with words of new meaning, and the arrival of "escalating" rather than "ascending," of "transportation" rather than "movement," of "sophistication" rather than "refinement," and of "medication" rather than "treatment" should not go unnoticed in relation to cultural change. These all constitute the unstructured nature of the future. Perhaps the so-called Age of Aquarius is really the age of Mill, with deep concerns for distribution which are expressions of values and norms.

Acknowledgment

This paper is published with the permission of the Directors of Pilkington Brothers Limited and Dr. D. S. Oliver, Director of Group Research and Development.

ISBN 0-201-04096-4

II. 6. Bringing the Feminine into Forecasting

Foreseeing and Learning

RITVA KAJE

Introspection

I am a woman. The workings of my mind are such that I have difficulty in seeing and addressing the world in terms of issues and problems. For example, the theme of this collection, The Nature of Futures Problems, is not natural to me; I would be more comfortable with either The Nature of Futures or The Futures of Nature. Moreover, I am the kind of person who, at every possible instance, tends to consider and perceive "what futures ought to be like" rather than what they most likely will be. And this naturally drives me to inquire, "What can we do about it?"

One thing we should try to do is at least provide useful forecasts in time to secure effective action. But how do we become better forecasters? I have chosen to single out this question rather than the initial one, since our theme is futures research. Incidentally, on any of the issues mentioned above, my prescription is: Bring in the feminine or Yin, as the old Chinese would put it — i.e., identify, acknowledge, accept, and deliberately develop the feminine qualities of all things.

Our world develops like our minds work, and vice versa. In Western civilization today, and in the entire world guided by it, the development is trending toward increasing emphasis on the masculine quality — or Yang — in all things. This represses, suppresses, and gradually destroys the now dormant feminine qualities. This is the lamentable nature of our future as I perceive it. Yet, Yin is vital and necessary for what I think futures ought to be: wholesome people and communities with wholesome lives in a wholesome world.

My psychological type happens to be such that it is vital to me to meet with man, either the analytic and well-focusing man within myself — my animus, as a Jungian psychologist would put it — or physical man, with the most masculine left half of the brain working of his mind. I should so much like to meet the minds of the other writers of this collection that I am tempted to respond to the problems raised and the issues defined in their papers. My natural response, however, would take the unacceptable form of an explosion, as I would attempt to reach everyone at once. I am prepared to propose a comprehensive and universal "answer" — that we have to bring in the feminine — as a "good solution" to the various "problems" they propose. Presumably, at some point or time, the problem-definition "particles" which other writers have disseminated would bump into the light or waves or flows or forces from my own problem-solving explosion (subsequently our

Futures Research: New Directions, Harold A. Linstone and W. H. Clive Simmonds (eds.)

ISBN 0-201-04096-4

readers would no longer agree that the explosion was mine at all; they would say that the other writers provided not only the kindling spark but the answers as well). Through the meeting of "questions" and "answers," learning takes place, and there is much enjoyment in learning, much more than in possessing problems or solutions!

However, there is more to the choice of communication media than this effectiveness; there is the transmission of signals, and an explosion is not good for that, since it blows the fuses. Therefore, this writer succumbs to the tradition of printed communication and will retire to her preconceived sequence of verbal language, borrowing only from Sir Geoffrey Vickers for a spark plug, besides acknowledging D. J. Loveridge's thesis via this introspective preface.

In Response to Vickers

In speaking about "social order," you suggest the *principle of relatedness* — a characteristically feminine principle. Apparently, we do not master that principle too well if we are indeed as entrapped by our own designs as Sir Geoffrey suggests and thus helpless in facing the consequences. In other words, we have not felt our way too well with coupling, uncoupling, sharing, and complementing our cultures and subcultures with each other or when attempting coordination and integration. And this is true about any and all levels of human coexistence — from individual to international to global. The achieved state of our social systems is so foreign to that for which we claim to be aiming, that we must not have even been *diffusely aware* of some of the possible consequences as we pursued the anticipated ones with determination. It may also be that our single-minded determination prevents us from seeing better and from feeling the possible consequences.

And how did we anticipate these consequences? By logical reasoning (plus, in some cases, the element of wishful thinking[1]). Selecting an illustration from Sir Geoffrey's article, we must ask ourselves whether it was not simply logical to expect that more individual freedom would result from the shift of the necessary functions to technological and bureaucratic automation and formalized democratic representation. Western civilization has been blinded by the principle of Logos, following it as a plough in a field. This is a characteristically masculine principle and in opposition to the principle of relatedness (the two are paired in this way by Esther Harding in *The Way of All Women*). An extreme state would be what Sir Geoffrey calls a "cultural vacuum" — i.e., a state where there is no relatedness or social order that one can relate to.

Naturally, the two approaches should complement each other in guiding our inquiring systems, organizational designs, and management action. Consider the case of technology assessment. The assessment aspect calls for consideration of relatedness: you cannot assess a consequence of the studied technology as good or bad unless you relate it to people. For whom is it good? For whom is it bad? Who

---

[1]Which is not earthbound either.

ISBN 0-201-04096-4

will gain, who would be the victims? In practice, we see that the first tentative map of the consequences themselves is traced most conveniently by means of logical thinking. But here again your imagination would be aided greatly by a relatedness inquiry such as: "What would the consequences be as experienced by a given group of people?" To find this out, you may need empathy much more than logic!

The Nature of Futures: The Feminine is Missing

We want to look into the feminine for its eventual incorporation into forecasting activities: What is it actually? What else but relatedness is "feminine"? Where and how can it be released? Expecting to search dark, and perhaps murky, waters, we will borrow some light. Two attractive torches are at hand: (1) The study of woman's mind with wisdom from a great little book: Irene Claremont de Castillejo's *Knowing Woman; A Feminine Psychology*. Marital and other serious man-woman relationships are, of course, a helpful context for a study of woman's mind; (2) The ancient Chinese way of perceiving everything in this world as either Yin (feminine) or Yang (masculine).

In the following discussion I present my own selected list of "feminine" qualities with their "masculine" counterparts, deriving ideas from both of the above-mentioned sources as well as from personal life experience and professional practice experience — as a woman in a man's world and as a go-between in two worlds, one arctic and closed to learning, the other sunny and open to learning and development. My Yin/Yang chart is for the reader's checking and for a starter in the development of your own more-sophisticated Yin/Yang chart.

In the middle, where there is a perfect meeting of the feminine and the masculine, we find the ideal. I have tried to name some ideal states in order to illustrate what I mean. In principle, the ideal states can be neither attained nor fully described (if they could, they would not be ideal).

Even a brief look at the chart makes it clear that we are well-furnished with masculine contributions to any human endeavors. On the Yang side are found all those contributions that are encouraged and rewarded in Western civilized communities. Further, we are alienated from the feminine sphere of our lives individually as well as collectively. For example, consider daily food intake in urban communities. How well does it connect us with Mother Earth? Do we have a feeling for the land and the seas through shopping and eating our food?[2] The same goes for our design for physical environment and organizations. Again from the chart we see the key words from the previous section written in response to Vickers' paper.

Consider, then, a typical Western well-educated woman. Does she clearly outweigh men in regard to Yin? Not at all. We note too many women (in women's movements) who have completely lost the view of the feminine. On the other

---

[2] J. Coates, talking and writing about technology assessment, has frequently listed the many ways by which our technology brings us out of touch with our natural world and our own nature.

ISBN 0-201-04096-4

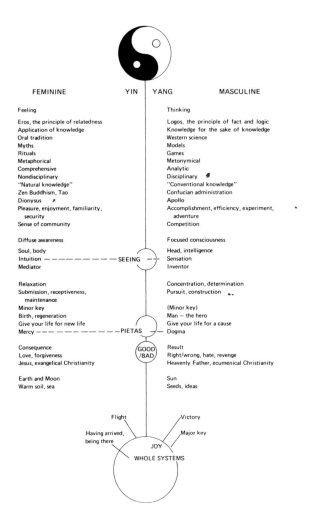

FEMININE   YIN   YANG   MASCULINE

Feeling   Thinking

Eros, the principle of relatedness   Logos, the principle of fact and logic
Application of knowledge   Knowledge for the sake of knowledge
Oral tradition   Western science
Myths   Models
Rituals   Games
Metaphorical   Metonymical
Comprehensive   Analytic
Nondisciplinary   Disciplinary
"Natural knowledge"   "Conventional knowledge"
Zen Buddhism, Tao   Confucian administration
Dionysus   Apollo
Pleasure, enjoyment, familiarity,   Accomplishment, efficiency, experiment,
  security   adventure
Sense of community   Competition

Diffuse awareness   Focused consciousness

Soul, body   Head, intelligence
Intuition — — — — — — — — SEEING — —   Sensation
Mediator   Inventor

Relaxation   Concentration, determination
Submission, receptiveness,   Pursuit, construction
  maintenance
Minor key   (Minor key)
Birth, regeneration   Man — the hero
Give your life for new life   Give your life for a cause
Mercy — — — — — — — — PIETAS —   Dogma

Consequence   GOOD   Result
Love, forgiveness   /BAD   Right/wrong, hate, revenge
Jesus, evangelical Christianity   Heavenly Father, ecumenical Christianity

Earth and Moon   Sun
Warm soil, sea   Seeds, ideas

              Flight   Victory

        Having arrived,   Major key
        being there
                            JOY
                     WHOLE SYSTEMS

hand, we know men who have a well-developed inner sensitivity to this view. Yet something from our domestic experience whispers that women more likely than men will be able to provide our systems with Yin qualities.

A frightening thought: even if we found a way to the presumably dormant feminine, she may have been petrified already with no return — a petrified sea.

Hopeful signs are present, however, in the Western world. Over the last ten years starting on the West Coast of the United States there have been men and women deliberately searching for wholeness in their lives — through meditation, through religious or sexual practice, through bodily sanity and enjoyment. A few of them have indeed acquired new lives. What is the new therein would, frequently, fall on the Yin side of our chart. Thus, individuals have not lost their reservoirs of

ISBN 0-201-04096-4

feminine: Yin is still there to be found in "liquid" form waiting to be tapped. Moreover, it is predicted that, by the year 2000, American Christianity will transform itself into Buddhist Christianity.[3]

Let us next consider organizations. How are their pools of femininity? Are the bureaucracies of business, government, education, and research petrified? In the literature, there is an awareness and search for something similar to my call for more femininity, although every writer has a different word for it.[4] In practical management development, however, there are few individuals such as C. West Churchman and his "school" at the University of California, and the Management Systems Oy group in Helsinki, who would attempt to raise general awareness about the nature of whole systems management in any of these terms.[5] However, there are spontaneous successful examples in our time of whole systems management — as there have been at other times in history.

Mao's China has served as an interesting large-scale "experiment" in recent years of deliberately developing a whole societal system with explicit concern for both Yin and Yang. But will Mao's China survive Mao? If it does not, will we learn from its Western-style disaster better than we have been learning from its wholesome progress?

A historical tradition of whole systems regulation is found elsewhere too, but it has not been transferred to us — communicated to us, Westernly civilized conquerors. In the case of the Chinese it may be important that the Chinese tradition for thousands of years was voiced and documented in script, besides being transferred by the more subtle media of a culture.

Does India have too much Yin today? The nature of Western futures is the excess of Yang. Yin has to be deliberately sought to complement aggressive (masculine) initiatives and pursuits. We do know that India is supplying the West with one guru after another, a way of enhancing Yin. Yin/Yang charts — this one and those produced by readers thereafter — can be used as suggested maps to indicate where one might look for feminine qualities or a key which would open a useful lookout window for someone else into the feminine. The fact that the feminine is so ignored, repressed, or dormant may require special consideration. We may not be dealing with a simple "walk-up" window. Perhaps the sleeping beauty has to be kissed.

Earlier I asked you to look at the entire cluster of words, concepts, and descriptors on both sides of the chart, thus giving you a general impression. However, the usable unit is one entry, or a Yin/Yang pair of entries. The application to Vickers' problem about social order and the cultural vacuum focused on the

---

[3]See Charles Gaston Areand, "The Paradigm Shift to a Mind-Expanding World View: H. G. Wells' Theocracy and Its Fellow Travelers," which surveys some of the literature on this theme (to be published in *Technological Forecasting and Social Change*).

[4]A reviewer of this article offered three literature references: Herman Kahn's "Post-Sensate Society" (*The Next Two Hundred Years*), Victor Ferkiss' "New Holism and New Immanentism" (*Technological Man*), and Theodore Roszak's "Ideas on the Unfinished Animal."

[5]See Churchman's article in Part III.

ISBN 0-201-04096-4

principles of relatedness and Logos. A harmonious balancing of the two dimensions on a line is essential in "problem solving." Obviously, different lines are applicable to different problems, and one will not always find an applicable pair of concepts on a preconceived chart. The particular selection in our chart reflects questions that have been intriguing the author personally over the last several years. For discussion on the art of forecasting, only two lines will be singled out: "intuition-sensation" and "diffusion awareness-focused consciousness." Before moving on to forecasting problems and leaving the reader to grapple with his future problems and Yin/Yang charts, a word of caution is in order: it is fascinating to learn about the feminine and masculine through intensive experience of physical man-woman relationships on all levels of individual existence – sexual through intellectual. Applications are evident everywhere, most of all in interpersonal relations at work which lead to new policy. It is also fascinating to learn from analogies between different levels of human existence: individual, group, organization, society, culture, civilization, humanity – but we should not take these analogies too literally. Let the connection remain diffuse – i.e., a loose and liquid association; one should be fully relaxed and spontaneous about the analogies, barely aware that they are being used.

What Happens in Forecasting?

An anecdote: Riding as a passenger in a car in Helsinki one day, M was reflecting on what he saw through a side window. P, the driver, recorded what M said, but did not comment very much. There was the M/S *Marcus* from Greece unloading coal from Poland at one of the piers. To return to the open sea, she would have to go through the passage under the bridge which was also within M's sight. M: "I would hate to be in the captain's boots when the M/S *Marcus* has to set sail in a strong wind. It is going to crush the drawbridge when moving out." Two days later a newspaper headline reported: "M/S *Marcus* damaged. Bridge closed to traffic for two months. The ship collided with the bridge as it was about to leave Helsinki in a heavy wind." P was frightened to learn this news. How could M see into the future this well? M is an able physicist who understands the behavior of the winds as well as the construction of ships and bridges. Simply looking at the ship and the bridge is enough to indicate to him how they are constructed. It occurred to him that the bridge was foolishly built. It is unlikely that M could have seen a *Marcus*-type vessel steered through the passage, but he does have a good feel for sailing and steering vehicles of various kinds. Besides, he could indeed calculate how the ship would move under given wind conditions and what would be the probability of collision. But clearly this could not be done in a flick of a second – nor are there computers that could do so.

M's mind could not possibly operate in a sequential way in this situation. There must have been a diffuse awareness which associated his previously acquired knowledge about the physics of the situation with the present brief observation to

ISBN 0-201-04096-4

produce that "blackish bluebird" of insight.[6]   Knowledge had to be maintained in a "liquid" way in the individual's mind — i.e., diffusely. In other words, his physics lessons had penetrated and become part of the sea of diffuse awareness and free association.

All passers-by have their own diffuse awareness, many have good eyesight and are fast, intelligent observers; yet they are not making connections such as M made concerning the M/S *Marcus* and the bridge. Thus, I know that I would never be able to predict a collision such as this even if I were asked to do so and got paid for it. I also have peculiar insights and make accurate predictions at times that make me feel somewhat like a witch; there is plenty of diffuse awareness in me too, but the best I could do in terms of ships and bridges would be inadequate. Something is missing.

I think that in M's case it takes, on the one hand, a gut feeling or diffuse awareness to make the difference (the bird) and, on the other, something else (the egg for hatching): apparently *specific* knowledge which *adequately* responds to the physical observation through the car window and is maintained on such a level of consciousness that it is readily available but free from focus, having no fixed location among the "lockers of the brain." With a correct call word it is extracted appropriately to match the unexpected situation (this is analogous to having a good sense of humor and a readiness to use it at the proper moment). Originally M had acquired his physics knowledge from books and experiments — these are the necessary "eggs." Such knowledge is needed in the forecaster's mind. It has entered through focused consciousness and becomes useful only through refocusing. The single, best descriptor of such phenomena would be "association." It overcomes the limitations of space, provided there is a proper balance between the focused and the diffused. This balance is what other passers-by did not have. Such learning and knowledge as that of M about physics, the prerequisite for useful seeing — insight of forecast — I shall talk about in the next section in connection with the abiliy to see and foresee. Seeing, and learning which enhances it, have been discussed here as they take place in individual minds.

Bring the Feminine into Forecasting

The great Jungian psychologist, Irene Claremont de Castillejo, in her book *Knowing Woman* describes as "diffuse awareness" the state of mind toward which women are naturally predisposed, while the "focused consciousness" mode is an equally characteristic predisposition of male minds. Thus, they become her definition of the feminine and the masculine, respectively. An easy connection is made at this point with Loveridge's thesis,[7] as it is a popular notion today that for women the right half of the brain dominates and the left for men. In response to this thesis we note that it is imperative for forecasting to incorporate a comprehensive

---

[6]This imagery derives from a fairy tale by C. West Churchman.

[7]See the preceding paper by D. J. Loveridge, "Values and Futures."

"imagination" of the right half of the brain to complement the analytic verbally conceptualizing left half. We sometimes spontaneously call for raised awareness and sometimes for more focus. My message is: the former is in much shorter supply and we therefore have to deliberately search for it and incorporate it in our forecasting. The message is simply not that "therefore, women should be the forecasters" (although that is an interesting implication). Assuming that the feminine pool is there, I will discuss two major functions for the feminine in forecasting: *mediating* and *meeting*. It will be convenient to discuss mediating in the context of seeing or perceiving, and meeting in relation to the phenomenon of learning.

The Feminine in Mediation

Let us discuss seeing or perceiving rather than forecasting and images of the future, as there is no time dimension in seeing. In other words, the prerequisite of seeing appears to be that the very limitation of time is overcome. Future is, of course, inherent in the present, the continuum being made possible through the gene pool and genetic code, as well as through cultural inheritance and learned images of history. Recollecting the anecdote about the ship and the bridge, the seeing and the learning can be seen as inverses of each other. Knowledge material was brought forth to see. This would not have been possible without an earlier learning process. In other words, we have a two-way diffusion process which involves a "feminine layer of the human mind" which performs the mediating function. There are clearly deeper mind layers, and at some point we begin to consider them as the unconscious. If the (knowledge) material were there, it would still have to pass through the diffuse awareness layer to reach any focused consciousness. The layers of the mind certainly have their different content, but the diffuse awareness — the feminine — serves as the mediator. We might interpret "knowledge" as "memory," "dream material," "symbols and images," "Soul" or "one's Self," "archetype," etc., and we could replace mediating by "reflecting," "dreaming," "creating art," "extrasensory experiences," etc.

M's insight achieved communicable expression in a verbal utterance. In addition to verbal language there are other avenues of communication: artistic expression and spatial arrangements including the creation of ethnic domains (the primary illusion of architecture), the nonverbal language of body movement, facial expression, and so-called psychosomatic symptoms, which represent the body's way of focusing on undesirable situations. We know that dreaming, dancing, and painting mediate materials from the deep collective unconscious, and there is no reason to believe that the other mentioned expressions would not fulfill a similar task. The most obvious mediated images which should be of interest to societal forecasting are utopias in the forms of novels, poetry, and drama, "visionnaire" painting, and people's "revolutionary" music. But equally powerful outlets of the feminine may be found in anecdotal story telling, children's plays, diary writing, etc.

The reason for failure of mediation can be found in submergence and cultural suppression of the feminine in Western educational systems and social status

ISBN 0-201-04096-4

systems. How then can the feminine be released and activated to serve in this role?

Meditation is a deliberate and effective means of arriving at a "feminine" state of mind. For the Buddhist this is a way to the sources of "natural knowledge." Meditators sometimes describe this as a state of "decentralized focus" — i.e., with many simultaneous foci. Bodily relaxation may be attempted in a deliberate way for the same purpose — e.g., yoga and breathing exercises. Some individuals attain a similar state of mind — heightened spirits and enhancement, excitement, or enchantment of body and mind — through exercises such as overdoses of sensory and intellectual stimuli, physical exhaustion resulting from voluntary physical activities, sauna, fasting, sexual intercourse, and asceticism. Fever dissolves a Western mind, as we well know, and shamans appear to develop a feverish state for this experience. Collectively, a related phenomenon is experienced through the sharing of hardship or any intense experience.

In most cultures, alcohol and drugs have been used to enhance as well as to suppress "seeing" (the latter is apparently the motive for alcoholic housewives).

Returning to the anecdote, we find that M was idle — i.e., he was not concentrating on any one thing. He said later that many things were on his mind and he was quite stressed. Apparently the key is the relaxation of the upper restrictive layers of the human mind. This would suggest simply a technique of upsetting these upper models, images, and structures; in other words, become confused or surprised, pushed off the normal tracks of thinking and expectations, and forced to look out through new windows. Another means is to replace the old mental maps by experiential and fairy-tale material, by myth, through involvement and associations.

In the case of group organizations there are also the behavioral and spatial fixations: conventional procedures, pecking orders, petrified organizations, structure, etc. Relaxation in this context means a realization that the system is not actually functioning any more according to the models and images held. It would suggest a gradual inquiring process which probes how the real system behaves, while the old structures are left to whither away naturally. In applying any of these procedures one must be aware of too much femininity — e.g., too much confusion — and strive for a balance which simultaneously brings forth masculine concepts such as structures and models.

It is obvious that anxiety, fear, and anger may block off the feminine by "blinding" the mind. The prescription is avoidance of insecurity, stress, and pressure. At other times the blocking is in the perceiver's mind and reflects his prejudices and beliefs. A common major obstacle is the natural resistance to relax in public. If you relax your control, you will perhaps reveal more of yourself than you intend to. And there is a natural and well-founded fear to see one's own self, even in private — the fear of finding one's self different from what has been assumed. The greatest source of insecurity must be the feeling of being lost and unfamiliar with one's own self. The prescription is development of sensitivity, friendship, and acceptance of all group members including yourself.

ISBN 0-201-04096-4

It is a common notion that outsiders see better. They are also not as threatening. This is a reason to hire a consultant to see how the organization actually operates and to help develop it in a desirable fashion. And it is the reason to have a foreigner look at the state of the nation. To make this seeing possible, you have to let him view it, review it, allow him an exposure to it. Since the outsider is with us for only a short period of time, the organization's life must be exposed or made visible in an unusually intense way to the consultant observer. We must prescribe means to "make the system visible," and we are thus right back to the very nature of seeing as exemplified in the anecdote. There must be, in other words, a meeting of intuition and sensation, or Yin and Yang. The prescriptions for improved seeing may be summarized as follows:

- Increase sensitivity to all those spontaneous diverse expressions from within and beyond your own diffuse awareness and that of your neighbor — individual and collective. In other words, listen better in order to hear more, and listen to your own body as well.
- Solicit verbal and visual, artistic and nonartistic, communicable expression for any and all people in the system to reflect feeling. Record; keep a diary; force expressions out.
- Do not disregard the noises or notions that seem trivial and obvious when they are spelled out. They should become obvious.
- Collect both spontaneous and solicited expressions from all parts of the system. Display them, make the system visible.
- Believe: In most social systems, there is enough awareness and enough vision. It simply has to be brought forth for focused consideration and action.
- Believe: The system is there to be seen, and the future is present.

Learning

Conception of an image of the future and its presentation in a communicable form are creative acts. Learning is also a form of creativity. A person changes when knowledge is imparted. Change means arriving at something that has not existed previously. In nature, creation always takes two:

Egg cell	Sperm cell
Placenta	Fetus and enzymes — the triggers
Soil, appropriately tilled and fertilized, or: Mother Earth	Seeds and the sun
The Feminine, Yin	The Masculine, Yang

ISBN 0-201-04096-4

Jean Sibelius made the same observation about the creation of music: two were necessary — inspiration and labor:

| Inspiration, spirit | Labor, determination |

In the ship-bridge case, the conception of the image of a future was "triggered" by the observations:

M's pool of internalized	M's observations and M/S
knowledge	*Marcus* and its environment
Diffuse awareness	Focused consciousness

In the classroom we know that motivation of the students and the teacher, pleasant, peaceful spatial arrangements, convenient scheduling, and an atmosphere of healthy competition with minimal fear of punishment are also critical elements for learning, in distinction to the substantive material (i.e., ideas, observations, techniques, etc.) to be learned.

Let us now consider forecasts as the material to be learned or internalized. People must experience a need for them, find the propositions relevant, their advocates credible, and the planners competent. Moreover, when the forecast material is to be communicated effectively, there must be a receptiveness at the "right moment."

Learning situation, motivation,	Forecasts
need, problem awareness	Insights
Questions	Utopian images of the future
Right place, time, and	Plans
audience	etc.

We can actually prescribe much more for a productive learning situation. The conditions for mediating are obviously also good for the diffusion of knowledge into a receptive and caring mind. The difference between seeing and learning (in my use of the terms) is primarily one of direction. So, we can look back to the previous section for our prescriptions of a situation generative of creative insights. For example,

Meditative
Bodily relaxing
Physical exercise
Intense stimulation
Experiential
Sex, sauna, fasting, asceticism
Challenge, hardships
Confusion
Some structure — cozy, safe, and secure (like home)
Open, easy
FRIENDLY

ISBN 0-201-04096-4

We have thus created another Yin/Yang chart. The essential message for forecasting and futures studies — as with learning — is that there should be a meeting of the two.

As a closing example, let me suggest the activities of the Club of Rome. While their publications may be criticized for narrow-minded or poorly based model making on the Yang side, they should be credited for working quite well on the Yin side. They have

> Shaken up, upset, attacked some commonly held images
> of the future
> Created doubt and confusion
> Roused other model makers and futures students
> Raised awareness
> Aroused crisis experience
> Maintained platforms of discussion
> Created receptiveness (for better forecasts, models,
> and visions)

It is characteristic of the traditional Western type of discourse that these Yin contributions have been largely disregarded in comparison with the monumental efforts to refine the substantive models (the Yang response). Within the Club of Rome, however, there is a warm Yin pool.[8]

---

[8]Editors footnote: The readily perceivable shift in emphasis from the initial Club of Rome studies (e.g., *The Limits to Growth*) to the recent work on values (e.g., *Goals for Mankind*) could be cited as movement toward a balance of the type described in this paper.

ISBN 0-201-04096-4

III. Managing Complexity

III. 1. Introduction

HAROLD A. LINSTONE

> The man of system . . . seems to imagine that he can arrange the different members of a great society with as much ease as the hand arranges the diffi-cult pieces upon a chessboard. He does not consider that the pieces upon the chessboard have no other principle of motion beside that which the hand impresses upon them; but that, in the great chessboard of human society, every single piece has a principle of motion of its own altogether different from that which the legislature might choose to impress upon it.
>
> Adam Smith

The five articles in this Part were originally prepared for a lecture series on Managing Complexity held at Portland State University, February 27-28, 1975, under the auspices of the University and the S & H Foundation. The purpose was to:

> acquaint faculty, students, and the Portland community with new and innovative concepts which open entirely new vistas to discipline-oriented academia and tradition-oriented public.

Since "managing complexity" appears to be one of the central challenges of the future,[1] the insights developed by the speakers are of profound significance and relevance in our present endeavor.

We find that the first two articles are directly related to the material in Part II, while the subsequent three are in the vein of Part IV. In other words, Churchman and Michael deal with foundation questions; Bellman, Von Foerster, and Holling turn a new eye on systems. Difficulties in futures research and difficulties in systems study are closely intertwined. This has already been apparent in Parts I and II. The relation will be most clearly enunciated by Sahal in Part IV when he observes that

> A systems-oriented framework is a prerequisite to the study of futures,

and

> A futures-oriented framework is a prerequisite to the study of systems.

After reading Parts III and IV it will be very clear, however, that the contributors are leading us away from the "first-generation" view of systems — 1940 to 1965 vintage — and in a new direction.

---

[1]Others in our kind of society include the maintenance of an individuality and a group identity within this complexity.

Futures Research: New Directions, Harold A. Linstone and W. H. Clive Simmonds (eds.)

ISBN 0-201-04096-4

In Part II, Mitroff, Loveridge, and Kaje led the reader to focus on the individual and on the internal experience: the individual personality type and its relation to solving the wrong problem, the individual behavior pattern and its relation to policy planning, the needed balance in activities associated with the dichotomy between left and right brain halves, etc. In this Part, Churchman beautifully states his philosophy of the importance of the unique individual and his inner world. As Adam Smith did two hundred years ago (in the quotation at the beginning of this Introduction), Churchman warns us that the analyst who has not himself focused on the process of individuation, the understanding of the self, will not be able to model social problems meaningfully. Heinz Von Foerster is equally forceful in proclaiming the importance of the individual: society should be subservient to the individual, and not vice versa. The observer must be brought into the act of management; he is part of the system and responsible for his actions. It is an open question whether the most advanced Western societies are actually moving closer or further from this concept of self-managing systems. On the one hand, we see subtle indications of surrender of responsibility by the individual to "others": if the child learns little, it is the school's fault; if the adolescent becomes a criminal, it is society's fault. On the other hand, greater participation in decision-making in the "precursor" Swedish society is observed by Bäckstrand as well as by Cetron and Clayton in Part V.[2]

The emphasis on ethics and morality exhibited by both Von Foerster and Churchman is striking. Churchman even views the discounting problem (see H. Linstone, Part I) in this light. Morality for him means a *negative* discount rate — i.e., recognition that the next generations should be more important to us than we are. Both Von Foerster and Holling see it in the rule to act so as to increase the options of future decision-makers.

Michael perceives planning as a learning process which features two aspects: (1) the creation of "myths" about social realities — i.e., humanly constructed futures alternatives, and (2) the process of "emergence" — i.e., the holistic characteristics which cannot be anticipated from any study of the system elements. The systems approach can assist in two ways: (a) description of the stable parts of social systems, and (b) rules of transformation (at least for the stable components). Like Mitroff, he stresses the need to include the planner in the invariably subjective descriptions, transformations, and design process generally. He, too, warns against the Pygmalion complex (see H. Linstone, Part I), terming the created "myths" *temporary* so that they are not mistakenly interpreted as the one and only new reality. The learning process implies tolerance for committing errors — including Mitroff's Error of the Third Kind. The expressed need here for the creation of temporary "myths" and error tolerance is in obvious conflict with the traditional organizational process model (see Part IV, Introduction).

---

[2]G. Bäckstrand, "The Public and the Future," as well as M. Cetron and A. Clayton, "Investigating Potential Value Changes," in Part V of this volume.

ISBN 0-201-04096-4

Bellman places the role of mathematics in large systems into perspective, and Holling leads us to the borders of mathematical terra incognita. We are just discovering that complex social/biological systems are not really malleable under the hammer of traditional mathematics — i.e., calculus, differential equations, and optimization methods. According to Bellman, new mathematical approaches are needed, and "almost everything remains to be done." Holling then shows us that a partially or totally unknown world (as reflected in Michael's "myths" and emergent system properties, for example) requires policies quite different from the familiar optimization which guides management in a completely known world. In particular, tolerance of failure is concretized in a strategy which minimizes its cost instead of its probability of occurrence. He aptly describes this as a "safe-fail" strategy in contrast to the "fail-safe" strategy of the totally known world. Organizations are clearly unprepared for such an error-embracing planning process.[3]

A final thought. When Churchman paraphrases Kant — "two things fill my heart with never-ending awe: the complexity of the total social system forever and the self within," when he defines maturity as the ability to hold conflicting world views simultaneously *and be enriched thereby,* it becomes obvious that we are in the presence of a mind set far removed from the "barbarism of specialization" bemoaned by Ortega y Gasset in 1930. He then wrote that, learning more and more about less and less, the modern scientist

> knows his own tiny corner of the universe [and] is radically ignorant of all the rest . . . He is a learned ignoramus, which is a very serious matter . . . Anyone who wishes can observe the stupidity of thought, judgment, and action shown today in politics, art, religion, and the general problems of life and the world by the "men of science" and, of course, behind them, the doctors, engineers, financiers, teachers, and so on . . . The most immediate result of this *unbalanced* specialization has been that today, when there are more "scientists" than ever, there are much less "cultured" men than, for example, about 1750.[4]

The contributors of this Part show that true systems thinking does not follow this familiar pattern at all.

---

[3] Cf. Allison's organizational process model, Part IV, Introduction.

[4] Jose Ortega y Gasset, "The Revolt of the Masses," New American Library, New York, 1950 edition, pp. 80-83.

ISBN 0-201-04096-4

III. 2. A Philosophy for Complexity

C. WEST CHURCHMAN

I should warn you in the beginning that there are two strange characteristics of philosophers. One is that they dearly love to ask questions, and if they sniff out that there is going to be an answer somewhere they are going to be very unhappy. So if you sense that I seem to be approaching a conclusion and get as far away from it as possible, you sense correctly. The other is that they equally like to point out that nothing is new about complexity. It has been going on for a very long time, and other eras in history seem to reflect the same concerns that we have in the 1970's about the idea of complexity.

There are three key words that I will make the theme of my remarks, and they are the only technical words I will use. One is *ontology,* which is the philosophy of reality. It is basic because we really want to know if complexity exists. Is there complexity in the real world? That is the ontological question. The second term is *epistemology.* For the philosopher this means the theory of knowledge: the question of how we know certain things to be true and other things false. Our question is: If the world is complex, then what is our theory of knowledge which will enable us to face that complexity? And the third term is *ethics.* The ethical question is: Is complexity a valuable thing in our society, or an evil thing, or neither?

I am interested in how the world is going to manage its affairs, and these three branches of philosophy are intended to give me the base for management thinking about this crucial problem.

I will begin with epistemology, because we have now quite a literature on the epistemological ideas of complexity. The first point is differentiation between complexity and simplicity. This differentiation is based on the notion that to know something we have to know it in a simple form. And the primary knowledge task that the manager faces is to go from complexity to simplicity and from simplicity to knowledge. A word of caution: I am not saying that is the answer — there are no answers here. But that is a classical approach to complexity. It consists essentially in trying to take the complex and get it into a simple form where we can understand it. Now Holling (in a subsequent paper) presents a perfect example of that, although he hides from us the enormous complexity that lay behind his research. With a few charts he excites us about budworms and other things in the forest. His is a classical approach to getting into a state of knowledge by taking the complex and putting it into the simple. "It takes a genius to create simplicity out of complexity." One of the great geniuses of all time is Spinoza, and his *Ethics* is essentially based on this epistemological theme. He considers all the complexity that we face in life, filters it down to the elementary postulates that make up the beginning of his book, and comes out with a very simple theme

Futures Research: New Directions, Harold A. Linstone and W. H. Clive Simmonds (eds.)

ISBN 0-201-04096-4

for everyone of us — namely, that the ethical mode of life is understanding. That is the only message you need — if you are a Spinozist. So out of the total complexity comes this genius' creation of simplicity.

But this is not the epistemology that we are trying to use today in Systems Science. We are not essentially struggling to cull the simple truths from the complexities. Rather, the spirit of our age is to hit complexity straight on, taking it for what it is. So complexity comes to be a characteristic of another mode of attack on knowledge — namely, letting everything that is there be examined and trying to put complexity together into a system which we call a model. For example, complexity is partially measured by the number of variables in the model. Consider the growth of this measure. When we first started doing operations research in the 1950's, the biggest linear program we could handle contained about 15 variables and a few constraint equations. I understand that in 1975 there was a linear program that had 2 million variables and 35,000 constraint equations. Such an approach to understanding complexity makes little attempt to sift out simplicity. Rather, it takes the world to be the way all those variables are, and does not try to deduce some simple truths.

Another meaning of complexity says that it consists in the complex interaction between the variables. We have come to be aware that, when you change a variable in a system, the impact on many other variables throughout the system occurs either immediately or with a time lag. For example, Forrester's World Dynamics model essentially had only five basic variables in it — not very "complex" in terms of the number of variables; but when you think of the interactions in the model, it appears quite complicated. Thus, DYNAMO, which is the simulation acronym for the model, could be thought of as a fairly complicated model in this second sense.

Another meaning of complexity recognizes that we live in a world of uncertainty. In making historical references in the first definition of complexity, I referred to Spinoza. For the second and third, which relate to large-scale model building, I referred to no historical figure. I think this is one thing which is truly modern: very large-scale model building. In the case of uncertainty, however, the historical roots are many. I will select one figure, Carneades, who lived in the post-Aristotelian period. It was Carneades who emphasized the point that no assertion is ever known with certainty. We live as human beings in a universal uncertainty, and uncertainty about everything that is happening to ourselves and in the outside world. But, said Carneades, that does not stop us from making assertions. In fact, the only certainty we have is that we will go on making statements even in a world of uncertainty. But Carneades argued that some statements are more appropriate than others. So he suggested a measure of confidence in the assertions we make, which is based on the word "appropriate." The word in English had exactly the same root as probability. In fact, all probability theory is simply an extension of Carneades' idea that we need to be able somehow to measure the appropriateness of the statements we make. Accordingly, our world becomes complex to the extent that it is uncertain for us. The obvious suggestion here is that we need to

ISBN 0-201-04096-4

develop a calculus of uncertainty. We can measure unexpectedness, say, on a scale ranging from zero for the completely unexpected, or the impossible, to one, for the completely certain.

Thus we have developed, in history, a theory of probability, and, more generally, of one type of uncertainty.

But there is much more fundamental uncertainty about our understanding of the world that is not reflected in probability theory. This has to deal with data — the information we use to build our models, to describe the parameters that drive the models. We need that kind of information if our models are going to have any kind of content. But the character of information in our understanding of the world is totally different from the rather simplistic notion of information that empiricism gave us. Empiricism says that if you want an answer to the question, "Are all swans white?" then look at some swans. And if all of them should turn out to be white, then you are on the right track. But if you suddenly go to Kyoto, Japan, and happen to see the black swans, that's done it. There is a black swan (unless the Japanese are painting them). So, not all swans are white. That is simplistic.

But systems scientists cannot proceed in that manner. To illustrate, suppose we would like to know the cost of the new Systems Science Program at Portland State University. President Blumel[1] has praised the program, but if I were on the Board, I would like to know, "What is the program costing?" If you were an accountant you might add up all the salaries, equipment, computer time, student pay, and all the rest of it, and say that that figure with an overhead is the cost of the program. But, from a systems point of view, this procedure would not be right. Epistemologically, that is not the cost of the program. The real cost is the lost opportunity of all of the individuals who are in this program at Portland State. What could they be doing now if they were not doing this? We need to estimate the value of the activity they could be doing, because they are losing the opportunity of doing it by being in the program. It is the lost opportunity that makes the cost. That is why we are so unpopular as systems people. We go into a room, and they are arguing about which programs to have at Portland State. And we keep saying, what other programs could we have? Those are the ones we need to talk about.

Now you can see why empiricism does not work for us. Where do you go to look for cost? What do you look at? You have nothing to look at; you must *think* about lost opportunities. In other words, you need a large value-loaded model to estimate those lost-opportunity costs.

For example, if you wonder whether Forrester's model reported in *The Limits to Growth* used good data or not, the answer is no. There are no models around today that use good data, in the sense of being epistemologically sound. Now what do we do? We use past data. We use the period which, say, *The Limits to Growth* does — i.e., from 1900 to 1970. Many things happened in that period,

---

[1]Of Portland State University.

ISBN 0-201-04096-4

but surely there was a lot of mismanagement. If we use historical data, they are partially generated out of bad judgment. And if we use those historical data to make forecasts into the future, they are bad data.

But how do we get the necessary data? I do not want to discourage budding systems scientists. We can have a procedure for estimating opportunity costs in Operations Research. If we want to know the costs of holding inventory, we cannot get them out of the accounting books. What we do is to talk to the smart controller, who seems to have some grasp of the financial system, and we talk and talk and talk, or rather we listen and listen and listen to him, because 95% of what we get is irrelevant. But out of all the talk we cull an estimate. That is the number we use, relying on our own judgment. It is a guess based on the best judgment we can make. But, of course, it may be terribly wrong.

Now you may be a systems expert and ask: Why do you not talk about sensitivity analysis? The answer is: I have not because some of the data have to be critical. If they are not, then we are really not doing anything. If none of the data matter at all, we might as well forget the whole story. So, I do not think the answer lies in sensitivity analysis.

Thus, the real epistemological complexity lies in the essential properties of your information needs. We are not laboratory technicians with good measuring devices in front of us.

Now is the time for an ontological interlude in this symphony. If the previous movement depresses you, this music is a little sweeter. So I will bring out the violin section accompanied by a few cellos, and point out that in classical rationalism the question of complexity had a beautiful solution. Descartes realized he was dealing with a very complex question. His question was: Is there any proposition I can know with absolute certainty? He realized he lived in a complex world, and somehow, while he was conducting the search for the unqualifiedly true proposition, he needed a mode of living, and some solid support. The answer is the Guarantor. His task was to prove the existence of a benign God. If we are the children of a benign God, then the problem of complexity is not even threatening. It depends upon how you define "benign," to be sure, but I am not going to go into all that detail. The point is that God will take care of us poor children in a messy world no matter how messy it may be. Because He is benign, He is not evil. So you now have the opportunity of being a reactionary (and there is nothing wrong with that) and of returning to the classical rationalism of the seventeenth century, and to your own satisfaction prove the existence of a benign God. In such a case, the complexity is there; but it resides in the infinite wisdom of the deity and not in your rather limited capabilities.

That is the ontological interlude: it says you have an optimist option. Any time somebody is in a gloomsday mood, you can reflect on that question. If you do and succeed, then you have the epistemological, ontological, and ethical answer. The key historical figure in this discussion is Descartes, because in the *Meditations* and *Discourse on Methods* he was living through that same experience of existing

ISBN 0-201-04096-4

in a complicated world and finding some way in which he could feel the guarantee.

Now the interlude is over, and we are back to present-day society which has not opted to go that route — not, I might argue, on any rational grounds that I have been able to find. It is still an option, not by any means closed, even though some of the uglier people in the scientific community may say, "I will not entertain that hypothesis because there is no test of it." The problem of the Guarantor is still with us! Is there any guarantee that human development and progress is going to take place? If there is — that is a God.

But now I will come back to today, and leave the world Godless for the time being and talk about the ethics of complexity. Is it good, or is it bad, that we live in a complex world? I am assuming that ontology has given us the answer that we live in a complex world, and so has epistemology. First we have the simple-minded, gloomy side that says complexity is bad. Why? Because, it will kill us all! If you look at a future population chart, pollution increases drastically and kills much of the population. Complexity is bad because it frightens me, or complexity is bad because I want it to frighten me. Whatever your answer is at this level, you must become part of the general gloomsday philosophy. I am not going to talk about that, because it is not very interesting although highly publicized.

I will talk instead about the bright side of complexity. Complexity is good! I will play this tune with a little bit of tongue-in-cheek. The theme here might be called the Club of Rome syndrome. Being very concerned about the future of the world, the group asked Hasan Ozbekhan to write a position paper. In that paper Ozbekhan first introduced into Systems Science literature the French word "problematique," standing for the complexity that I mentioned earlier, the inter-action of the world's problems. I might say, parenthetically, at this point, that many systems scientists and a lot of people in the world do not recognize this to be true. The Battelle Memorial Institute has a project called Dematel, in which they asked the world's experts to identify the world's problems, and the experts identified forty-seven of them. (It is a mystery why these things always come out to be prime numbers.[2]) They then asked experts in the world of transportation, education, etc., to fill in that forty-seven by forty-seven matrix with numbers from 1 to 7 indicating the interaction of the pairs of problems. I said to them, "My God, what are you doing that for! The only way to fill in that matrix is to put nothing but sevens in it." They said, "Yes, we know that, but look at how the experts of the world do it." True enough, many of them quite frankly saw no connection at all between energy and education. I do not know how they think the school build-ings are lit, or how they think in general.

But back to the Club of Rome's attitude. It says, in effect, that the world is in a complicated situation, that complexity is there, and, therefore, we need, in effect, the best minds to try to tell us how to get out of it, how to progress, how to get

[2]**Editors' Note:** True to form, the recent Stanford Research Institute's "Assessment of Future National and International Problem Areas" for the National Science Foundation identi-fied forty-one problems! (Cf. Teige, Harman, and Schwartz, Part V.)

ISBN 0-201-04096-4

ahead, and how to make things easier. Now when you get into that syndrome complexity is pretty good because planners become very important. For a while we did not know whether we were important: in the 1950's and 1960's everyone was muddling around with queuing theory and inventory theory, and trying to solve little problems of little companies or little problems of little governmental agencies, and so on.

But now, by God, we are hired by the Club of Rome and we can really take the whole world on. And as we do it, the titles of our books reflect our modesty: *The Limits to Growth;* Mesarovic's *Mankind at the Turning Point;* Stafford Beer's *Platform for Change;* and finally, Russ Ackoff's *Redesigning the Future*!

I really think the world is getting great for us planners. But that's just a facetious side, and I do not think that you have to take that point very seriously. What these "holistic" people are doing in the world today is making us pay attention to the future generation, as a moral obligation on our part. Now I am dead serious. There was a time in my young life when I was struggling with the question, "What is morality?" I came to the conclusion that morality is what a future generation would ask us to do if they were here to ask us. I believe that the voice of future generations is a morally critical voice today, because a lot of things we are thinking about today have their implications for the future generation. Consider nuclear energy production and its waste. We do not know what to do with the waste now. The salt mine is no longer a necessarily good solution. Some people think it should be taken to the Antarctica and sunk in the snow. One suggestion is that, since we do not know what to do with it, what about orbiting it, and let some smart technologist of the future take care of it. They will figure out what to do with our waste! That is a serious space application. I feel that it is clearly immoral. It is immoral because future generations would very likely ask us not to do this if they were here to ask us. We may have to do it, incidentally, but at least we have to admit we are being immoral in doing it.

Linstone talked about discounting the future (Part I). Any positive discount, I think, is immoral. My children are a lot more important than I am in my life and their children's children are still more important, and so on. The value of future generations keeps increasing, and becomes an amplifier rather than a diminisher. The bright side is that we are being made aware, in the 200-year projection, of the things we are doing today and their implications for future generations. We are facing the problem of how we are going to assess values that are out there a hundred years from now. Given our incapabilities of assessing our own values, that is a tremendously complex problem. It still does not diminish its importance, and, therefore, I think that complexity is really on the bright side of making us face up to it. There is a gloom side which says we cannot cope with the problem. So you can present the issue dialectically in your mind between the bright side, in that we are deeply concerned, and the gloomy, because we do not know how to handle the problem.

Now I come to another bright side. A vast portion of economic literature

ISBN 0-201-04096-4

involves aggregation. Economic models have to aggregate a number of things, and one of the things they aggregate is you! In great globs you are aggregated into statistical classes. There is nothing more frustrating than the damn statistician! You can get up on the Golden Gate Bridge. You have been thinking for months that you will take your life. You finally go and stand on the bridge, and as you are falling, some statistician says, "Yes, that fits right into the probability distribution." That is the moral of your glorious suicide, ruined by these aggregators! They ruin our lives in very, very deep ways because they aggregate. Aristotle is probably at fault, or at least I will blame him. He receives so much credit — it cannot hurt to give him a little criticism. He is trying to figure out how logic works, and he knows pretty well in his own mind that if all men are animals, and all animals die, then all men will die. Then he thinks about Socrates and how he would do in a syllogism. So it turns out that Socrates is man, all men will die, therefore, Socrates will die. At that point in history, Socrates was made into a class. That was deadly, but people have been doing it ever since. They have been taking us unique individuals, classifying us, and making decisions about classes. Not about us as individuals — but on us as classes! They forget that there is another side, another kind of reality. We are back to the ontological problem. There is something just as complex as classes, just as real, and that is our own inner self. The self, the individual, the psyche, the soul — not the brain, not the mind, but *self.*

Is this the first time it has been said in history? No! It goes back to Indian philosophy, to the compassionate Buddha, to the whole mythology of self in Hindu philosophy. It is said over and over again in poetry and drama. One of my favorite characters is Immanuel Kant. Kant, after writing his *Critique of Pure Reason,* which deals with empirical science, decided that something had been left out. His own language is different, but he finds that there is another aspect to reality which he calls "the will." He could have just as well called it the self, for that matter. He then develops in his second critique, the *Foundation of Metaphysics and Morals,* a story about that world — *The Kingdom of Ends.* In *The Kingdom of Ends,* we are all wills — nobody is a class. Nobody is a man, woman, adult, black, white, etc.; we are all wills, not distinguishable by any class categories. Here is a man who spent his life in what we would today call hard science. He worked in physics and astronomy, wrote a basic text on the philosophy of science, etc. In the 1780's he comes to the realization that something in his life has been left out. For all the complexity lies on the phenomenal side, there still is another world. At the end of one of his books, there is this statement: "Two things fill my heart with never-ending awe: the starry heavens above, and the moral law within." If I could paraphrase that, without ruining Kant's original saying, I would do it as follows: Two things fill my heart with never-ending awe: the complexity of the total social system forever, and the self within. No one should stand up and say, "Look, you have to forget that self within; we have other problems — pollution, poverty, etc. — on our hands." The inner world is just as important, but is it as immense as the

ISBN 0-201-04096-4

starry heavens? Yes it is! I think it is just as immense, just as awesome, and just as compelling. In modern phenomenology the call for attention to the inner self is to be found in Husserl and Heidegger, and in psychology, especially in Carl Gustav Jung and the Jungians, but there are many other people writing on the same theme, the development of the self.

In *Two Essays on Analytical Psychology,* Jung says that, until you have gone through the process of individuation, which is his label for the understanding of the self, you will not be able to face the social problems. You will not be able to build your models and tell the world what to do.

For the Christians among the readers, I will cite Matthew, chapter 25, as well as tell a little story. Some of my students were at Laguna Beach (California) trying to help the community in its desperate plight. It really is a community that has a desperate plight, since it is torn apart at its very foundation. Some people in a lovely little town on the Pacific beach south of Los Angeles want to put up high-rise developments. Some people see development as the end of old Laguna: the artists will be gone, and shops and hotels will take their place. Then there are the hippies, some living off drugs and painting pictures, and the three rich-man ghettos, where you have to have a card in hand in order to enter. So the community is torn apart.

The students and others were trying to help the community pull together. When I visited them, they had a little place in the center of town they called the Volunteer Post, where people could drop in and talk about their problems. Even the police chief occasionally dropped by. That day they had a schizophrenic on their hands, a very disturbed young man. Eventually he went out to get us some coffee, and they said to me, "We've been talking to this guy all day long. It seems to us that this big city of Laguna Beach is being neglected because we are spending all our time with one disturbed man." I then got out Matthew, chapter 25, and read it. It says that the King on Judgment Day turns to those on his right hand saying, "you fed me when I was hungry, you clothed me when I was naked . . .," and so on, and they say to him, "Lord, when did we do any of these things?" The answer is, "Even as you did it onto the least of these, my brethren, you did it onto me." One case.

Thus, from that perspective of the unique individual, it is not counting up how many people on this side and how many on that side. All the global systems things go out: there are no trade-offs in this world, in this immense world of the inner self. You do not trade off your evil by going out and doing good. Forgiveness happens, but that is not a trade-off. All our concepts that work so well in the global world do not work in the inner world, which is essentially a world that is ineffable for the English language. We have great trouble describing it very well in scientific language, but it is there, exists, and is important. I know what the global planner's answer will be: How am I going to put the two together? How am I going to put an individual person into the model? Of course, the answer is, You are not going to do it! "Well, what am I going to do? *Are* you telling me that I have to

ISBN 0-201-04096-4

pay attention to the unique individual, or *aren't* you telling me that? Anyway, I don't know how to do it because I have to handle 300 years and billions of people and you are telling me that I have to handle the unique individual. Tell me what to do." The philosopher is *not* going to tell you what to do. I warned you at the beginning, I am not going to answer any questions, so I am not going to answer that one.

Hegel was one figure in history who had a suggestion. He suggested in his writing that the mature individual is the individual who can hold conflicting world views (*Weltanschauungen*) together at the same time, and act, and live, and that his or her life is enriched by that capability — not weakened by it. If you can think about that — that will be the end of my message here. That is complexity, that is really complexity! To be able to see the world globally, which you are going to have to be able to do, and to see it as a world of unique individuals — a Kingdom of Ends, each individual infinitely valuable in itself, not to be "compared" excepting perhaps through some key words. The key words for that world are: faith, hope, and love. With those in hand, and Paul's message, complexity can be handled if these exist. If they don't, it can't be. But these come out of the inner self; do not try to define them, please. If you do, realize that you are ruining them. You cannot define hope. But if it is not present in today's society, then according to Paul, a systems man, the whole of human destiny will fail.

The title of this paper is "A Philosophy for Complexity," and what I have been trying to do is to develop for you a kind of mode of questioning, essentially using historical literature as a basis. I have simply been generating many questions so that you can reflect on the issue better. Wherein is its reality and our way of perceiving it? How do we understand complexity? And, what is the value of complexity?

ISBN 0-201-04096-4

III. 3. Planning's Challenge to the Systems Approach

DONALD N. MICHAEL

I want to share with you some of my "thinking in action": where I am in my struggles to understand some of the issues of effective long-range social planning.[1] I invite you to share my struggle and help me think about how to get on with it. I cannot talk about Planning's Challenge to the Systems Approach or even the planner's challenge to that approach. What I am going to talk about ought to be of concern to all planners, and it is to some. But much of what I will be exploring I am certainly not going to represent as the conventional position or preoccupation of the activity or its practitioners. I will talk about *my* challenge to that approach. Nor do I really mean to "challenge." Instead, I seek your help as systems analysts and systems designers.

To put it another way, I am uncertain about what planning should be in the kind of world I would like ours to evolve into. I am uncertain partly because I am not at all clear about what values and ways of being a future world might have and how I would feel about them if I were living in it. What this means, essentially, is that working our way from where we are to where we might be is a learning activity. I think of planning as a mode of learning rather than as a kind of engineering. (I will return to this point later.)

Let me now indicate what, it seems to me, are some of the necessary characteristics of a planning perspective. Doing so will lead into how the systems analyst, the systems designer, and the systems approach might help the planner. For me, planning is *one* way of trying to *cope with* or *live with* societal complexity. There are other ways: the religious way, the political way, the esthetic way, and so on. Planning could very well partake of these, but the point here is that planning is not the only way to try to live with or cope with societal complexity. Note, too, I emphasized planning as a way to "cope with or live with complexity," rather than a way to eliminate complexity. (This, I think, is in keeping with the concept of safe-fail, which Holling offers us in a subsequent paper.) Planning ought to be a way of moving with complexity so that the complexity is enriching rather than destroying. If we look at planning this way, what are some more specific implications of the position?

From this perspective one can perceive two aspects to social complexity. One is a regulable aspect, and the other is a turbulent aspect. To be perceived as regulable

---

[1] These thoughts will be fragmentary and sometimes probably contradictory, but what in them is coherent and useful will probably turn out to have been better and more usefully expressed in one or more of West Churchman's writings. I am enlightened, dismayed, and delighted — all at once — when I read or talk with him to find out he has usually been there first.

Futures Research: New Directions, Harold A. Linstone and W. H. Clive Simmonds (eds.)

ISBN 0-201-04096-4

is to be perceived as capable of maintaining relationships through time — i.e., part of our world that is perceived by us, whatever the basis for that perception, as having continuity, expectedness, reliability, stability. The other aspect we perceive is the turbulent — that part consisting of the unpredictable, the unanticipatable, sometimes the unlocatable sources of change.

Turbulence, as I use the idea, is partly a product of ignorance. That is, if we had certain information we might, in principle, be able to do something so as to transform turbulence into part of the regulable — not necessarily that we would want to, but that we could, if we wanted to. The other aspect of turbulence I will call "true" turbulence. By "true" I mean that the circumstances or outcomes are unanticipatable, even in principle. Mutations, emergent social processes, new theory, new art styles are examples. One cannot anticipate their characteristics. (When I come to emerge in societal processes, I will say more about this.)

Possibly the most impressive, certainly one of the most obvious examples of what I am calling true turbulence — its unpredictability and unanticipatability — is that of the "great man." One can argue whether society makes great men or great men make society. Either way, individuals make an unanticipatable difference, for, as West emphasized, a person consists of much more than his/her surface and rational characteristics. A person is a vast universe, a cosmos of the unconscience, and this is hidden from us. It is this unconscious that is the source of inspiration and vitality that subtains our activities, our wills, our wishes, and our directions. But this unconscious self does not operate according to the logics of our systems design or language, nor is it reducible to any linguistic or mathematical mode. So, great persons arise partly out of the thrust of their unconscious and out of whatever appeal they have to the unconscious of others, and because part of the source of their greatness derives from the unconscious, their coming and sequences are unanticipatable, unpredictable. They produce turbulence and are in part the product of turbulence. So too, to a greater or lesser degree, with all events, made by or significant for human beings.

Let me mention another aspect of what I mean by planning in preparation for examining what kind of help it would be good to have from the systems approach. Planning should increase our options for human development. It need not do this solely by increasing the predictable and decreasing the turbulent. Some planning efforts would be for the purposes of increasing turbulence in order to open up unpredictable ways that lead to further human development by decreasing gratuitously constraining stability.

The conclusion from all of this is that planning must be a learning process; it cannot be a social engineering process. Engineering is based on reliable experience, which, in turn, derives from replicable experiences. We act most of the time as if our experience with our pasts and presents were replicable, and that is partly what gives our world its stability. But this assumed or imposed reliability also can and does lead us into counterproductive and unproductive beliefs and actions. The planning tasks, then, are to *learn* what, at a given time, can be accepted as reliable;

ISBN 0-201-04096-4

what can be regulated to make it reliable, what cannot be regulated, and what we should not attempt to regulate in order to make it reliable. But we do not know how to accomplish any of those tasks in our kind of world. There is an irony to planning: you do not need it when most of the world is stable; but you do need it when there is much turbulence. However, when there is much turbulence, the reliable experience is lacking that is necessary for engineering – regularizing – the human situation. So we have to learn what is worth paying attention to that can be transformed, that can be made reliable, and what ought not to be made reliable, what should be left to grow its own way so that we can discover what it creates by way of richer human beings. Thus, planners, plans, the systems approach, and the products of the systems approach all must be part of the societal learning process. And all those people who are planners and systems analysts must become learners.

What are they to learn? I think they are to learn new myths regarding the constitution of social reality. They would learn what these new myths might be by making fundamental contributions to their creation, and by being part of their content.

I am not using "myth" deprecatively. I will try to clarify the way I am using "myth" by indicating my view of the nature of "social reality." These are not uniquely my ideas. They represent the accumulated understanding of anthropologists, psychologists, historians, and philosophers. The point is – the myth about reality that I would like you to sustain at least while listening to the rest of what I say – that we *create* our social reality. And part of what we create when we create our social reality are the conditions for demonstrating to ourselves that it is real. We create myths, in other words. About who we are, and what we are, and why we are. Let me quote from two scholars in this area. What they have to say is central to the kind of ideas I want to share with you about the relation of planning and the systems approach:

> It is important to keep in mind that the objectivity of the institutional world, however massive it may appear to the individual, is a humanly produced, constructed objectivity. . . The objectivity of the social world means that it confronts man as something outside of himself. The decisive question is whether he still retains the awareness that, however objectivated, the social world was made by men – and, therefore, can be remade by them. . . Typically, the real relationship between man and his world is reversed in consciousness. Man, the producer of a world, is apprehended as its product, and human activity as an epiphenomenon of non-human processes. Human meanings are no longer understood as world-producing but as being, in their turn, products of the "nature of things."[1a]

[1a]P. L. Berger and T. Luckmann, "The Social Construction of Reality," Anchor Books, New York, 1967, pp. 60 and 89.

Evidence from every corpus of knowledge about human behavior supports this. So myth – the "humanly constructed objectivity" – determines what we pay attention to and why. And myth engenders action that reinforces myth.[2] Myths also exclude alternative ways of being and doing and perceiving. You recall the injunction, "Seek and you shall find." That is exactly what myth making does. There seems no way around it – except through "enlightenment" or transcendence or madness, but these are not the circumstance of planners or their clients – at least not now. If you will, then, the myth I am asking you to subscribe to here is that this is the way human beings are.

Let me describe one other characteristic of the social world before indicating the kind of help I would like from the systems analysts and designers. This other characteristic of the social world is the process of emergence. "Emergence" refers to the unanticipatable characteristics of superordinate regulative processes that grow out of the circumstances that were there before they came to be. These regulative processes are the network of relationship-maintaining processes that pattern our social intercourse. They are the *whole* that is greater than the sum of the parts. Emergent properties cannot be predicted from the parts. You cannot predict a new theory from what we know; you cannot predict the properties of a machine from physical and chemical characteristics of the materials comprising the machine; you cannot predict the content of a book from the words, or its vocabulary from the laws of syntax. And so on and so on. This is true in art, in science, in social forms, in perception. What happens over time in the human condition is that ways of being and doing, the regulative processes, the stabilizing processes, evolve beyond the parts that make them up. It is the synthesis between thesis and antithesis that Hegel was talking about, and the synthesis is not predictable from the characteristics of the thesis or the antithesis. Certainly, this is partly because unconscious processes invariably and powerfully operate in the creation of and response to the events human beings live in. But somehow a new synthesis happens. And we get, for example, a market economy, utterly unpredictable if you were a feudal lord. Heaven only knows what we will get some time in the future out of today's turbulent interaction of events, and persons, and processes. So, there is an emergent property "attached" to our condition, a transforming property that is particularly important in periods of high change like this. Through most time and most societies regulative systems have been adequate to keep the parts going in a predictable, accountable, reliable way. Ours is in a period of change, but it is not just a movement of the pieces, so to speak. Our period is probably emerging by way of new myths to new forms of regulative stability. But when and to what, nobody can know. This, then, is the kind of myth about social reality I work with when I think about the problems and possibilities of using the

---

[2]In dynamic societies these actions and the conditions produced by them eventually undermine the dominant myths. A more familiar example of this process is that of paradigm change in science as delineated by T. Kuhn, *The Structure of Scientific Revolutions,* 2nd ed., University of Chicago Press, Chicago, 1970.

ISBN 0-201-04096-4

systems approach for helping to cope with and live with societal complexity.

In this light, what do I think I need and would like other planners to seek from the systems approach? To begin with, I would like the systems approach to provide me with two kinds of descriptions, two kinds of understanding. One is a description of the social reality, the social processes, that characterize the perceived stable parts of the human condition. The other is the transformation rules to help me understand what kinds of temporary regulative processes might provide a felicitous transformation period from where we are to some emergent society. For these to be useful to me I need descriptions of the social world that *include* the human beings who contribute to the regulated aspects of the world and to its emergent aspects through the application of the systems approach. That is, these descriptions need to include descriptions of the planners and the systems creators, their accepting or rejecting clients, and the consequences of the relationships among them. For, by the very fact of their creativeness, those contributing to the analysis and design of social systems must be self-conscious about themselves as biased intervenors into social reality. Let me offer some examples of how this is so and, hence, why it is necessary to include the planner, the systems analyst, and the designer, and their clients, in the very descriptions of the stability characteristics and the transformation processes of social reality provided by the systems approach.

In the first place, systems descriptions, if they make or are intended to make a difference, are neither passive nor neutral. Systems descriptions are active; they are influential. What I am emphasizing is that I want something from systems people that will influence me to use it. And for me to use it means that I think it or its application will also influence other people. Now, systems images that influence do so partly because they satisfy the reality description requirements of their consumers. Hence, they are not neutral.

Let me give you an example drawn to my attention by my colleague, Duane Elgin. The President's Commission on Population and America's Future generated a nice systems description of where the centers of population growth are expected to be in the United States. By providing that systems description they very likely increased the likelihood that those will in fact be the centers of population growth, because those people who seek to benefit from population growth will focus their activities in those places, thus making the population grow.

Systems designs are also arbitrary, a point that has been emphasized in many ways, many times. I include it here as part of my general argument. The point is, of course, that we cannot attend to everything; so we attend to what is important. But perceived importance is certainly dependent on the socially rewarded skills of the person doing the attending. One attends to those things that make a difference in one's life. So the systems analyst and/or designer attends to those things that are stable enough to represent as a system; i.e., they maintain their relationship through time. And the systems analyst seeks out such stability and represents it as a system because that is what a systems analyst is rewarded for doing — rewarded in the psychological sense. "This is who I am," says the systems

ISBN 0-201-04096-4

analyst, "the person who can reveal and relate these interactive stabilities." Typically, then, the systems analyst or the systems analysis excludes those very instabilities that disrupt that which the systems people are trying to represent as a system. And in our time that excludes an awful lot because there is an awful lot that is in the process of being transformed!

Another reason why the description of social reality must include the systems planner and designer in the system that is being represented is that part of the system that must be modeled are the processes that result in the use or non-use of the knowledge about the system. The effect of the system image on planning depends, obviously, on whether people, including planners, use the image or not. This being so, one must include in the system description the knowledge utilization processes concerning the use of the system description; i.e., what happens when the system image is presented to the planner or the planner's client. How it is used, or not used, or partially used influences the "reality" – i.e., the system in which all parties are part. We are beginning to understand this knowledge utilization process, and that understanding illuminates our misconceptions about the putative attractiveness of new knowledge. There is widespread belief that, if you "build a better mousetrap, people will beat a path to your door." Quite the contrary, build a better mousetrap and you will have to pull people kicking and screaming through your door even to look at it. For many reasons, most people most of the time do not use new knowledge, and this can and often does include planners and systems people. Therefore, what the planner needs from the systems approach is a "reality" that includes what happens to the systems approach when s/he tries to use it – just because its use is not a foregone conclusion.

Moreover, if the systems approach is to be influential – that is, if it is to be useful to planners – then the systems analyst and designer must include themselves as part of the system's transforming process. By creating an image of a system, the analyst or designer contributes to creating a myth, a "reality" that channels the actions of people, including their own actions and those of planners. Thus, systems people must include themselves as societal "input generators"; they are creating a system out of a nonsystem or out of an earlier version of a system. (By nonsystem I mean that which was not recognized as a system until the systems designer painted it, sculptured it, equated it out of the blooming, buzzing confusion we live in.)

In this activity, systems analysts and designers are also systems *transformers* through their representations of the systems that grow from the planners' actions in response to the system that *was* earlier provided by the systems analyst. That is, if systems people represent an earlier reality in an influential way, then, as a result, they contribute to the creation of a new reality. The systems designer always represents a previous social reality, because by the time the image is used there is another social reality. But the designer is also a systems transformer by the very act of doing this. S/he provides something which, if it is influential, alters that social reality. Thus, part of the system, both the stable and the transforming aspects, will be what they will be because of the altered reality created by the

ISBN 0-201-04096-4

systems analyst and the planner in the act of convincingly (i.e., influentially) describing the system. At the very least the planner has to be convinced. That is, s/he needs a convincing systems design and analysis, to have the incentive to act, to intervene. The planner needs a myth to believe in, to be inspired by, to be guided by.

In part I have been anticipating my second request for help from the systems approach: a description of the system's transforming processes by which the social system that is described learns to become another system. The system approach ought to be able to provide some understanding of the relation between societal being and becoming − the learning process. In different words, the planner needs systems designers and analysts who are knowledgeably, actively, cautiously, and with a great deal of anguish, acting as myth makers. That is, by creating their systems as their myths, they may contribute to the stable component of the social system. This, then, could be used as a reference, a comparatively solid base, while we learn to become something else as we live in the turbulent component of our world. People gain the vitality and assurance to act through such stabilities. What happens is that the representation, the system image, is seen as natural − this is the way things are; this is how things fit together; this is why it is good this way. Thus people may be focused and stimulated by such myths.

Let me exemplify this by reminding you of two powerful myths which grew from primitive to quite sophisticated models. People, believing in them, acted them out and reinforced them. Seeking, they found. One was the myth of the market economy, that there really was an automatically regulating system, "the hidden hand." People acted out that myth, that model, that "systems analysis," and it became for a long time a basis for societal regulation.

The other myth started out, significantly, as a description by political scientists of how the political process operates in the United States; it is called disjointed incrementalism. This means that each agency and effort goes its own disjointed way, a little bit at a time, moving backward crablike, looking at where it has been, not at where it is going. It started out as a description, but it ended up as the theoretical justification for interest-group pluralism and engendered a belief that that is the natural way for people to behave efficiently and effectively in an open society.[3] (It also ended us up, I think, in some of our present mess because disjointed incrementalism has been essentially indifferent to the requirements for a *shared future*.) At any rate, these were/are two powerful myths created by earlier generations of systems designers and analysts, though they did not call themselves such.

One highly desirable consequence of all this would be the possibility of reducing undesirable turbulence by providing a myth about what it is "natural" to do, or to be, according to which people would then want to act. Then, to the extent that

ISBN 0-201-04096-4

[3] T. J. Lowi, *The End of Liberalism: Ideology, Policy, and the Crisis of Public Authority*, Norton, New York, 1969.

people behave that way, maybe turbulence would be reduced. Sir Geoffrey Vickers, a deeply perceptive explorer of societal regulation, once observed that the reason that people are a lot more reliable than random events is because they *want* to be.[4] And people want to be reliable in terms of what they think is natural and right, and what they think is natural and right has to do with the myths they subscribe to about reality and self and their relationships. What I am proposing here is that a crucially important role for the analyst and the designer is to create such potentially stabilizing myths — but in a *temporary* form. What is needed here is a state of mind, a state of being, in which system makers see themselves as creating viable and humane but temporary myths, rather than seeing themselves as describing "objective reality." Both feet planted firmly in midair. Because once one moves away from recognizing the need to live in a world of temporary myths, one runs the grave risk of coming to believe that the myths one creates are *the* reality. Then the opportunity is lost for the kind of learning that planning should try to facilitate.

Now to be the kind of person who truly accepts his responsibility as that of creating certain kinds of temporary realities requires knowledge of and access to self far beyond that possessed by most people in this society. Not that it is not there to be uncovered in most of us; rather, most of us have it pretty well hidden, repressed, covered up. It requires such knowledge and access because being a creator and participator in temporary myths in a turbulent world lays very heavy personal demands on the systems person and the planner. I will mention two requirements: living with uncertainty, and embracing error.

The experience of uncertainty, as I am using the word, is not that dealt with in economics or decision theory. I mean psychological uncertainty: the uncertainty that arises when you know that you do not know; when you know that there is no honest way to put a number on something, no subjective probability to be assigned. It is the uncertainty that comes when you realize that you do not understand your situation well enough to be in control of it. All one can do is live in it and learn from it and try to create possibilities and see what happens to them as one goes along, whether they add to one's life and the lives of others or they do not. But living this way, especially as a professional using the systems approach — an approach that is supposed to reduce uncertainty — calls for a special sense of self-worthiness.

Error embracing is *the* condition for learning. It means seeking and using — and sharing — information about what went wrong with what you expected or hoped would go right. Both error embracing and living with high levels of uncertainty emphasize our personal as well as societal vulnerability. Typically, we hide our vulnerabilities from ourselves as well as from others. But if we are going to create and live in temporary myths, we must understand our repressed fears and anxieties

[4]G. Vickers, *Freedom in a Rocking Boat: Changing Values in an Unstable Society,* The Penguin Press, London, 1970.

ISBN 0-201-04096-4

about being vulnerable and learn to live with them and use them creatively.

Geoffrey Vickers[5] distinguishes two conditions of social change. One has to do with change that arises when you have a sure base to work from; when the myths of the society are strong, its creativity grows from that vitality. Examples are the Renaissance and, in some places, earlier periods in the history of the United States. The other kind of social change occurs when the myths come apart, and change is the response to having little one can cling to. The latter condition seems to be ours. Under such circumstances there is an enormous incentive for the planner to seek assurances from the systems person and for the systems person to want to provide them. Both would like to believe that "this is the way things *are*." Then they can, in high spirits, expect to build on those assurances. I am arguing that this is the wrong way to go. What both the planner should be seeking, and the systems person seeking to provide, are temporary platforms, places to move on from, to learn from, to check where we might be going to. Realizing this tentative situation, this situation of having both feet planted firmly in midair, is to my mind *the* chief challenge for both the planner and the analyst/designer. And it is a challenge we presently do not know how to meet. If the challenge can be met, we will have to *learn* how to do so. We will have to learn how to create the myths that make such learning possible.

ISBN 0-201-04096-4

[5]ibid.

III. 4. Large Systems

RICHARD BELLMAN

Introduction

Let me begin with the following story.

Gertude Stein was dying. Gertrude Stein, as you may recall, was a hippy of the 1920's. She said, "A rose is a rose is a rose," and naturally acquired quite a reputation for wisdom. Her faithful acolytes felt that as she lay dying she would see even further. Her friend, probably Alice B. Toklas, said, "Gertrude, Gertrude, what is the answer?" Gertrude Stein opened her eyes for the last time and said, "What is the question"?

We cannot expect easy answers to hard questions.

In this paper, I want to pose some questions. It would be well if I gave answers, but it will be sufficient if I give some directions.

Problems of Society

It is clear that society needs some guidance. It is a good society, probably the best we have had so far. But it is obvious that it cannot run itself.

We are fortunate people. Society needs trained people, and we are trained.

What systems am I thinking of? I am thinking of the economic system, the city, the fundamental tool of civilization, energy, the environment, health, education, and welfare. I am sure that you will think of other systems.

Every business represents a system. Indeed, it represents many systems. Usually, they are in the same direction but not always.

What Can Mathematicians Do?

But what can a mathematician do? He wants to be relevant, but obviously classical mathematics not brought up to date is not relevant. Fortunately, there is a great deal that we can do.

We do not want him to be a sociologist. He has neither the training nor the inclination. We do not want a society run by mathematicians and computers, nor do we want a society without mathematics and computers.

Communication

Let us begin with the observation that in six thousand years we have not learned to make a good teapot. In other words, we do not know yet how to transmit liquid from one place to another. How much more difficult is it to transmit ideas? It is obvious that in twenty-five years we have not learned how to use a computer. In

ISBN 0-201-04096-4

other words, we do not know how to communicate with a computer, either from a man to a computer or from a computer to a man. We do not understand how to communicate ideas.

This has become clear in many areas of artifical intelligence. For example, machine translation has failed almost completely. In general, we do not know how to use experts. We do not understand how to communicate ideas across fields.

Mathematicians know some of the answers, but how do they communicate them to the nonmathematicians? It is a very interesting and nontrivial question. Anybody who has tried to use a computer understands the many difficulties that arise.[1]

Structure

Obviously, each system has a different structure. The mathematician can use his knowledge of algebra and topology to good avail here.

It is very important to know what are the different systems, and what their structures are. We can expect that different systems will require different methods. As a matter of fact, different systems may require quite different conceptual approaches. It is appropriate to quote Emerson: "A foolish consistency is the hobgoblin of small minds."[2]

It is also important to study the levels of various decisions. This means that stratification and the theory of types will play a significant role. The logician can participate very meaningfully here.

Mathematical Models

The mathematician is a keeper of abstractions. There are people who say that they are very practical and that they do not use theories. This is not so. As Boltzmann said, "There is nothing as practical as a good theory." Everybody uses theories, some explicitly and some implicitly. One of the functions of mathematics is to make assumptions explicit.

One of the functions of the mathematician is to construct various mathematical models of the process under consideration. These models are to be used by the major decision maker for decision-making. It is his responsibility to look at the assumptions and see whether he agrees with them.

It is important to realize that the same process can give rise to many different mathematical models, and the same mathematical model can be treated by several different methods.

---

[1] R. Bellman, Communication, Ambiguity and Understanding, *Mathematical Biosciences,* in press.

[2] R. Bellman, *Local Logics,* 1975 International Symposium on Multiple-Valued Logics, Indiana University, Bloomington, Indiana, May 13-16, 1975.

ISBN 0-201-04096-4

Mathematical Theories

The mathematician must have various mathematical theories at his disposal. He has to deal with the future, which means uncertainty, and he has to deal with decision-making. This means that he should be familiar with classical probability theory, which handles one type of uncertainty, and also with such modern theories as the theory of fuzzy systems of Zadeh. For decision-making he should be familiar with dynamic programming and control theory.[3-5]

Curse of Dimensionality

The difficulty with mathematical models is not too few data, but too many data. We have given this difficulty the name of Curse of Dimensionality. Many interesting problems concerning the use of data arise in this way. These problems have not been worked on to any extent.

This is particularly the case with modern computers. They give a great deal of data. Unless the mathematician arranges these data, the major decision-maker will either ignore the data or use the wrong data.

Simulation

By "simulation" we mean constructing a model of the process and testing various policies for operating the system. This procedure allows effective use of computers, and this is particularly important at a time when the computers are getting faster and the fast storage is getting bigger and cheaper. It must be understood that simulation is difficult. Although many people have written about it, it remains an art form.

Simulation permits the testing of various policies in electronic time. It means that digital computers can be well used.[6,7]

If the model is made too large, we learn nothing. If the model is made too small, we learn nothing. In many cases we learn most from the construction of the model.

[3]R. Bellman and S. Dreyfus, *Applied Dynamic Programming,* Princeton University Press, Princeton, New Jersey, 1962.

[4]R. Bellman, *Introduction to the Mathematical Theory of Control Processes,* Vol. 1, Academic Press, New York, 1968.

[5]R. Bellman, *Introduction to the Mathematical Theory of Control Processes,* Vol. II, Academic Press, New York, 1971.

[6]R. Bellman, "On Top Management Simulation," in Elizabeth Marting (ed.), *Top Management Decision Simulation,* American Management Association, New York, 1957.

[7]R. Bellman and C. P. Smith, *Simulation in Human Systems – Decision-Making in Psychotherapy,* John Wiley & Sons, New York, 1973.

ISBN 0-201-04096-4

Opportunities

What the foregoing means is that there are tremendous opportunities for the young mathematician. Almost everything remains to be done, and it is very important. It also means that there is little point in going to the literature. These are new problems.

ISBN 0-201-04096-4

III. 5. The Curious Behavior of Complex Systems: Lessons from Biology[1]

HEINZ VON FOERSTER

The topic of this paper is the management of complexity. More precisely, I would like to discuss the behavior of complex systems in the biological context as related to the management of complex systems in the social context. The question to be considered is: What lessons can be learned from biology that are applicable to the management of complex social systems?

Some years ago, I could have responded to this question by filling pages with charming metaphors and anecdotes of the superficial parallelisms between living organisms and social organisms. I could have used the standard analogies — for example, the parallel between the brain and mankind. There are now about 4 billion people in the world — this is 4×10^9 people. The brain has about 10 billion or 10×10^9 neurons. So the ratio between the number of people on the globe and the number of neurons is about 1 : 2. I could argue, for instance, that a neuron has an average of 3000 connections to other neurons in the brain. I could argue that individual people during the course of their lives have approximately the same number of connections to other persons. I might also refer to the other metaphor that is used quite frequently, that the brain is the manager of your body.

There are many of these parallels between social and biological systems, and they are quite interesting. A new paradigm is emerging, however, which is changing the way in which we view biological and social organizations. Our appreciation of the similarities and differences between biological and social systems is changing, and as a result all these superficial analogies collapse. We find that these analogies not only can be misleading, they can even be dangerous.

As an example of the dangerous consequences of taking these metaphors seriously, consider the following metaphor with which you will probably be pestered throughout your life. This is: "A cell is subservient to the good of the body as a whole, and so is an individual subservient to the good of the nation." Belief in that metaphor has led to societies such as Germany during the Hitler years, where, I can tell you, this phrase was painted on the walls. And when the individual is nothing, and the nation is all, what do you do with individuals? Of course, you can just dismiss them, you can put them into ovens, or you can exterminate them with Cyclone B as was done in the concentration camps. This metaphor must be reversed; the society should be subservient to the individual and not the other way around.

---

[1]I dedicate this piece to Ann Corrigan, whose sensitivity for the thoughts I wish to express, and for the language in which these thoughts should be expressed, made it possible that they are now expressed at all.

Futures Research: New Directions, Harold A. Linstone and W. H. Clive Simmonds (eds.)

ISBN 0-201-04096-4

To fully appreciate this point, one has to realize the autonomy of the living organism. I am an autonomous entity; my cells are not. My finger is not autonomous, my arm is not autonomous. I would be autonomous even if I had passed through a severe brain operation. I wish to refer here to a point made by C. West Churchman in a preceding paper; that is, do not forget the "self." The self is precisely that autonomous entity which is the living organism.

If we still wish to use the living organization as a parallel for the organization of the living — i.e., the social organization — then we will have to ascend to much higher levels of abstraction, or we will have to go to much deeper levels of epistemology. My strategy here will be to present, in three steps, several subtleties that arise from a deeper consideration of the parallels and differences between biological and social organisms. I will first point out a peculiar culturally embedded cognitive dysfunction which inhibits some of us from viewing the management of complexity in a productive perspective. I will show that this cognitive dysfunction is being weakened by the emerging paradigm to which I have made reference. In step two I will address the topic of this paper directly — namely, the topic of management. I will interpret a managerial act as a cognitive act by showing that underlying both these processes is the fundamental concept of computation. I will then allow myself a short digression into mathematical formalism in order to show what properties are associated with these operations of cognition and management. Finally, in step three, I will consider some managerial and ethical consequences of these subtleties. It will be shown that managerial problems and ethical problems are closely related.

It is becoming increasingly clear that the crucial problems of today are societal. These problems arise from the tremendous complexity of the modern society. However, the conceptual problem-solving apparatus that Western culture has developed is incapable not only of solving the societal problems, but even of perceiving these problems. The blind spot which does not allow us to perceive the complex societal problems has two roots. One is the traditional reductionist approach to problem solving; the other is the traditional explanatory paradigm of causation. Both of these are now under assault.

As Linstone has stated (Part I), the traditional reductionist approach destroys the problem it wants to explain. In this approach, if you have a large complex problem and you do not understand it, you chop it into pieces. If you do not understand these pieces, you chop again. You continue chopping until the pieces are small enough and simple enough to be understood. Thus reductionism always leads to success, but the result is that you know everything about nothing. On the other hand, if you take the approach of holism, considering larger and larger systems, you eventually know nothing about everything. But if neither way is to be recommended, what then must we do? We must not chop, we must learn how to see. The point I am trying to make is that we do not know how to see. This is because of another preoccupation of our Western culture — namely, the explanatory paradigm of causation.

ISBN 0-201-04096-4

Causation is inoperative particularly in explaining the behavior of social systems. This is because the law that supposedly transforms the past cause into the present effect is itself changed by the very effect it produces. In other words, consider the system-theoretic concept of a nontrivial machine. A nontrivial machine has the property that, whenever it carries out a computation, it becomes a different machine. Thus it is very difficult to predict a nontrivial machine. The usual way in which we accomplish this is to trivialize the human being. When children come into school they are unpredictable; you do not know what they will say when you ask them a question. You trivialize them so that they become predictable citizens; they come up with the "right" answer. But if we truly want to understand society, we will have to understand the nontrivial machine.

This observation that the paradigm of causation prevents us from seeing was first brought to my attention by Carlos Castaneda, who has reported his experiences with one of his teachers, a Mexican brujo named Don Juan. Don Juan wants to teach Castaneda how to see. But Castaneda experiences great difficulties, because he always wants to explain things, and things he cannot explain, he cannot see. So Don Juan always tells him, "Now Carlitos, do not explain things, look what you can see!" Carlitos still experiences difficulties, and he has explained these difficulties now in four volumes,[2] and they are very enlightening with respect to what it means to *see*. Unfortunately, at that point both he and we have a blind spot. But this blind spot is not simply that we do not see; rather, we do not see that we do not see. That is a dysfunction of the second order; and a therapy for a dysfunction of the second order must be a therapy of the second order.

The popularity of Castaneda's books persuades me to think again of Magoroh Maruyama's idea of an emerging new paradigm.[3] One aspect of this paradigm is the idea that properties that were thought to reside in objects are becoming recognized as properties of the observer. An example is the property of "obscenity." There is now a tremendous effort, even in the Supreme Court, to determine what is obscene. Recognizing obscenity, however, is a property of the observer and not of the object being observed. If you show a picture to Mr. X, and Mr. X says, "This picture is obscene!" you know something about Mr. X but very little about the picture.

A second example is the property of order. Recognition of order, like obscenity, is a property of the observer and not of the observed. To make this point clear, consider the two sequences of numbers in Fig. 1. The top sequence is nicely ordered, while the sequence underneath appears random. But the second sequence can also be considered perfectly ordered, if the observer is able to perceive

---

[2]C. Castaneda, *The Teachings of Don Juan: A Yaqui Way of Knowledge*, Simon and Schuster, New York, 1968; *A Separate Reality: Further Conversations with Don Juan*, Simon and Schuster, New York, 1971; *Journey to Ixtlan: The Last Lessons of Don Juan*, Simon and Schuster, New York, 1973; *Tales of Power*, Simon and Schuster, New York, 1974.

[3]M. Maruyama, "Toward Cultural Symbiosis", in E. Jantsch and C. H. Waddington (eds.), *Evolution and Consciousness: Human Systems in Transition*, Addison-Wesley, Reading, Massachusetts, 1976, pp. 198-213.

ISBN 0-201-04096-4

it. The numbers in the second sequence have been placed in alphabetical order according to the names of the numerals.

1 2 3 4 5 6 7 8 9
8 5 4 9 1 7 6 3 2

Fig. 1

This example may be presented somewhat more rigorously. The order of a sequence may be defined to be the length of the description of that sequence, given a particular language. For example, a Turing machine could be used to compute a sequence, given an input tape which we will take as a description of that sequence. The length of the input tape would be a measure of the order of the sequence with respect to the language of that Turing machine. A Turing machine to compute the first sequence (up to an arbitrary length) of Fig. 1 would require only a short description: that is, "The next number of the sequence is 1 + the previous number." In the case of the second sequence, the description is just "alphabetical." In a random sequence one must name all the numbers in the sequence and the description becomes very long (as long as the sequence).

A third example is that of complexity. Complexity can be defined as the length of computation that is necessary to produce a particular arrangement. Alternatively, and at one level higher, computation can be measured as the length of the algorithm used to compute the organization or arrangement of a system. Clearly, this measure of complexity is highly dependent on the language being used and, therefore, on the perceptive system of the observer.

This idea that properties are computed by observing systems and do not reside in observed systems leads to another point – namely, that a very basic concept of Western culture is crumbling: it is the concept of "objectivity." Briefly stated, objectivity is the premise that the properties of the observer shall not enter into the description of his observations. This is nonsense, however, because without the observer there are no descriptions. The observer's faculty of describing enters, by necessity, into his descriptions. Some philosophers believe, therefore, that one should negate objectivism and use subjectivism. However, if nonsense is negated, nonsense is again obtained. Neither objectivism nor subjectivism are legitimate approaches. But if objectivity and subjectivity are unacceptable, then how can we deal with observation? This question leads to my next point, step number two in my proposed strategy.

When I was first considering the topic Managing Complexity, I decided to look into a dictionary for the definition of "to manage." I found that "to manage" is "to direct or control the use of; to handle; to wield." To manage is "to exert

ISBN 0-201-04096-4

control over, to make submissive to one's authority, discipline and persuasion."
According to this definition, management reduces the degrees of freedom of the
system being managed. I also looked into the Indo-European roots of this verb to
obtain a clue to the deeper meaning of "managing"; this root is "to do with your
hands, to 'handle', or to 'unhandle' "; a related word is "manacle," which is
defined to be "a device for confining the hands, usually consisting of two metal
rings that are fastened about the wrist and joined by a metal chain." That is
management.

This view of management, however, comes from the old paradigm. A different
perspective has recently been offered (see papers by Michael and Holling). This is
the view that management must increase, not decrease, the degrees of freedom of
the system to be managed. This is a complete reversal of the description of management within the old paradigm and suggests that we are moving toward something
new.

Two operations are involved in management; one is the perception of the current
state of the system, and the second is an action or operation upon this state in
order to change it. I now wish to equate the managerial act with the cognitive act.
But what is cognition? Since "cognition" is a monolithic concept, it is necessary to
put that monolithic concept into a form that is accessible to our conceptual tools.
Such a form is shown in Fig. 2, where cognition is interpreted as "computing a
reality."

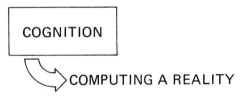

Fig. 2

You may have two objections to this interpretation of cognition as "computing
a reality." First, why "computation?" I assure you that computation is not at
all associated with purely numerical quantities. Computation is a very general
expression for all reorderings and rearrangements. Second, why "computing *a*
reality?" There is just the *one* reality. Again, this is the old paradigm speaking.
The new paradigm recognizes that there is not just one reality; rather, we must
recognize that there are many realities (see Michael). The reality of a Navajo, the
reality of a multimillionaire, the reality of a slum dweller, are quite different
realities. Cognition is the computation of just such *a* reality.

One may argue that one does not compute wrist watches, nor the galaxies, etc.;

ISBN 0-201-04096-4

what one may do is to compute a *description* of these objects. I yield to this argument and propose that cognition is to be considered as computing descriptions of a reality, as shown in Fig. 3. These descriptions of reality are what Don Michael has referred to as "myths." We are computing myths of a reality.

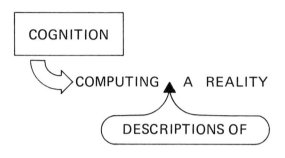

Fig. 3

A neurophysiologist will inform us that the process of visual perception begins with the rods and cones, which compute a description of the image being projected onto the retina. Behind these rods and cones are neurons which compute descriptions of the descriptions that have been computed by the rods and cones. The bipolar cells compute descriptions; these descriptions are sent to the ganglion cells which compute descriptions of the bipolar descriptions; the ganglion descriptions are then sent to the lateral geniculate nuclei; and so on. Visual perception, therefore, is a process of computing descriptions again and again and again. To account for this process, I propose that cognition be interpreted as computing descriptions of descriptions of descriptions, . . . , in an infinite recursion, as shown in Fig. 4.

Fig. 4

ISBN 0-201-04096-4

It should be noticed that, in Fig. 4, "reality" has disappeared. Reality is embedded in the recursion itself. This suggests that "reality" is not to be confused with "apples," "chairs," "tables," etc. Reality is something else; it has a different logical structure.

To go one step further, computing descriptions can be considered to be a computation. Cognition, therefore, can be interpreted as computations of computations of computations, . . . , in an infinite regress, as shown in Fig. 5.

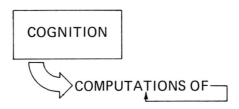

Fig. 5

The act of management involves perception of a state of the system followed by a reordering of the system into a different state. Management, like cognition, is a computation. Just as cognition has been shown to be computations of computations, etc., the act of management can be interpreted as management of management, etc. (see Fig. 6). This is a second-order description of management. The concept of recursive management corresponds to a point that has been made by Don Michael in a preceding paper — namely, that the manager must be a part of the system being managed. This is exactly the case of living organisms; they are their own managers. There is no "something" that manages the whole system. The system manages itself; therefore, it functions. It is a heterarchical, not a hierarchical, organization.

Fig. 6

I will now take a brief excursion into mathematical formalism, in order to investigate the properties that appear in these recursive computations. The tool used to handle recursive definitions is called recursive function theory; an example of a recursive function is given in Fig. 7. Here a function Y is defined as a trans-

ISBN 0-201-04096-4

form on some variable X_1. The transform T is any function – squaring, cosine, sine, etc. X_1 is defined as the same transform T performed on X_2. X_2 is T performed on X_3, and so on. The result of this recursive definition is that Y equals the transform on the transform on the transform, in an infinite recursion.

$$Y = T(X_1)$$

$$X_1 = T(X_2)$$

$$X_2 = T(X_3)$$

$$\cdot$$
$$\cdot$$
$$\cdot$$

$$Y = T(\underbrace{T(T(T,,,,}_{Y})$$

Fig. 7

Please note that a result of this recursive definition is that the independent variable, X, is gone. It has been computed away by a recursive computation. In the example of cognition and management, it is the "reality" that is computed away by the recursive computation. But can this infinitely recursive equation be solved? Certainly it can. Y is defined to be "the transform on the transform, etc., etc.," as shown in the last equation of Fig. 7. But that part of the right-hand side of the equation which has been marked by a bracket is also "the transform on the transform, etc., etc."; hence, the bracketed part is equal to Y. Thus Y is equal to $T(Y)$; Y is equal to the transform on itself (see Fig. 8).

$$\overline{Y} = T(\overline{Y})$$

$\overline{Y}$ Eigenvalue

Fig. 8

ISBN 0-201-04096-4

Some of these functions which are transforms on themselves have solutions that are stable; some have solutions that are unstable. I have put a bar on top of the Y in Fig. 8 to denote that these are values for which stable solutions exist. These stable values are called *eigenvalues*. For example, the eigenvalue of the square-root function is 1. If you take any positive number X_1, and compute its square root X_2, then compute the square root of X_2, and so on, the sequence of numbers will converge to the number 1. Another example is the differential operator, whose eigenvalue is the function e^x. The derivative of e^x is e^x. Eigenvalues, therefore, are mathematical representations of self-computation.

We now understand that cognitive acts are recursive computations in which, in some instances, stable states are reached and, in other cases, instabilities appear. Cognitive acts might also demonstrate multistable states or, as Ashby has called them, polystable states.[4] Increasingly complex systems may be constructed by using nonlinear combinations of such stable points.

I would like now to turn to step 3 of my strategy, and draw some managerial and ethical conclusions to the ideas presented above. We have discussed the emergence of a new paradigm containing a different perception of social and biological organizations. We might say that the old paradigm was the management of observed systems. The new paradigm is the management of observing systems. This new paradigm brings the observer into the act of management in the form of recursive management.

The concept of recursive management closely parallels an idea that has been presented by Gordon Pask.[5] Pask makes the following distinction. There are two ways in which an observer interacts with the system. One is when the observer enters the system by stipulating the purpose of the system. The second type of interaction is when the observer enters the system by stipulating his own purpose. This is second-order management. This latter type of management is crucial to the management of social systems because, if we do not allow the observer to enter the system by stipulating his own purpose, then it will be the system that will stipulate the observer's purpose. We have all seen the results of such an approach; we have all heard the statement: "I am not responsible for my deeds, I was ordered to do them." The system is no longer an autonomous system in which the actor is responsible for his actions; it becomes a heteronomous system in which the actor always makes someone else responsible for his actions. With the advent of the concepts of autonomy and self-management, therefore, we have reached the last level, the ethical level.

But what is ethics, and how is it related to the problem of managing complex systems? Ethics is the conceptual machinery for computing morals. Morals are devices for managing behavior. Ethics, therefore, is a general theory of management. The ethics of the old paradigm tended to compute proscriptions, that is,

---

[4]W. Ross Ashby, *Design for a Brain,* Chapman & Hall, London, 1960.

[5]G. Pask, "The Meaning of Cybernetics in the Behavioral Sciences," in J. Rose (ed.), *Progress of Cybernetics,* Vol. 1, Gordon & Breach, London, 1970.

ISBN 0-201-04096-4

"DO NOT's". The ethics of the new paradigm is prescriptive; that is, it says "DO" and not "DO NOT." This is quite a different ethic. From this ethics of the new paradigm, I would like to propose a new managerial categorical imperative, a "DO" imperative, which is: "Act always so as to increase the number of choices."

ISBN 0-201-04096-4

III. 6. The Curious Behavior of Complex Systems: Lessons from Ecology

C. S. HOLLING

I want to address the subject of the curious behavior of complex systems by focusing on the following questions: How do systems cope with ignorance? Or cope with the unknown? Or cope with the unexpected? To consider these questions, I will cover briefly three areas. First, because the question of coping with the unexpected relates in some sense to the stability and instability of systems, I will describe the types of mathematical paradigms of stability behavior that have been developed for ecological systems. I will draw from these mathematical paradigms some essentially simple ideas. Second, I will review a number of real-world examples through the filter of the conclusions emerging from these mathematical analyses, in order to determine to some degree how systems cope with the unexpected. Finally, I would like to discuss several different conceptual paradigms that relate to the theme of coping with the unknown and draw some conclusions with respect to the management of complex systems.

How have we coped with the unknown? By and large, we have coped with the unknown by trial and error. When a problem arises, we mobilize the best knowledge we have at the moment to implement a trial solution. If implementation of this trial solution produces an error, then we learn from that error and revise our original solution. We implement the revised solution, and continue testing and revision until finally we obtain some solution that adequately resolves the problem.

This trial-and-error method, however, is becoming dangerous. The scale of the trial solutions being implemented today is becoming so large that the consequences of an error would be more than the natural and social systems could bear. Nuclear engineers, for example, can say quite happily, "Of course, we have tested the individual components of our nuclear energy plant to various sorts of destruction." But when these pieces are organized together into a complex system, there is no way that we can have any confidence that the probability of failure has been reduced to zero. Moreover, if the trial solution fails, the consequences would be extremely serious.

Some nuclear engineers discussing this issue around the strange word, "hypotheticality," coined by Professor Wolfe Haefele.[1] His point, and the point of the nuclear community, is that the traditional kind of scientific approaches cannot in principle apply to this issue of coping with the unknown. He believes strongly that

---

[1]Formerly Director of an Institute of Nuclear Engineering in West Germany at Karlsruhe and now Deputy Director of the International Institute of Applied Systems Analysis near Vienna.

Futures Research: New Directions, Harold A. Linstone and W. H. Clive Simmonds (eds.)

ISBN 0-201-04096-4

this issue lies in a "hypothetical" area in which there are no signposts from past experience. Yet in his field in particular — and, I would add, in my field of resource and environmental science — it is the *central* issue. The central issue in these fields is not how to mobilize our knowledge to the best advantage, not how to cope and organize our known, but rather how to cope with the unknown. The domain of our ignorance is vastly greater than the domain of our knowledge, and if we implicitly or explicitly plan on the presumption of sufficient knowledge, we can be certain that failures will occur.

The issue of how systems cope with the unexpected concerns the stability behavior of systems. The natural systems we are living with today are ones that have survived. This is obvious, for the systems that have not survived are not here today. The systems that have survived have done so in the face of unexpected traumas and perturbations, including climatic shifts and geomorphological changes. These systems have not predicted future events or changes but somehow were designed so that they could absorb those unexpected traumas and rise triumphant over them. So the issue of hypotheticality and how systems cope with the unknown involves the ability of systems to remain stable in the face of unexpected events.

Since the 1920's attempts have been made to model simple ecologic systems in order to explore their stability properties. These models have mostly used rather simple mathematics, a few differential equations or sometimes difference equations, relatively few state variables, and simple functional relations among the variables. Lotka and Volterra[2] developed some simple, coupled differential equations relating the change in population of one species of animals to another. These may be two species competing for a common resource or one species being a predator and one a prey. The Lotka-Volterra model generates a neutrally stable system whose behavior has been plotted in Fig. 1A. This plot gives a phase plane representation of the model in which time has been collapsed. The X population might be a predator and the Y population might be a prey. As seen in Fig. 1A, the neutrally stable system has the property that the system's behavior cycles: given any starting point, the system eventually returns to that point. This kind of stability is that achieved by a frictionless pendulum.

The Lotka-Volterra model is extremely simple. No ecological system behaves in that way whatsoever.

About the same time as the development of the Lotka-Volterra model, two Australians, Nicholson, a mathematician, and Bailey, an ecologist, developed a model using difference equations, and, therefore, incorporated an explicit time lag.[3] No time lag exists in the Lotka-Volterra model. The Nicholson and Bailey model produces, not neutrally stable orbits, but unstable conditions in which, given any starting point, the system eventually spirals off until one or the other of the

[2] A. J. Lotka, *Elements of Mathematical Biology*, Dover, New York, 1956.

[3] A. J. Nicholson and V. A. Bailey, "The Balance of Animal Populations — Part I, *Proceedings of the Zoological Society of London*, 1935, pp. 551-598.

ISBN 0-201-04096-4

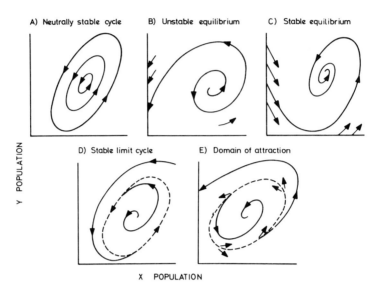

Fig. 1.   Some examples of phase plane behavior shown by different ecological models.

populations is extinct (Fig. 1B). The Nicholson and Bailey assumptions and the resulting system behavior are also unrealistically simple. Incidentally, if a lag is introduced into the Lotka-Volterra model, the same global instability results.

For many years ecologists with real-world experience refused even to communicate with mathematicians who produced such naive and unsophisticated models. This situation changed, however, with the appearance of the computer, a tool that could allow modeling of at least some of the complexity of ecological systems.

May has reviewed the modeling literature in order to encapsulate this tradition of mathematical analysis but also to enrich it with the knowledge accumulated over the years.[4]   When May included more realistic representations of how organisms interact with themselves and their environment, he generated behavior like that depicted in Fig. 1C. This kind of behavior produces a stable equilibrium within a wide range of parameter values; that is, wherever one starts in this space, eventually one ends up in one unique equilibrium state. That equilibrium state need not be a point; in fact, realistic ranges of parameters are more likely to produce a stable limit cycle (see Fig. 1D). The key point is that this type of system is globally stable; wherever one starts outside the limit cycle, one spirals into it, and wherever one starts inside the limit cycle, one spirals out to it. It should also be noted that these descriptions of stability behavior assume a deterministic universe.

---

[4]R. M. May, *Model Ecosystems,* Princeton University Press, Princeton, New Jersey, 1973.

ISBN 0-201-04096-4

More recently, models have been developed that are some variant of a class of simulation models, in which there are more than just two state variables, in which increasingly the spatial heterogeneity of the system is captured, and in which the functional relationships are built on the basis of a rich background of experimentation. In short, in these models there has been an effort toward incorporating complexity, realism, and some degree of precision. These models behave in a quite different way from those presented above.

Again considering just the deterministic and not the stochastic models, the behavior of these simulation models can be described in a simple form as follows (see Fig. 1E). No longer do these systems demonstrate global stability; rather, there is a region such that, if the system is outside that region, it spirals to some other point or region. In the case of Fig. 1E the system would spiral to the extinction of one population; in richer models, it might spiral to another stability region. The only time a system would move to some stability condition is if it were within the stability condition's region or domain of attraction, and as long as the system was in that domain of attraction, it would move to that stability condition. The stability condition need not be a point as shown in Fig. 1E. Often it is a limit cycle or even a stable trajectory.

This kind of behavior is strikingly different from the behavior demonstrated by the models discussed previously, and this difference is significant. The essence of this difference is that in the systems illustrated in Fig. 1E, if the state variables are perturbed in some totally arbitrary manner, then the system will recover and will remain qualitatively the same as long as the perturbation keeps the system within the domain of stability. But if the system is near the boundary of the stability domain, then the slightest disturbance will carry the system over that boundary into another stability region, which may or may not result in the ultimate extinction of a population. These systems are locally, but not globally, stable.

These models work very well for a simplified mathematical view of the world, but how does the real world operate? Unfortunately, if we wanted to find some real-world examples that closely mimic the global assumptions of these models, we would search to the end of time and never succeed. More happily, we can find some examples that roughly approximate these models. One of the key requirements of such examples is that the real-world system should be reasonably contained so that there are no major influences from the outside. Moreover, while these systems cannot be expected to be entirely deterministic, they should be buffered to some extent from the more extreme kinds of stochastic events – e.g., climate.

Aquatic systems – particularly fresh-water aquatic systems – satisfy these requirements to a large degree. There is a natural boundary in these systems which somewhat isolates them from the outside world. The properties of water provide significant buffering of climatic effects. The greatest body of fresh water in the world is the Great Lakes, and there happens to be a particularly rich set of data about this system, going back to the late 1800's, which concerns essentially the

ISBN 0-201-04096-4

harvesting of fish. In the 1880's, there were about fifteen different species being harvested. Beaton and Smith have conducted an exhaustive analysis of these fish harvest data,[5] and all species conform to the same pattern. If the data are plotted from 1880, all fifteen species show at first a high, sustained, and modestly fluctuating yield (see Fig. 2). Three quarters of these species then show a drop of two to five orders of magnitude which occurs over a one- to three-year period. Extinction occurs in some instances, but in many cases a low level of population is reached. Furthermore, the population is maintained at that low level even when the fishing pressure is released. At the same time, of course, there have been changes in the Great Lakes due to pollution, but in a significant number of cases — the herring, sturgeon, and others — these events took place well before 1935 when the major pollution changes began, and all these early changes in fish population show this consistent pattern.

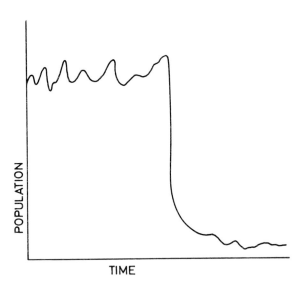

Fig. 2. A stylized representation of population changes in several fish species in the Great Lakes.

The only way this kind of pattern could appear is if there were multiple stability regions and if at some point the fish population flipped out of one stability region into another stability region which supported a lower population level. The only possible way to move the system back to the previous stability region, with the

[5]S. H. Smith, "Species Succession and Fisher Exploitation in the Great Lakes," *Journal of the Fisheries Research Board of Canada,* Vol. 25, 1968, pp. 667-693.

ISBN 0-201-04096-4

higher fish population, would be through some explicit intervention that would lift the system over the ridge, the separatrix, and pop the system back into the original domain. Simply lifting the fishing pressure would not be sufficient.

A number of other similar examples for fresh-water systems could be given, including lakes in Scotland and salmon on the West Coast. Rather than present these examples, I would like to discuss in greater detail another example, a terrestrial system. I have chosen this example because it has a high degree of complexity and spatial heterogeneity so that a richer understanding of the stability properties of real-world systems may be developed. This example concerns an insect pest problem, the spruce budworm, which infects the whole middle half of the continent of North America. Analysis of tree rings has allowed the pattern of outbreaks of this pest to be traced back to the 1700's. Outbreaks last from 7 to 16 years, with a 34- to 72-year inter-outbreak span (Fig. 3). During the inter-outbreak periods the budworm is present in barely detectable densities which, when appropriate conditions occur, can increase explosively over several orders of magnitude during a 3- to 4-year period.

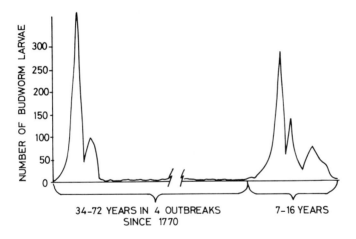

Fig. 3. Population changes of the spruce budworm.

In addition to the advantages of the complexity of this example, there is a particularly rich set of data on the spruce budworm that has been collected over the past 30 years by the first interdisciplinary team in ecology. On the basis of this extensive effort, it is fairly clear that the major characteristics of this system can be captured from the actions of six variables: budworm, birch, spruce, balsam, weather, and natural enemies (see Fig. 4). Considering only the trees, it happens that balsam can out-compete spruce and birch and, therefore, if no other variables

ISBN 0-201-04096-4

intervened, and assuming no unexpected events, the forest would eventually become a monoculture of balsam. However, the forest is very diverse, and this is due in large part to the budworm. Balsam is preferentially attacked by the budworm, spruce to a degree, and birch not at all. The result of these interactions is a dynamic rhythm of shifting competition in which for long periods the balsam are growing most successfully until suddenly the balance of competition shifts, the balsam population drops, and the spruce and birch populations expand.

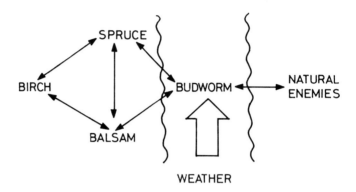

Fig. 4. Key variables of the budworm/forest systems.

These variables, however, are not sufficient to describe the system. While good foliage and mature trees are necessary conditions for the outbreak of the spruce budworm, they are not sufficient conditions. Sufficient conditions are the proper foliage state plus the appearance of certain weather patterns. If for two or three years the springs are warm and dry, and there is adequate foliage, the budworms will multiply rapidly and an outbreak will develop. But even these variables are not sufficient. Study of the data suggests that in the inter-outbreak period the budworm is in a stability region, with a very low equilibrium point, which is made possible by certain natural enemies — parasites and insect predators but particularly vertebrate predators. With these six variables, the essential dynamics of the system can be captured.

    Just as there is a specific behavior in kind, so there is in space. The particular area we have studied covers 40,000 square miles, most of the province of New Brunswick. There is tremendous spatial heterogeneity in the forest and in the characteristics of the budworm outbreak.

    Let us now look at the pattern of behavior of the system in space and time. Figure 5 shows a sequence generated from a simulation model. The X and Y dimensions are geographic dimensions. The vertical dimension in this case is the number of budworm eggs, although a number of other state variables — e.g.,

ISBN 0-201-04096-4

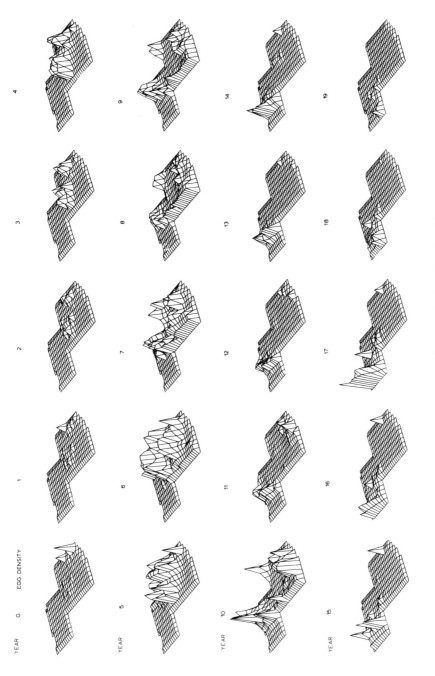

Fig. 5. Annual egg density patterns for a typical outbreak with no management.

foliage, – could be plotted. It should be noted also that this sequence represents the case of no management of the forest. The sequence begins at the start of an outbreak which becomes a major infestation by year 4. This spreads and begins to collapse in the center because of tree mortality by year 7. Thereafter the outbreak gradually subsides to return to endemic condition by year 19.

Because of the existence of a rich set of data covering a 30-year period, the results of this simulation model can be validated, and indeed the pattern shown in Fig. 5 is the pattern that is found in the real world. The real-world system shows enormous variability in time, and heterogeneity in space.

The question to be considered now is: Can this system be represented in the form of phase plane behavior similar to the models discussed earlier? This task is a little difficult because there are, in fact, 75 state variables, and I cannot produce a 75-dimensional space on paper. But by a series of compressions, including making weather deterministic, the system behavior can be described roughly, using two state variables (Fig. 6). One of the state variables is the budworm population; the other state variable is a combination of foliage conditions and age classes of trees.

Exploration of the phase plane behavior produces the following results. First, there are two stability domains or regions as shown in Fig. 6. If the system starts anywhere in the shaded region, budworms will become extinct locally. Of course, budworms may enter the system from outside through dispersal and re-establish their populations, but if there was no exogenous recovery and if the system began in the shaded stability domain, the population would become extinct. Plotting the typical outbreak pattern produces a trajectory that looks like a large limit cycle (A, Fig. 6). At the top of the cycle there are large numbers of bugs and the foliage is in good condition, but then the budworms eat all the foliage and both populations collapse, first the foliage and then the budworms. After the budworm population collapses, a long equilibrium period follows (shown at the bottom of the limit cycle) until the system pops back into the cycle with an outbreak of budworms. If the system began at a different condition, the cycle would be different; for example, B (Fig. 6) shows a small limit cycle with a 15-year periodicity. Cycle A is cycling on the generation time of the trees, while B is cycling on the time constant of the foliage production.

If various trajectories resulting from different intitial states of the system are mapped, we find that some move to the smaller limit cycle while others move to the larger limit cycle. If the entire map of trajectories is filled, a separatrix or stability boundary appears, which takes the form of a funnel (C, Fig. 6). This particular stability region is produced in part by vertebrate predators, which have significant impact only on low densities of budworms. The result of the impacts of these predators on the budworm population is this little stability pit, and when the budworm population starts to collapse because the foliage has been eaten, it gets sucked into that vortex or pit produced by the predators and becomes locked into an equilibrium condition. But as the foliage recovers, the diameter of this stability pit becomes smaller and smaller until a chance weather condition might

ISBN 0-201-04096-4

occur that could flip the system out of what is now a very small stability pit. Even without this occurrence, the pit will eventually collapse completely and change from a pit into a pimple, with the system spinning off into an outbreak. So we see that a richer representation of stability behavior can be obtained from this real-world example.

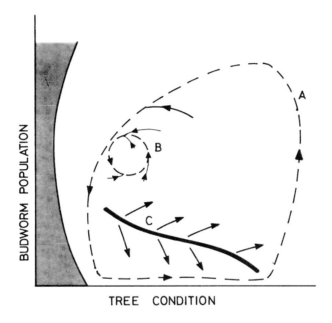

Fig. 6. Stylized representation in a phase plane of the budworm/forest system.

The above simulation results describe the conditions in an unmanaged world. For 30 years this region has been sprayed with insecticide − a rather intelligent and sensitive use of insecticide, economical and sophisticated. The result of this management policy is shown in Fig. 7. Essentially the policy is successful in partially protecting trees but at the price of maintaining persistent semi-outbreak conditions over larger and larger regions. It has locked the managers into a policy in which there is an incipient volcano bubbling, such that, if the policy failed, if by some unexpected event this policy could no longer be implemented, then there would be an outbreak of an intensity and extensity that has never been seen before.

In fact, that is the present situation. The government, of course, has banned insecticides of various classes, which has forced the use of more expensive but less environmentally disturbing insecticides. The use of more expensive insecticides results in a management effort that is just on the edge of economic infeasibility.

ISBN 0-201-04096-4

124

C. S. Holling

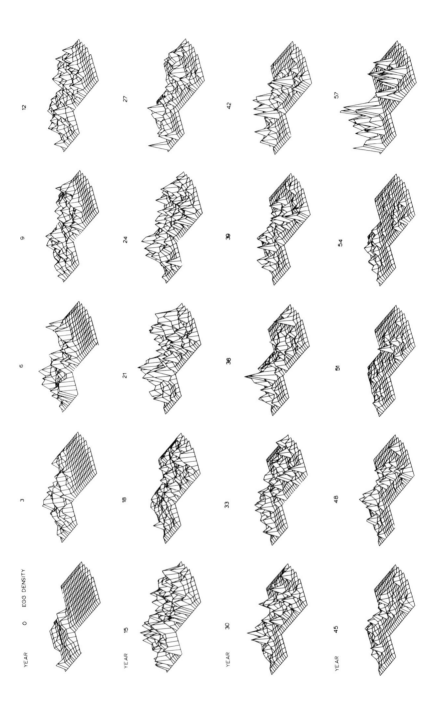

Fig. 7. Representative egg density patterns with historical management simulated.

ISBN 0-201-04096-4

The unexpected has been encountered. It has been encountered in two forms: the unexpected failure to implement certain policies and the unexpected shift of social objectives. Thirty years ago nobody would have cared if all the DDT in the world had been dumped on the Province of New Brunswick. Now the world does object, society does care, and this is an example of the point I have been pursuing. This point is that some management activities, whether it be fishing in the Great Lakes or spraying in New Brunswick, can lock one into a situation in which options rapidly foreclose and in which one becomes incredibly sensitive to the unexpected appearance of the unknown. That unknown might be an unexpected shift of societal objectives, or it might be an unexpected change in economic or other forces so that one cannot act to achieve societal objectives. It might be the unexpected appearance of functional relations that come from nowhere or were not included in the original analysis because nothing was known about them.

Many other examples could be given here, including ones concerning the plains of East Africa, the moors of Scotland, and certain marine systems, but space limitations prevent examination of these cases. The lesson learned from all these examples, however, concerns the existence of multiple stability regions which can move with time, and the key point that stability is not measured in terms of minimized fluctuations but in terms of persistence, in the sense of being able to absorb unexpecteds. Thus the spruce budworm system, which appears at first to be highly unstable with several orders of magnitude shifts, is in another sense a highly stable system. It is highly persistent. Furthermore, the diversity of species in this forest, upon which the forest and recreation industries are based, exists precisely because the budworm population experiences such wild oscillations.

The result of these insights is that questions about the stability of systems are turned around 180°. The questions that now are posed relate not to equilibrium states but rather to the domain of stability that surrounds these states. We are less interested in forces that lead to convergence to equilibria than we are in forces that lead to divergence from boundaries. We are less interested in the unique characteristics of the equilibrium condition than we are in the size of the stability domain. When we ask these questions, we find that an act of management – e.g., fishing – can move a stability region or can cause it to shrink, so that some climatic shift or other unexpected event that previously could be absorbed when the system was in a large stability domain can no longer be handled. One might argue that the situation in the Great Lakes was the result of pollution, or the lamprey, but it was the result of none of these. These are the proximate causes, not the ultimate causes. The ultimate cause was the management activity that, in an equilibrium sense, was quite optimal and efficient but which led to an unexpected constriction of the stability domain so that the unexpected event that previously could be absorbed flipped the system into another stability region. Traditional management, contrary to what was previously believed, does not assume global stability, but it does presume that management, which is largely equilibrium-focused, does not have any effect on the size of stability domains. This is an unwarranted assumption,

ISBN 0-201-04096-4

especially considering the state of our ignorance. The result of this assumption is that we encounter strange worlds where for years we seem to be meeting our objectives, but meanwhile the stability domains in which we are operating shrink. An unexpected event then occurs, and suddenly we are in a qualitatively different world.

One of the lessons learned from these studies is that variability in itself contributes to this ability to persist in the face of the unexpected, this "resilience" property of systems. This idea of stability, therefore, is a different conceptual view from the traditional, equilibrium-oriented concept. This new conceptual view produces different key questions. The first question, which is the classic question in stability theory, is: "How do ecological systems fluctuate in response to disturbances?" A new and more interesting question is: "How do they persist in response to fluctuations?"

To give a brief example which relates to these two questions, consider the Managua earthquake. How did that system respond? The Managuan society was a culture in transition; when the earthquake occurred, enormous fluctuations resulted. The police did not function, communication was cut, and so on. Nevertheless, the system persisted because people were able to draw support from the remnants of their extended family. One can hypothesize what would be the result of an earthquake of similar intensity in San Francisco. It could be argued that the fluctuations resulting from that earthquake would be much less; the police, fire systems, and communications systems would function effectively and efficiently. But the more interesting question, in terms of resilience, is that if both societies were subject somehow to the same *fluctuations*, would San Francisco persist? I suggest that San Francisco has a rather small domain of stability, with a very deep pit, so that as long as it is inside this domain it is very efficient and damps oscillations. But given large enough fluctuations, San Francisco would be more likely to flip out of its stability domain than the highly "inefficient" system of Managua.

The primary issues arising from the two key questions are as follows. How can we categorize the kind, intensity, and duration of disturbances? How can we adequately handle the spatial and temporal units of a system? We do fairly well in the temporal domain but not in the spatial domain, where we must resort to brute force and numerical cranking. How can we classify and compress variables in systems that are insanely multidimensional? Since the questions we are asking are essentially qualitative, how can we define approximately the qualitative states of existence of a system? Such a definition will involve boundaries and stability regions. How can we begin to disaggregate the concept of resilience into components so that we could design a system by incorporating appropriate components of resilience? Finally, how can resilience be measured?

A preliminary disaggregate of resilience has been formulated by my colleague Bill Clark. There are three primary components in this disaggregation. The first component is called boundary maintenance. This component relates to those

ISBN 0-201-04096-4

functions that are independent of outside influences and considers those endogenous events or measures that produce certain characteristics of the stability region and certain degrees of persistence of qualitative states within that region. But if the system does leave this stability domain, it may be able to return, because the system in reality is not isolated and may have some relationships with its environment that allow it to recover and move back into its stability domain. This is the second component of resilience, called the restorative component.

The third component, called the contingent or conditional component, is the most difficult to comprehend. Consider the phase plane representation in Fig. 8. In Fig. 8A, the system is such that, if it were to leave its stability domain, it would move eventually to an equilibrium point B between X' and X''. In Fig. 8B, the system will move to an equilibrium point B upon leaving its stability domain, but here the equilibrium point is outside the interval X' to X''. For a given system, the position of this equilibrium point B will be determined by certain endogenous conditions. The difference between the two cases is that, in Fig. 8A, the system can be restored from B to its stability domain A by changes in Y alone. In Fig. 8B, moving only one variable is not sufficient; the system can be restored only through simultaneous movement of both variables. In some sense, therefore, the contingent components of resilience are a measure of the cost of recovery.

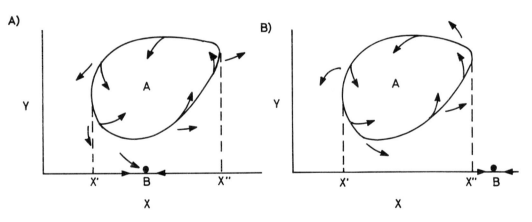

Fig. 8. Position of an equilibrium relative to a domain affects the ease of recovery.

Resilience, therefore, involves the resistance of a system to leave a given state, which can be descriptively defined as reversible or prescriptively defined as desired, together with the ease of returning to that state once having left.

Finally, consider one point on the prescriptive side. What conclusions can be drawn from these ideas for the management of complex systems? Imagine three

ISBN 0-201-04096-4

systems (Fig. 9) that can be characterized in terms of the degree of our knowledge of the world in which these systems reside. Figure 9A is a "known" world, Fig. 9B a "partially known" world, and Fig. 9C an "unknown" world. Each system can be described in terms of its phase plane behavior, and each system has more than one stability domain. What would be our objectives if we had to deal with problems in these three different worlds?

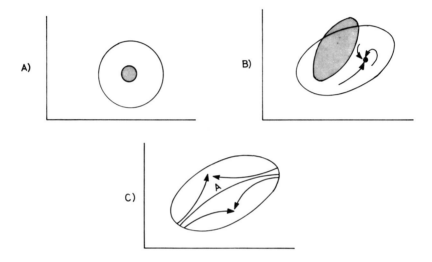

Fig. 9. Diagrams of policies for a "known," "partially known," and "unknown" system.

In a totally known world, we know that the policies we have designed will not change or shrink the stability domain. Therefore, if we are designing for safety, we should design policies so that the system will reside in the middle of the stability domain (Fig. 9A, shaded region). This is the traditional method of designing for safety. One determines where the limits of the stability domain lie and then tries to operate within some smaller region, so that if a mistake occurs, the system can return to the smaller domain.

In a partially known world (Fig. 9B), there is no way of knowing if a policy will cause evolutionary and sequential constriction of the stability domain. Prior to management, the shape and size of the stability domain has been created through a long evolutionary history during which shifting variables have pushed the boundaries out to a certain point and stabilized the boundaries at that point. If a management policy is established to restrict the system to a smaller stability domain, then those elements that previously kept the boundaries out may weaken, and the boundaries may begin to shrink. In such a world, we must presume, for

ISBN 0-201-04096-4

safety reasons and because of our (partial) ignorance, that the boundaries will shrink; to prevent the boundaries from shrinking we want to allow the system to monitor the boundaries so that its own forces will keep them from shrinking. Thus the safety goal in such a world would be to retain the same residence properties of the state variables which existed before management. That is, if before management was initiated, the system tended to reside in a certain area of its stability domain (the shaded region in Fig. 9B), then management policies should be designed to keep the system in that area, or as close to it as possible. This is quite a different objective from that which is appropriate for a totally known world.

In a totally unknown world, the situation is slightly more complex (see Fig. 9C). In this world there exists a stability region with a separatrix A embedded in the region. The key point for this unknown world is that not even the societal objectives are known. We do not know if we want to be above or below the separatrix. The only certain statement is that these societal objectives will inevitably shift. If the society begins to move along some trajectory, then inevitably some of the consequences of being on that trajectory will be perceived and will result in a shift in social objectives. In a totally unknown world, therefore, it is desirable neither to be as far away from a boundary as possible nor to be diffusely represented within the boundary. The proper strategy in an unknown world is to move along an internal stability line, a separatrix A, that allows a maximization of alternative options. From this line, and this line only, the society can jump in any direction it might wish.

Thus in designing for safety, if we presume that we have sufficient knowledge about our systems, and if in fact our world is partially or totally unknown, then our management policies will inevitably result in unforeseen and undesirable consequences. The type of approach applicable in a totally known world assumes that the probability of failure of a designed system can be minimized to a manageable level without increasing the cost of failure. The types of approach applicable in a partially or totally unknown world make no such assumption; rather, these strategies (Figs. 9B and 9C) assume that the probability of failure can never go to zero. The strategies applicable in a partially or totally unknown world do not attempt to minimize the probability of failure but rather to minimize the cost of failures. The approach taken in a totally known world is a "fail-safe" strategy; the approach taken in a partially or totally unknown world is a "safe-fail" strategy.

Acknowledgments

The thoughts expressed in this lecture have emerged from a number of cooperative projects undertaken with colleagues at the Institute of Resource Ecology, University of British Columbia, and at the International Institute for Applied Systems Analysis. I owe a particular debt to Bill Clark, Wolf Haefele, Dixon Jones, Carl Walters, and Ralf Yorque.

ISBN 0-201-04096-4

IV. Questioning the Methodology

IV. 1. Introduction

HAROLD A. LINSTONE

Im Ganzen liegt das Dämonische

Goethe

The only ideology [Ivanko the bureaucrat] worships is the maximum satisfaction of his personal needs; and his needs are infinite and in conflict with his resources, which, no matter how great, are always limited. His practical activity is directed at constant expansion of these resources...

The Ivankiad
Vladimir Voinovich (1977)

Mathematics has exhibited two glorious virtues: it has proved to be an exceedingly powerful tool in the development of modern science and technology, and it has provided an ideal source of intellectual games for *homo ludens*.[1] Mathematical *modeling* ignited modern astronomy and physics and provided the underpinnings for engineering. Undoubtedly the most inspired invention for the modeler has been the computer. It has expanded modeling from a rather academic pursuit to a quasi-industry: there is a plethora of think tanks and a cornucopia of canned models. Reports, newsletters, and meetings spew forth impressive, albeit often useless, quantitative analyses.

Institutionalization of an activity is inevitably accompanied by a subtle shift from problem or substance focus to methodology or technique focus. An organization tends to fit the problem into its modus operandi rather than fit the organizational process to the problem. We see this in modeling: relatively few models are truly problem-specific or based on substantive theory. Although models usually originate in a problem-specific context, they assume a life of their own. Input-output analysis was originally based on a theory of economics. Today it is used in entirely different fields without a theoretical basis. System dynamics began in the bowels of electrical engineering. Forrester then ingeniously applied it to the firm (industrial dynamics), urban modeling (urban dynamics), and world modeling (world dynamics). If one looks at a system dynamics diagram and removes the words, it is impossible to tell whether it concerns a global problem, a city, or a factory. Therein lies both its seductive (and deductive) beauty and its danger — false simplification.

Starting with a kit of tools, the modeling process is no longer dependent on the unique entity being modeled, but on a set of rules independent of this entity. I can select a tool from the kit, but I do not fashion a new tool to deal with the problem at hand. Consider some implications:

---

[1]This label, meaning "Man the Player," has been popularized by John Huizinga (*Homo Ludens,* Beacon Press, Boston, 1955). Being an intellectual game, mathematics has not, of course, been as popular as physical "games" such as sports and warfare.

Futures Research: New Directions, Harold A. Linstone and W. H. Clive Simmonds (eds.)

ISBN 0-201-04096-4

133

1. Structural modeling[2] imposes a structure on the subject; its effect is more often mind-confining than mind-expanding.

2. The computer assumes that every input can be quantified; Zadeh developed his Fuzzy Set Theory to help squeeze qualitative input into quantitative form. It should, incidentally, be stressed that qualitative mathematics per se may prove to be a very fruitful direction of study, an example of the "tremendous opportunities" suggested by Bellman in Part III. Although the man in the street may identify mathematics with quantification, the scientist hardly has any excuse for such misconception. Topology illustrates the point — it is a branch of mathematics concerned with the characteristics of "geometrical figures that persist even as the figures are subjected to deformations so drastic that all their metric and projective properties are lost."[3] Topology thus leads us in a totally different direction than calculus and numerical analysis; it leads to the study of form and morphogenesis. The recent work in "catastrophe theory" of René Thom is relevant in this context.

3. The "first-generation" systems approach is reductionist in nature; it only superficially views the system as a "whole." Consider a standard definition such as that of Hall and Fagen:

> A system is a set of objects together with relationships between the objects and between their attributes.[4]

To Sahal this is an aggregate. By way of contrast, note the holistic definitions of Weinberg:

> A system is a way of looking at the world.[5]

and of Rapoport (quoted by Sachs):

> A system is a portion of the world that is perceived as a unit and that is able to maintain its "identity" in spite of changes going on in it.[6]

A system seen as a "whole" is much more than an aggregate of related elements, and its behavior can never be understood merely by studying the aggregate.

The following table may be helpful in clarifying the differences between, say, aggregate structural models and reasonably holistic models:

---

[2]In a recent survey, nearly one hundred structural modeling techniques were uncovered (G. Lendaris and W. Wakeland, Report 77-6a, "Structural Modeling: A Bird's Eye View," included as an appendix in H. Linstone, George Lendaris, Christian Putz, Devendra Sahal, Wayne Wakeland, and Mark Williams, Report 77-6, *The Use of Structural Modeling in Technology Assessment, Progress Report — February 1977,* Systems Science Ph.D. Program, Portland State University, Portland, Oregon.

[3]R. Courant and H. Robbins, *What Is Mathematics?* Oxford University Press, New York, 1941, p. 235.

[4]A. D. Hall and R. E. Fagen, "Definition of System," in W. Buckley (ed.), *Modern Systems Research for the Behavioral Scientist,* Aldine, Chicago, 1968, p. 18.

[5]G. M. Weinberg, *An Introduction to General Systems Thinking,* Wiley-Interscience, New York, 1975, p. 52.

[6]A. Rapoport, "Modern Systems Theory," *General Systems Yearbook,* Vol. 15, 1970, p. 22.

ISBN 0-201-04096-4

Subject	Structural Model	Quasi-holistic Model
Orchestral symphony	Score	Karajan recording
Building	Blueprint	Scale model
Human being	Anatomical chart	Ape
Human society	Hierarchical organization chart	Primitive tribe

Sahal maintains that the study of whole systems *as whole systems* is necessarily self-referential and that it cannot be done *in vitro* but only *in vivo*. This statement has enormous implications for modeling. It means that no "model" can ever be fully holistic and that futures research must be satisfied with less than true holism. However, it certainly need not — indeed must not — surrender to reductionism. The dangers of the latter should be, but too often are not, self-evident: solution of the wrong problem (Mitroff's Error of the Third Kind, Part II), suppression of creativity, and omission of qualitative perspectives vital to better understanding of the "whole system" behavior.

For example, there exist many transportation network models; none properly consider the substitution of the movement of ideas for that of goods and people, — i.e., communications for transportation. There exist numerous input-output matrices for Western countries; none trigger insight on a postindustrial society based on different values. There exist many models of the United States governmental structure; none describe holistically the impact of basically new structural alternatives such as decentralization or regionalization. *In vitro* modeling is, to a large extent, responsible for the overdetermination of the future and the foreclosure of possible actions lamented by McHale (Part II).

What can be done?

McLean suggests that multiple structural models avoid the traps, protecting us against reification (or implicit total acceptance) of any one model. We might well ask whether one and the same team can develop a true diversity of models as he recommends. Hemingway could not possibly write like Thomas Mann, Puccini like Richard Strauss. There are exceptions — Picasso clearly used a multiplicity of styles with great facility — but they are rare. In any case, Sahal and Sachs insist that the multiple model approach does not go far enough — several deductive models do not conjoin to produce a holistic or *in vivo* perception. Sachs also insists that "the inquirer has to become part of the planned reality." Mitroff and Blankenship have lent support to this argument previously in their paper on guidelines for holistic experimentation.

> The subject (general populace) of any potential holistic experiment must be included within the class of experimenters; the professional experimenters must become part of the system on which they are experimenting ...

ISBN 0-201-04096-4

The reactions of the subject to the experiment and to the experimenters (and vice versa) are part of the experiment and as such must be swept into its design.[7]

We have another echo here of Von Foerster's "observing systems" — properties thought to reside in the object really reside in the observer.

Sachs uses the words "mathematical method" to mean the paradigm of inquiry derived from rationalistic philosophy; Skolimowski talks about the bias toward "formal models." Both imply a correspondence to the "rational actor" model of Graham Allison. Sachs and Skolimowski, like Allison and Churchman,[8] are convinced of the inadequacy of this approach for complex systems that are not purely technological. The value of Allison's "organizational process" and "bureaucratic politics" models (Table 1) in providing more holistic insight is surprisingly easy to demonstrate. They add highly relevant perceptions about the past and present which can hardly be elicited by the modes of inquiry habitually used by analysts (Lockean, Leibnizian). Thus they can assure a much more meaningful foundation for futures research.

The significance of the organizational process model is readily seen in the following historical examples:

Pearl Harbor: A case of the dominant inference pattern: in the face of clear and diverse messages and official warnings ten days before December 7, 1941, the modus operandi of the United States military establishment in Hawaii remained the same.[9]

Energy: Key roles played not only by OPEC but by the Seven Sisters (major oil companies), who have, according to Blair,[10] exercised near perfect control of supply and marketing, frequently proving stronger than national governments and international governmental organizations.

Apollo Project: Impact of the search for missions by the United States Air Force and United States Army was important.

Drugs: The New Drug Application (NDA) is the key instrument in obtaining Federal Drug Administration (FDA) approval of a new drug.

[7] I. I. Mitroff and L. V. Blankenship, "On the Methodology of the Holistic Experiment: An Approach to the Conceptualization of Large Scale Social Experiments," *Technological Forecasting and Social Change,* Vol. 4, 1973, p. 345.

[8] See discussion of Churchman's Inquiring Systems and Allison's models by H. Linstone in Part I.

[9] G. T. Allison, *The Essence of Decision,* Little, Brown & Co., Boston, 1971, p. 88.

[10] J. F. Blair, *The Control of Oil,* Pantheon Books, New York, 1977.

ISBN 0-201-04096-4

ISBN 0-201-04096-4

Table 1

Allison's Three Models

	Rational Actor	Organizational Process	Bureaucratic Politics
Basic Unit of Analysis	Action as choice of total system	Action as organizational output in framework of present capabilities and constraints	Action as political resultant (bargaining, compromise)
Emphasis in System View	Quasi-technological	Social	Behavioral
Organizing concepts	Unitary decision maker (e.g., government)	Constellation of loosely allied units topped by leaders	Players ("where you stand depends on where you sit")
	One set of goals (e.g., national)	Problems factored; power fractionated	Parochial priorities and perceptions
	Problem as seen by unitary decision-maker	Parochial priorities	Goals include personal interests
	Solution a steady-state choice among alternatives	Goals are constraints defining acceptable performance of organization	Players' impact based on relative power
	Action a rational choice based on goals/objectives, alternatives/options, consequences, and value maximizing selection	Sequential attention to goals	Action channels structure the game
		Standard operating procedures (SOP)	Rules sanction some tactics (bargaining, coalitions, bluff) but not others
		Programs and repertoires	
		Avoidance of uncertainty	
		Problem-directed search	
		Central coordination and control	
Dominant Inference pattern	Actions are maximizing means to achieve ends	Behavior of organization at time t similar to $t - 1$, at $t + 1$ similar to t	Action resultant of bargaining game among individuals, groups

Table 1 (continued)

Allison's Three Models

	Rational Actor	Organizational Process	Bureaucratic Politics

General propositions	Likelihood of any action results from a combination of relevant values and objectives, perceived alternative courses of action, estimates of various sets of consequences, and net valuation of each set of consequences
	
	Increase in costs of an alternative reduces likelihood of its selection
	
	Decrease in costs of an alternative increases likelihood of its selection
		Standard routines: program is a cluster of SOP's satisfying rather than maximizing (first acceptable rather than best alternative)
		
		Long-range planning institutionalized, then disregarded
		
		Incremental change
		
		Trade-offs neglected
		
		Organizational health implies growth, imperialism
		
		Administrative feasibility a major dimension
		
		Directed change possible when organization is in crisis
			Peculiar preferences and stands of individual players
			
			Styles of play vary
			
			Face of issue differs from seat to seat
			
			Fuzziness useful to get agreement
			
			Focus on immediate decision rather than on doctrine
			
			Views:
			    Looking down – options
			    Looking sideways – commitment
			    Looking up – show of confidence
			Frequent misperception
			    Misexpectations
			    Miscommunications

Source: G. T. Allison, *The Essence of Decision,* Little, Brown & Co., Boston, 1971.

ISBN 0-201-04096-4

Similarly, the bureaucratic politics model uncovers vital system insights:

New drugs:

MER/29, an anticholesterol drug, was approved by the FDA on the basis of falsified data — e.g., suppression of data on recognized harmful effects — in the NDA provided, according to Fine, by a laboratory head in a department of the drug manufacturer.[11] Thalidomide was not approved by the FDA despite heavy industry pressure, owing to the strong will of Dr. Frances Kelsey of the agency to resist inadequate data.

Apollo Project:

The positions and ambitions of Senators Lyndon Johnson and John F. Kennedy, as well as the negative stand of President Eisenhower, were crucial factors in activating the program.

Domestic economic legislation:

Franklin Roosevelt and Lyndon Johnson exhibited remarkable skill in manipulating Congressional leaders in support of domestic economic legislation.

Vietnam:

A critical factor influencing decisions was the fear of successive presidents that history might record them as responsible for the first war lost by the United States.

Soviet government:

See Voinovich quotation, p. 133

Those who have tackled decision questions via the three models soon realize that investigative reporting is a potent complement to systems analysis.

It is quite obvious that such insights are of potential value in technology assessments (TA) — an important aspect of futures research. In a recent evaluation of TA studies it became apparent that the best TA's are problem-focused and not methodology-focused.[12] The technology is well embedded in a holistic setting. The failure of reductionist, "first-generation" systems analysis is discussed here by Skolimowski. One could argue with his statement that "TA is a peculiar kind of theory which tries to *constrain* action." It happens that this is the view of much of the science establishment and of industry. Technology assessment is seen as a necessary evil in the same class as Environmental Impact Statements and New Drug Applications. But one can heartily endorse two other Skolimowski statements:

Real assessment begins where expertise ends,

and

There is no algorithm for judgment in any sphere of human activity.

---

[11]R. A. Fine, *The Great Drug Deception,* Stein & Day, New York, 1972. Approval of the drug was later withdrawn after users developed side effects (e.g., cataracts, ichthyosis).

[12]H. Linstone, George Lendaris, Christian Putz, Devendra Sahal, Wayne Wakeland, and Mark Williams, Report 77-6, *The Use of Structural Modeling in Technology Assessment, Progress Report – February 1977,* Systems Science Ph.D. Program, Portland State University, Portland, Oregon.

ISBN 0-201-04096-4

We consider the Allison models as an example of a "second-generation" systems approach. Erich Jantsch has suggested that holism can be approached in modeling by concentrating on the levels beyond cause-and-effect models — beyond Newtonian mechanics and statistically preprogrammed system models, i.e., beyond econometrics. He reveals three higher levels:

- Adaptive, evolutionary, morphogenetic dynamic models (e.g., role playing, ecological models, Prigogine's "order through fluctuation" principle).
- Moral action models (e.g., learning games, inventive system models, "live" simulation).
- Creativity or *Zeitgeist* models (e.g., new cultural paradigms, generation of myths, religions, ideologies).[13]

We cannot expect to be successful at all these model levels, but they point the way toward holism in human system design (Table 2).

Maruyama has developed the second cybernetics concept, moving from deviation-counteracting mutual causal paradigms (maintenance of entropy) to differentiation-amplifying mutual causal paradigms (decreasing entropy). The latter concerns itself with self-organizing systems in which complex patterns are generated by simple rules of interaction (Table 3). The correspondence to Von Foerster (Part III) should be noted.

McLean sees three objectives in modeling: prediction, communication, and learning. We would suggest that learning is the most achievable, communication the most mishandled, and prediction the most dangerous. If planning is a learning process, as Donald Michael insists,[14] then no further justification for modeling is needed. Communication via modeling, particularly with the aid of computers, is often mishandled because it is misunderstood. For example, computer users assume that all those with whom they must communicate are of the same analytic type as they themselves are (see Part II, Introduction, Table 1), or, if not, that the others are "convertible" — an undesirable idea even if feasible. Communications must be adapted to the individual, not vice versa. This is a task for a communicator rather than a modeler, an artist rather than a scientist. Finally, in the matter of prediction we note Sachs' insistence that planners assume the objects of planning to be inductive systems. They are never entirely predictable. Although today's forecasters stress that they are not predicting *the* future, that they deal in alternatives, "what if's," and early warning, there is still a large body of clients expecting predictions[15] and considering, even demanding, accuracy as the measure of worth of a forecast.

---

[13] E. Jantsch, *Design for Evolution,* Braziller, New York, 1975.

[14] D. Michael, *On Learning to Plan — And Planning to Learn,* Jossey-Bass, San Francisco, California, 1973.

[15] "I understand your three alternatives, but tell me now which is the most likely one, the one I should use."

ISBN 0-201-04096-4

Table 2

A Matrix of Dynamic Modeling Approaches. Progressing from the Lower Left (Field S_1) to the Upper Right (Field A_3), a Hierarchy of Dynamic Systems Principles Emerges, All of Which Play a Role in the Human World.

Perspective (level of inquiry) / Nature of System	*Rational* Change	*Mythological* Process	*Evolutionary* Evolution
Apperception Self-reflective consciousness (ternary)	A_1 Rational role-playing models	A_2 Learning approaches, gaming, moral systems approach	A_3 Formation of spiritual paradigms, cultural morphogenesis, syntony — *Creativity*
Perception Reflective consciousness (binary)	P_1 Mechanistic system models, rigid behavioristic models	P_2 Adaptive system models, homeostasis, ecological models, contingency models	P_3 Inventive system models, biological and social morphogenesis, coordinative models of relations — *Volition (moral action)*
Subjectivity Nonreflective consciousness (singular)	S_1 Newtonian mechanics, cause/effect models	S_2 Irreversible thermo-dynamics, statistical mechanics, econo-metrics	S_3 Dissipative structures — *Vitality (life-preserving behavior)*
	Causality (local determination)		*Probability (statistically programmed behavior)*

Physical systems

Biological/social systems

Spiritual/human systems

Source: George Braziller, Inc., from *Design for Evolution* by Erich Jantsch; reprinted with permission of the publisher. © copyright 1975 by Erich Jantsch.

ISBN 0-201-04096-4

Table 3

The Maruyama View of Cybernetics Concepts

	Stochasticism	Deviation-Counteracting Mutual Causal Paradigm	Differentiation-Amplifying Mutual Causal Paradigm
Entropy:	Increases.	Maintains.	Decreases.
Basic process:	Toward even distribution, homogenization.	Homeostasis, morphostasis, servomechanism.	Increase of heterogeneity, growth of patterns, morphogenesis, evolution, differentiation, symbiotization. Self-organizing noise.
Cause-effect:	Conditional probability.	*Dissimilar* initial conditions lead to *similar* results due to the difference-counteracting mutual causal loops.	*Similar* initial conditions produce disproportionately *dissimilar* results owing to mutual causal loops which amplify very small initial kicks.
Information:	Amount of information decreases owing to noise, overloading of channels, etc.	By making use of redundancy, loss of information can be counteracted.	Complex patterns may be generated by simple rules of interaction. It takes more amount of information to describe the finished pattern than to describe the rules of interaction. It is often impossible to infer the rules of interaction from the finished pattern. Amount of information increases.
Cosmology:	Decaying universe.	Convergence to pre-established goals, predictable equilibrium, or periodic oscillation.	Self-generating and self-organizing universe. No pre-established goal. No blueprint.
Research method:	Find probability distribution; determine conditional probability based on given initial condition.	Analyze causal loops. Find the range of initial conditions which lead to the same equilibrium or same periodic oscillation. (Note: Equilibrium does not mean homogeneity. It means *maintenance* of heterogeneity.)	Analyze causal loops. What makes difference is the circuitry of differentiation-amplifying mutual causal loops rather than the initial condition.

Source: M. Maruyama, personal communication.

ISBN 0-201-04096-4

Sachs' discussion of "unknowns which cannot be deduced from what is already known" reminds one of the United States Air Force label for unpredicted problems which arise in the development of a new technological system: "unkunks" (unknown unknowns). Something always goes wrong which has never occurred with the old systems. In politics we similarly find "unkunks" — the assassination of Abraham Lincoln and John F. Kennedy, the discovery of theWatergate burglars and of the coverup — near-zero-probability events which change the course of history. There is another side to this coin too. As Lord Keynes has observed:

> A large proportion of our positive activities depend on spontaneous optimism rather than on a mathematical expectation . . . Most of our decisions to do something positive . . . can only be taken as a result of animal spirits . . . and if [they] are dimmed and the spontaneous optimism falters, leaving us to depend on nothing but a mathematical expectation, enterprise will fail and die. The thought of ultimate loss is put aside as a healthy man puts aside the expectation of death.[16]

Churchman and Von Foerster presented us with a moral challenge: the objective of planning should always be to maximize the options of those who must make decisions in the future. It is a fundamental guideline which bears amplification. Stafford Beer has talked elsewhere about "abortive" planning, Maruyama about self-organizing systems. Sachs here uses the term "active adaptation," advising planners to "design strategies for coping with the unpredictable." He thus points us in exactly the same direction as Von Foerster's recursive management concept and Holling's "safe-fail" strategy for planning in a highly uncertain world (Part III).

ISBN 0-201-04096-4

[16]J. M. Keynes, *Essays,* quoted by 'Adam Smith' in *Supermoney,* Popular Library Edition (paperback), New York, 1972, p. 254.

IV. 2. Getting the Problem Right – A Role for Structural Modeling

MICK McLEAN[1]

Introduction

In recent years mathematical simulation modeling has become, rightly or wrongly, one of the most influential techniques used for thinking about the future. Furthermore, the methodological difficulties inherent in the modeling process represent to some extent a microcosm of those encountered in the more general domain of futures research. We shall therefore touch upon many of the points raised by other contributors; while we shall deal with several key issues in some depth, constraints of time and space force us to omit others.

In principle, mathematical modeling seems capable of attacking the problem of problem definition from the most basic of methodological standpoints. A model is an attempt to formalize the most significant features of a particular problem area, and thus has great potential as a means of *understanding* and communicating the nature of a problem. Mathematical models are most frequently applied in areas where problems are embedded in a complex *dynamic* situation whose evolution through time is governed by the mutual interaction of many diverse and heterogeneous variables. Such models are directly concerned with the definition of the underlying structure of complex systems and with the derivation of the behavioral consequences of such a structure. Ideally, modeling can come quite close to an approach which attempts to preserve, as much as is humanly possible, the essential wholeness of a particular problem. Of course, it can be argued that the attempt to force real-world situations into a mathematical framework imposes severe limitations on the kinds of problems that can be investigated (for further discussion of this point, see the paper by Sachs in this volume). The author would argue, however, that *any* exercise in thinking about the future, or indeed the present, involves the use of some kind of formal or informal model. To capture the full complexity of any situation, an array of such models will inevitably be required. Mathematical models need form only *some* components of that array; and they would, of course, highlight only *selected aspects* of the real system under study. This point is indeed central to the theme of this paper and will constantly recur as the argument progresses.

---

[1] An earlier version of this paper was presented to the Third International Symposium on Trends in Mathematical Modeling; Bariloche, Argentina, December 1976.

Futures Research: New Directions, Harold A. Linstone and W. H. Clive Simmonds (eds.)

ISBN 0-201-04096-4

The Purposes of Modeling

The basic motivation for building simulation models stems from the urgent need to understand how many complex social, economic, and technical systems *work.* Short-term forecasts may often be made on the assumption that certain social or economic trends will be maintained and that these "trends" can be estimated simply by looking at the past behavior of the key variables. For longer-term forecasts it may be all-important to identify *changes* in such short-term trends, and to do this it is necessary to acquire a deeper understanding of the underlying mechanisms which generate the historical behavior of the system. Thus, while the purpose of a simulation model is to reproduce the historical behavior of a system and project that behavior into the future for the purposes of forecasting, the focus of the modeling exercise should be the correct identification of the causal structure which produces that behavior. Knowledge of such an underlying causal structure is equivalent to the possession of a *theory* of the workings of a system. Now it must be accepted that for the wide range of socioeconomic phenomena in which the forecaster is interested there do not exist any completely adequate causal theories.

Given this situation, there are two courses of action open to the modeler. He can either attempt to build a model *only* on the basis of the available data relating to the behavior of the system, or he can attempt to construct a primitive theory based on plausible relationships between the model variables. By using the latter approach, the behavior of the system can be derived from the causal assumptions made and this *model* behavior checked against the available real-world data. Examples of both approaches are prevalent in the forecasting literature, the first being epitomized by the large number of econometric forecasting models,[2] the second by the "systems dynamics" approach pioneered by J. W. Forrester[3] and the multiplicity of models built with this approach.

In general, models constructed largely on the basis of statistical analysis of time series data are built to provide short- to medium-term *prediction.* For models based on an attempt to construct a theory, the resulting theory can be an end product in itself. The construction of such models is usually less concerned with prediction than with gaining knowledge — ideally practical knowledge for understanding the present and choosing and realizing the future. This kind of modeling is thus, as we claimed in the Introduction, more concerned with "problem definition" — setting a framework within which potential future problems can be investigated, than with the solution of such problems. It is with the potential of this approach to modeling that this paper is primarily concerned.

In providing an explicit framework for thinking about the future of a particular aspect of the real world, models also possess great potential for facilitating communication between disparate individuals and research groups working on common

---

[2] A useful survey of these models is given in R. J. Ball, "Econometric Models," *Mathematical Model Building in Economics and Industry,* Griffin, London, 1967.

[3] See, for example, J. W. Forrester, *Principles in Systems,* Wright-Allen Press, Cambridge, 1968.

ISBN 0-201-04096-4

problems. Ideally, computer simulation models can represent an improvement over "mental" models, which may be fuzzy, incomplete, and imprecisely stated.

Furthermore, if it is correct to suppose that the problems of the real world are not organized in the same fashion as the problems of the academic disciplines, then the full character of such problems can become evident *only* if a wide variety of causal relationships can be considered: economic, political, sociological, psychological, technical. Such an eclectic analysis can yield several different conceptualizations — models — of what it is that determines the nature and scale of the problems being studied. Some of these models may well be complementary, in which case a suitable array of mathematical models would provide a means for exploring determinants from a number of contrasting viewpoints. Some will not be complementary, indicating both the inherent complexity of the problem and the existence of fundamental theoretical and ideological viewpoints — different perceptions of the problem.

In addition, simulation models can provide a much more accurate assessment of the dynamic behavior implied by a set of assumptions about the structure of a system. This is perhaps the most basic and least disputable advantage of computer modeling. The digital computer can certainly and precisely derive the solution to a large number of complex equations; where those equations represent the causal structure of a system, the solution can be interpreted as an unambiguous projection of the future behavior of that system.

In summary, then, we can say that there are three main factors underlying the motivation for building computer simulation models: a model can be a device for *prediction* — that is, a method for deriving the future consequences of assumptions made about the present; a tool for *learning* about the way a system works; and a means of improving *communication* between different research groups and between researchers and the public.

Modeling in Practice

The question we must now address is whether conventional approaches to mathematical modeling do *in fact* both incorporate a multiplicity of differing disciplinary viewpoints and highlight possible areas of consistency and contradiction between the different possible perceptions of a problem area. A superficial analysis of recent major forecasting models is sufficient to suggest that this is not the case. For example, it can be argued that each of the large-scale world models so far completed has been based on a *single* conception of the problems facing the world: the early MIT world models and that of Mesarovic and Pestel being obsessed with physical limits, the Bariloche model focusing exclusively on the provision of basic needs for the world's population, and so on. In the context of models used for urban and regional planning, Sayer[4] has remarked on the conceptual supremacy

---

[4]R. A. Sayer, "A Dynamic Lowry Model," in M. H. Whithed and R. M. Sarly (eds.), *Urban Simulation: Models for Public Policy Analysis,* NATO Advanced Study Series, 1974.

ISBN 0-201-04096-4

of a very limited range of established models, which, despite their lack of confirmation, tend to structure and constrain researchers' perceptions of urban systems.

It can also be argued that this tendency for the constructors of mathematical models to sidestep the fundamental problem of problem definition is not accidental and due merely to a clumsy or malevolent application of modeling, but instead is inherent in the use of particular modeling methodologies. When a model is built to study a complex situation, two definite, if not distinct, research phases can be identified. First, there is the stage of problem finding involving the formation of a conceptual structure, which can then be translated into a set of mathematical equations which describe the system under study. In the second stage this structure is used to derive the consequent behavior of the system using complex mathematical techniques. Existing modeling technologies such as the wide range of available continuous system simulation languages (CSSL) have been developed to cope with the second stage of the modeling process and the second stage *only*. Thus, whereas advanced computational techniques have been exploited to explicate the system behavior from the system structure, the process of determining the system structure is not usually assisted by the use of such techniques or by the exploitation of the available computational resources.

Furthermore, the apparent simplicity and appeal of the CSSL's has shifted attention from the vital task of producing an *adequate* model structure. Their ease of use enables the modeler to produce a working model with a minimum of time, effort, and thought; and it encourages him to devote a disproportionate amount of time to the refinement and calibration of detailed numerical relationships. Once a dynamic model has been built with these techniques, its structure soon acquires an air of concrete permanence, and many man-years can be happily employed in the evaluation of minor amendments, experimentation with varied parameter values, and general tinkering within a given model framework. The similarity of the structures of the agricultural subsystems of many varied world models, as noted by Clark and Cole,[5] testifies to the hypnotic inertia of a certain choice of system representation.

One significant consequence of this pattern of model development is the tendency of models to become more and more complex as additional relationships and variables are added to the existing structure. Increasing complexity leads in turn to a reduced motivation to challenge the basic structural assumptions of the model; as the model grows larger and larger, the more important it becomes for the creators of the model to justify the time and effort expended in its construction. The very process of modeling thus comes to possess an inherent dynamic which discourages the modeler from ever questioning the extent to which the "right" problem has been solved, the most appropriate structure selected. Indeed, well-established techniques for the evaluation of model structure, such as sensitivity analysis, seem rarely to be applied until the modeling exercise has been completed

---

[5]J. Clark and S. Cole, "Models of World Food Supply, Demand and Nutrition," *Food Policy,* February 1976 (see p. 138).

ISBN 0-201-04096-4

and the model presented to the public. In the next section we shall try to outline a positive approach to modeling which does not incorporate the debilitating tendency to encourage dogmatic adherence to a single complex model structure.

The Case for Structural Pluralism

A central feature of such a method requires that the modeler can best contribute to the task of "getting the problem right" if he is prepared to work with many alternative models rather than with a single model and a set of "data." Insistence on a plurality of model structures should *not* be regarded as a demand for a preliminary phase in the modeling process which will later be replaced by a "correct" model structure. Structural pluralism must be an *essential feature* of any modeling exercise which claims to improve our ability to deal with real-world problems. Nor should the modeler rest content with a specious plurality of model structure created by minor structural modifications to a core model. Rather, the alternative structures should be developed in such detail that a problem already "solved" with the guidance of one model can be treated in a new and perhaps more detailed fashion with the aid of a fresh structure. The function of such concrete alternatives is to provide a means of assessing the adequacy of forecasting models in a manner that transcends mere comparison of the behavioral consequences of structural assumptions with available theory and data.

However closely a forecasting model seems to reproduce a historical situation, however obvious the assumptions embodied within the model, and however necessary those assumptions seem to be to both the users and the constructors of a model, its adequacy as a basis for forecasting can be asserted only after it has been confronted with alternative models. The construction and detailed development of these alternative models should, if possible, therefore precede any public pronouncement of the practical success or policy relevance of a forecasting model. This, then, is the methodological justification for a plurality of model structures; such plurality allows for a much sharper criticism of models than any comparison of a single-model behavior with historical data or the plausibility of a single set of structural assumptions with an accepted body of theory. The proliferation of alternative models is thus compatible only with an epistemological commitment that regards the current inadequacy of theories of socioeconomic phenomena as resulting from genuine theoretical differences of opinion.

Must Models Be Complex?

There is, of course, an apparent serious drawback to the methodology outlined above. That is the rather obvious point that it takes time to build alternative models. To deal with this problem it is necessary to return to a number of basic questions concerning the relationship between the adequacy and the complexity

ISBN 0-201-04096-4

of models. It has already been pointed out by Clark and Cole[6] that a primary requirement for a model to be of value is that it should be as simple as possible, the very purpose of modeling being the *simplification* and structuring of reality. Indeed, one of the most important theoretical advantages of model building, the way in which underlying assumptions are made explicit, is often vitiated in practice by the extreme complexity of the representations chosen. The more simple a model is, the more easily it may be understood by the audience to whom it is addressed. This means that not only are any policy recommendations derived from the model more comprehensible, but their derivation from the underlying assumptions of the model can be more clearly traced.

There is also good reason to suppose that, in common with many other forms of intellectual and economic activity, model building possesses an inbuilt tendency toward diminishing returns of scale. This feature is especially relevant when the model builder is concerned with a problem area categorized by a lack of a theoretical base or a shortage of time series data, or which features a high level of conflict between so-called "experts." Given this all-too-common situation, the building of a range of explanatory models can be a most powerful heuristic device. In such circumstances the production of a single, elaborate, untestable, complex dynamic model can be regarded as an almost criminal waste of scarce research capacity.

An analogy between this kind of model building and the seventeenth-century school of art and architecture known as "baroque" provides some interesting insights. The baroque school possessed two main characteristics: its deliberate intention as propaganda through its dramatic intensity and emotional appeal, and its heavily and sometimes grotesquely ornate style, with unnecessary features added for ornament rather than use.

These features, which in art or architecture might be merely ugly or overpowering, can, in forecasting, become quite dangerous. Undoubtedly computer simulation models do possess an appeal which is derived solely from the use of a computer. Whatever the detailed content of the models, the combined use of high technology and an apparently rigorous mathematical treatment has considerable advantages as an effective tool for propaganda. That the "success" of the Limits to Growth model[7] as a propaganda exercise was in a large measure due to the use of a computer has been acknowledged by the project's sponsors, the Club of Rome.[8]

It is somewhat more difficult to justify the second "baroque" parallel: the assertion that much of the complexity of model structures is designed for ornament rather than utility. It has certainly been demonstrated that many models can be

---

[6]J. Clark and S. Cole, *Global Simulation Models,* Wiley – Interscience, London, 1976 (see pp. 110-112).

[7]D. Meadows, D. Meadows, and J. Randers, *The Limits to Growth,* Universe Books, New York, 1972.

[8]H. Thiemann, Interview in *Europhysics News,* August 1973.

ISBN 0-201-04096-4

greatly simplified while still retaining the same behavior patterns.[9] It is often the case that modelers disaggregate their models (that is, add new relationships and variables) so as to anticipate the potential criticism that their models are too simple. This is, of course, a perfectly natural and practical step. On the other hand, it frequently turns out that many additions and amendments to the model make no significant difference to model behavior. When this happens it is again quite natural for the modelers to leave such changes in the model, despite the fact that they make no difference to the model results. In this way the model acquires a great deal of redundant complexity. An alternative approach would be to restore the model to its previous state after each apparently unnecessary amendment has been made, while retaining full details of any elaborations which were tried out.

Of course, the possibility that several of such "redundant" sections of the model interact in a synergistic fashion should be investigated before this course of action is taken. Thus, the final model would be as simple as possible, and charges of oversimplification could be defended on the basis of well-documented experiments performed during the process of model building. Few model builders have, in fact, adopted this approach.

Was WORLD-3 "Good Enough"?

As a limited evaluation of our proposed approach, let us consider the model that formed the basis of *The Limits to Growth.*[7] One of the key assertions of the constructors of this model was the fact that the behavior mode of the model was robust to almost any conceivable structural modification — that the basic pattern of world economic development was that of "overshoot and collapse." As a result of the more detailed mathematical assessment of WORLD-3 which followed the publication of *The Limits to Growth,* at least four authors[10-13] have been able to show that relatively minor changes to parameters and relationships in the model lead to radically different outcomes for the future of the world system.

Here we see a dangerous pitfall to the idea advanced by Gerhart Bruckmann of a forecast that is "good enough."[14] To all outward appearances the forecasts derived from WORLD-3 would certainly meet this criterion. Supporters of the Limits thesis have argued that it makes little difference whether the world economic

[9]J. G. M. Cuypers and O. Rademaker, "An Analysis of Forresters' 'World Dynamics' Model," Project Globale Dynamica, Report U16, (1973-05-01), Eindhoven, 1973.

[10]H. Scolnik, "On a Methodological Criticism of Meadows' WORLD-3 Model," Fundacion Bariloche, Argentina, 1973 (mimeo).

[11]P. J. Vermeulen and D. C. J. de Jongh, "Parameter Sensitivity of the 'Limits to Growth' World Model," *Applied Mathematical Modeling,* Vol. 1, No. 1, June 1976, pp. 29-32.

[12]D. Schindowski and C. Schönbeck, personal communication to the author, Institut für Raumplanung, Universität Dortmund, Federal Republic of Germany.

[13]H. S. D. Cole, Christopher Freeman, Marie Jahoda, and K. L. R. Pavitt (eds.), *Thinking about the Future,* Chatto and Windus, 1973. (Published in the United States as *Models of Doom,* Universe Books, New York.)

[14]G. Bruckmann, "Problems of Futures Research," paper presented to the Science Policy Research Unit, University of Sussex, March 1976 (mimeo).

ISBN 0-201-04096-4

system will collapse from a shortage of natural resources in twenty years or in two hundred years; the important point is that without drastic modifications of the present world system such a disaster is inevitable. Whether such catastrophe is inevitable or not has not yet been determined with any certainty; what *is* now certain is that the Meadows' model is not "good enough" to settle the question beyond any doubt. Here we see that even a comparison of WORLD-3 with alternatives which consist of minor structural variants of the original model is sufficient to provide an extremely powerful critical assessment of the adequacy of the model. It is possible to conjecture that an intellectual stimulus even greater than that of *The Limits to Growth* might have been provided if the talented team which produced WORLD-3 had *themselves* devoted some time to the production of a series of alternative models.

This task, as it turned out, was left to others. At an early presentation of the Limits model in Rio de Janeiro, a team of scientists from the Fundacion Bariloche in Argentina decided that a response was necessary.

The re-emergence of the view that world development can be seen as a race between population and scarce resources, first stated by Malthus early in the nineteenth century, was greeted with concern by the Latin American scientists. They believe that, although control of population and pollution and the rational use of energy and minerals are essential, these measures are only complementary to and dependent on more fundamental social, political, and economic changes required in the international system if the major problems of the world are to be challenged successfully. They identify the root causes of these problems in the uneven distribution of power, both between and within nations, resulting in oppression and exploitation. The deterioration of the physical environment is not an inevitable consequence of human progress but the result of a particular form of social organization.

The conceptual "model" of the Bariloche team thus involves a shift toward a society that is essentially socialist, based on equality and full participation of all its members in the decisions affecting them; consumption and economic growth are regulated in such a way both to increase the welfare of all the population and also to remain compatible with the natural environment. The team realized that it was not sufficient merely to *describe* their ideal society, it was also necessary to demonstrate that such a society could be viable in terms of the available economic and physical resources. The normative mathematical model[15] was thus built to demonstrate the possibility that all countries and regions of the world could move from their present situations toward a world in which all its people could be provided with their basic needs — a world free from hunger and poverty.

The results of the Bariloche model indicate that, with the exception of the Asian region, the basic needs targets can be met in the time span of a single generation — in Latin America by 1992 and in Africa by 2008. The major underlying

---

[15] A. O. Herrera *et al., Catastrophe or New Society,* International Development Research Centre, Ottawa, Canada, 1976.

ISBN 0-201-04096-4

assumptions of the Bariloche team were a completely equitable distribution of income within regions, the implementation of a radical and sophisticated planning mechanism for the allocation of investment, that there will be *no* resource shortages during the time span considered, and that technological progress will continue at the rate experienced during the last few decades.

This latter assumption is especially crucial: when the model is run, assuming that technological progress gradually declines, reaching zero in the year 2000, the results show a different picture. In this case only Latin America reaches the basic needs targets, and then over a longer time period; in Africa and Asia the economic system collapses. Debate concerning the future rate of technological progress was a key feature of many of the criticisms of the Limits to Growth thesis, and it would seem that the Bariloche model confirms the criticality of this key variable. Here we have an example of the perception of a problem which clearly only emerges when two alternative and distinct model structures are compared.

A Role for Structural Modeling

Thus we see that a methodological requirement for structural plurality cannot be ruled out on the grounds of the excessive demand for scarce resources required for the construction of a range of adequate alternative models. Nevertheless, we have also seen that existing techniques for dynamic modeling do not seem completely suitable for the efficient production of a variety of relatively simple model structures. At this stage it seems pertinent to examine the required properties of a modeling technology which would be suitable for the kind of *structural* modeling for which we have argued. First, the technique should be able to quickly display the behavioral consequences of a particular simple model structure. Second, there should be provision for equally rapid structural analyses to be performed which can relate the behavior mode of the model to the particular structural assumptions it contains. The combination of these two criteria would enable the modeler to build a series of models by using an iterative process where particular assumptions can be quickly assessed, and accepted or rejected, and by using structural analyses as guidelines for model development, rather than proceeding by trial and error. The kind of structural analysis we have in mind would include the identification of dominant feedback processes, stability and control analyses, sensitivity testing, and the full range of available techniques which are at present applied only to models that have already been completed.

These two fundamental criteria entail, in practice, a number of additional secondary requirements. The need to rapidly assess the adequacy of model structure, for example, imposes limits on the nature of the relationships which could be included in the model.

Often it would seem reasonable to allow only linear relationships, since this enables a model to be expressed in the extremely compact and easily manipulable form of an interaction matrix. This limitation would be far from serious for the following reasons. First, many of the structural features of models referred to

ISBN 0-201-04096-4

above are independent of the particular form of the functional relationship between variables; dominant feedback processes, for example, can be just as easily revealed in a linear model as in any other form. Second, as Young[16] and Clark and Cole[17] have pointed out, the overall response characteristics of large complex systems are often quite simple and can adequately be generated by a linear model. Third, as we have already mentioned, many models can be represented in a linear form if a sufficiently small time domain is selected; indeed, Rademaker[9] has pointed out that the behavior of Forrester's nonlinear WORLD-2 model[18] can be quite closely duplicated by an equivalent linear version of a model for a time span of forty years. Finally, we must emphasize that at the stage of model construction we are describing, the model structure would be far more sensitive to the choice of variables and interactions between them, than to the particular functional form of relationships used. Furthermore, it is worth noting that one of the most significant aspects of real-world nonlinearity, time delays, can easily be incorporated in an interaction matrix representation of a model.

A second requirement implied by our basic criteria would be that the modeler could best communicate directly with the computer via interactive computing. This would greatly facilitate and speed up the iterative process of model building outlined above. At present, interactive computing has been applied mainly to enable users of a model to experiment with decision-making within the context of the use of a large complex model with a *fixed* structure.

Such an interactive model-building framework would also need to incorporate facilities for the addition and deletion of model variables and the rapid amendment and recalibration of the model relationships. One significant "spin-off" from such a framework would be that, providing sufficient attention is paid to the design of the man-machine interface, the potential user of a model could participate directly in the modeling process. This would be in contrast to the currently most usual situation in which potential users of such models are presented with the system structure as a fait accompli.

Constructing an interaction matrix requires little technical skill; the potential user could suggest components for the model in terms of his own priorities and objectives, and the visual display could highlight the structural consequences of the inclusion of specified variables and interactions. Furthermore, this model-building situation would tend to encourage the development of alternative model structures. It is possible to imagine a scenario in which "experts" with divergent viewpoints could use a structural modeling framework as a forum for debate in which irreconcilable differences of opinion could be displayed by a range of alternative, yet comparable, models.

[16]P. Young, paper presented at the Warwick Conference on Modeling National Economics, 1973.

[17]J. Clark and S. Cole, *Global Simulation Models,* Wiley-Interscience, London, 1976.

[18]J. W. Forrester, *World Dynamics,* MIT Press, Cambridge, Massachusetts, 1971.

Progress in Structural Modeling

It would be misleading to suggest that the main thrust of our argument for structural modeling, as presented above, is a completely new development in the field of forecasting research. Indeed, many other researchers have been working along the lines suggested for several years. It would, therefore, be worthwhile to review progress and discuss briefly the current state of the art in this area. A more adequate coverage of this topic can be found in a recent paper by the author.[19]

There is a considerable body of both theoretical and applied work on the use of "directed graphs" for structural modeling. The theoretical background to this work is ably presented in the book on structural models by Harary, Norman, and Cartwright.[20] The practical application of this theory is epitomized by the work of Warfield[21] and other members of the Battelle Memorial Institute;[22] indeed, Battelle have been largely instrumental in the dissemination of the notion of Interpretive Structural Modeling. There are three main differences between this work and the requirements for such modeling outlined above.

The Battelle work has tended to concentrate on the use of "unweighted" and often "unsigned" binary graphs. This is the equivalent of studying only the existence or nonexistence of interactions between the components of a system. This restriction has been encouraged by their use of either manual or relatively simple computational techniques for the analysis of such models. As a consequence, the dynamic evolution of the systems described has not been investigated. Working along similar lines, Roberts[23] has for some time now been developing structural models to analyze the future demand for energy. In his work he pays a lot of attention to the problem of deriving an interaction matrix representation of a system from a collection of expert judgments; for him this problem is separate from the problem of analyzing the model once it has been constructed. Our approach has already incorporated a solution to the first problem in as much as we assert that the construction of a model should be an ongoing process synchronous with the analysis of that model.

Roberts' analyses depend on a rather cumbersome use of various mathematical theorems (some taken from Harary et al.[20]) concerning various stability properties of models. We describe the techniques as cumbersome, since, like Battelle, little use is made of automatic analyses, and mathematical sophistication and extreme

[19]M. McLean with P. Shepherd and R. C. Curnow, "Progress in Structural Modeling – A Biased Review," paper presented to the Third European Meeting on Cybernetics and Systems Research, Vienna, April 1976.

[20]F. Harary, R. Z. Norman and D. Cartwright, *Structural Models – An Introduction to the Theory of Directed Graphs,* John Wiley & Sons, New York, 1965.

[21]J. M. Warfield, "Structuring Complex Systems," Battelle Monograph No. 4, April 1974.

[22]M. M. Baldwin (ed.), "Portraits of Complexity," Battelle Monograph No. 9, June 1975.

[23]F. S. Roberts, "Signed Digraphs and the Growing Demand for Energy," The RAND Corporation, Santa Monica, California, R-756-NSF, 1971.

ISBN 0-201-04096-4

ingenuity substitute for computational power. His work nevertheless represents an extension of the Battelle work, since it is concerned primarily with forecasting the dynamic behavior of systems represented by structural models.

Since Roberts' analysis relies on rigorous mathematical theorems, in his early work he limited his model structures to "signed digraphs" — that is, models specified in terms of signed binary numbers only. The limitations of this kind of model for behavior mode analysis have been pointed out elsewhere,[24] the principal drawback being that using only binary numbers ensures that all feedback processes in such a model are of equal importance, whereas in real-world systems, some feedback loops can be described as dominant, the identification of such loops being an extremely powerful method of analysis.[25] Roberts has recently extended his methodology to include quantitative data but still relies on manual (noncomputerized) techniques of analysis.[26]

The work of Kane[27] is very similar in both content and purpose to that kind of structural modeling for which we have argued earlier in this paper. Kane has produced a combined methodology/programming language to deal with cross-impact matrices which represent the structural dynamics of a system. His computer language, called KSIM, is designed as an *alternative* to existing dynamic simulation languages, with the emphasis placed on ease of use and the ability to quickly assess the implications of structural changes. KSIM, however, provides no facilities for structural *analysis* to guide the improvement of models under construction.

KSIM is not, however, designed to run interactively, thus restricting the speed with which alternative structures can be examined. Furthermore, KSIM has another fundamental limitation built into the method by which system behavior is calculated. Kane makes the somewhat arbitrary assumption that all functional relationships expressed in the model take the form of a logistic curve; that is to say, all state variables in a system described by a set of KSIM equations are allowed to vary only between an explicit upper and lower bound. Now, while it is true that, as Kane asserts, "such growth and decay patterns are characteristic of many economic, technological, and biological processes,"[28] it is also undoubtedly true that many of the variables commonly included in the models of social and economic systems behave as if no such bounds existed.

[24]M. McLean, P. Shepherd, and R. C. Curnow, "Techniques for the Analysis of System Structure," Occasional Paper Series of the Science Policy Research Unit, No. 1, Univeristy of Sussex, February 1976 (see pp. 18-19).

[25]M. McLean and P. Shepherd, "Feedback Processes in Dynamic Models," to appear in *Applied Mathematical Modeling.*

[26]F. S. Roberts, "Weighted Digraph Models for the Assessment of Energy Use and Air Pollution in Transportation Systems," *Environment and Planning,* Vol. 7, 1975, pp. 703-724.

[27]J. Kane, "A Primer for a New Cross-Impact Language — KSIM," *Technological Forecasting and Social Change,* Vol. 4, 1972, pp. 129-142.

[28]*Ibid.,* p. 133.

ISBN 0-201-04096-4

The work of Moll and Woodside[29] has corrected two of the limitations inherent in KSIM. They have implemented an interactive computer package, XIMP, in which either KSIM or Roberts digraph models can be embedded. XIMP enables the modeler to both modify and run structural models on-line, and in addition contains facilities for parameter identification, tracking optimization, sensitivity analysis, and stability analysis. While XIMP has not yet been tried out as a vehicle for model development, it would seem that it has great potential for such use.

A survey of progress in structural modeling would be incomplete without some mention of the work at the Science Policy Research Unit (SPRU), of which the author is a member. A full description of this work is available (see McLean *et al.*[24]) together with an introductory article;[30] the concrete manifestation of our research is a computer modeling package, SPIN, which has been tailored for the type of structural modeling for which we have outlined a case.

Four aspects of the package are especially relevant to our discussion. First is the fact that the package has been designed specifically for the fast construction of alternative dynamic structural models. Second, we have concentrated on making the package easy to use to make the techniques available to the nonexpert modeler. Third, the package represents only a methodological framework; its only *essential* feature is the use of an interaction matrix representation of a linear model. Although it contains at present a number of techniques for the analysis of system structure which we have found to be of use for guiding model development, their use is optional and they can be replaced by others at the choice of the user. This flexibility reflects our greater commitment to an *approach* rather than to a particular set of methods. Finally, we would like to emphasize that our development of SPIN has been closely related to ongoing research at SPRU concerned with both the construction of new models and the analysis and evaluation of models already constructed by other researchers. This reflects our view that a sound methodological basis for systems research and modeling can best be established through confrontation with real-world problems, that there is no question of a trade-off between theoretical research and practice but rather a significant synergy to be obtained from their interaction. A recent article[31] describes in greater detail how these techniques can be applied in practice in a particular area.

Conclusions

This paper started by examining whether mathematical modeling could contribute to the problem of "getting the problem right" (see Simmonds, Part I). We

[29] R. H. H. Moll and C. M. Woodside, "Augmentation of Cross-Impact Analysis by Interactive Systems Analysis Tools," Technical Report No. S. E. 76-1, Department of Systems Engineering, Carleton University, Ottawa, Canada.

[30] M. McLean and P. Shepherd, "The Importance of Model Structure," *Futures*, Vol. 8, No. 1, February 1976, pp. 40-51.

[31] R. C. Curnow, M. Kaldor, M. McLean, J. Robinson, and P. Shepherd, "A Systems-Analytic Approach to General and Complete Disarmament," *Futures*, Vol. 8, No. 5, October 1976, pp. 384-396.

ISBN 0-201-04096-4

have tried to describe an approach to modeling which would seem to have considerable potential for doing just that; and we have reviewed the progress that has been made toward implementing that approach. One important reservation remains; this can perhaps best be expressed in terms of a philosophical analogy. Philosophers of science will perhaps recognize the ideas of Feyerabend[32] in our plea for structural pluralism. Perhaps a more significant source of inspiration can be found in the work of Popper.[33] While we would find many points of disagreement with the details of Popper's epistemology, we would concur with his emphasis on the importance of a self-critical and sceptical *attitude* as a prerequisite for the growth of knowledge. In forecasting, as in other forms of human enquiry, no technique can do more than facilitate the search for alternative conceptual structures; firm motivation to exploit that technique is also required. In addition, we feel that structural modeling is only one of a wide range of possibilities for thinking about the future – no single method can offer a universal framework. We would hope that the critical attitude required for the most fruitful application of modeling would also motivate the researcher to seek out and explore alternative modes of enquiry as well as alternative models. The promotion of a fresh spirit of enquiry in the practice of futures research is perhaps the most significant contribution that can be made by this symposium on the nature of futures problems.

[32]P. K. Feyerabend, "How to be a Good Empiricist – A Plea for Tolerance in Matters Epistemological" in B. Baurin (ed.), *Philosophy of Science*, The Delaware Seminar, Vol. 2, Interscience, New York, 1963, pp. 3-39.
[33]K. R. Popper, *The Logic of Scientific Discovery*, Hutchinson, London, 1959.

IV. 3. The Conception of Futures in a Systems Framework[1]

DEVENDRA SAHAL

Introduction

The basic viewpoint of this study is that an adequate conception of futures problems is impossible except in a systems framework. Conversely, systems cannot be adequately studied except in a futures framework. In the next section this theme is elaborated, followed by a discussion of the conception of futures in a systems framework outlined in its preliminary form. Underlying this attempt is the view that a failure to distinguish *wholism* from *holism,* the process of aggregation from that of evolution, counting from measurement, and the fitting of past observations from the prediction of future events, is a major obstacle to the study of futures. Further, the contemporary paradigm in the so-called mathematical general systems theory is of little help in understanding the nature of futures problems. The final section then considers systems theory in a futures framework. Some recent developments with important implications for systems theory and futures research are briefly discussed.

Holism and Evolution

The concept of a system is regarded here as based on the dictum that the process of whole-formation is of an entirely different kind when compared with the process of aggregation. An aggregate is a set of elements. A system is an *ensemble harmonique.* Unlike in an aggregate, the constituents of a system cannot be identified except with reference to the whole. A system cannot be deduced from the relationships among the constituents, while the relationships can be deduced from a knowledge of the system.[2] Of prima facie interest from a system viewpoint is the character of the whole. The systems approach, according to the viewpoint advanced here, does *not* seek knowledge of the interrelationships between the components. What it does seek is an understanding of the process underlying the structure as a whole. A systems approach is necessarily an approach *to* the whole *as* a whole. It is a *holistic* approach, in contrast to the *wholistic* approach to the phenomenon in terms of the relationships between its constituents.

The process of whole-formation is a process of structural change. Genesis by its very nature is epigenesis.[3] What it involves is a change in the complexity or the

---

[1] In my view there is neither *a* future nor *the* future.

[2] A. Angyal, "The Structure of Wholes," *Philosophy of Science,* 1939, pp. 25-37.

[3] J. C. Smuts, *Holism and Evolution,* Macmillan, London, 1926.

Futures Research: New Directions, Harold A. Linstone and W. H. Clive Simmonds (eds.)

ISBN 0-201-04096-4

systemic nature of the whole, a process very different from the process of additions to, and subtractions from, an aggregate. The concept is one of the process of evolution, which is very different from the mechanistic concept of locomotion.

The discussion thus far may be summarized in the form of a set of "laws" I have proposed elsewhere:[4]

- *An evolutionary process cannot be understood except in a systems framework.*
- *The concept of a system is meaningless except in an evolutionary framework.*

Further, if one were to regard the study of futures as a study of evolution, we have immediately a second set of "laws" as a corollary to the first:

- *A systems-oriented framework is a prerequisite to the study of futures.*
- *A futures-oriented framework is a prerequisite to the study of systems.*

Difficulties in developing such a framework are many. An examination of the contemporary paradigm of futures research reveals that it purports to study futures but is, in fact, past-oriented. The so-called "systems theory" purports to take a holistic approach but is, in fact, reductionist. Let me elaborate.

Conception of Futures in a Systems Framework

If there is a framework that is most unsuitable to conceptualization of futures problems, it is the one that is subject to the *ceteris paribus* clause. There is no conservation law which states that the future will equal the past. Indeed, just the opposite is the case. Thus, very often we have the fact that what would clearly seem to be an upper limit of growth turns out to be, in reality, a steppingstone for further development in the form of a phoenixlike rise of an S-shaped curve on the ashes of the old. Such a pattern may or may not be universal. But a characteristic feature of the evolutionary processes is that they are always subject to parametric shifts. It is, therefore, a fundamental requirement that any model of evolutionary process must itself be an evolutionary model.[5] Retrospective futurology is a contradiction in terms.

Orientation to the past in futures research is therefore unfortunate. Statements such as "growth of population is hyperbolic" or "technological substitution follows an S-shaped curve," in so far as they are based solely on a model's good fit to historical data, are trivial restatements of facts. And since there are as many

---

[4]D. Sahal, "Models of Evolutionary Processes in the Design of Engineering Systems," *Proceedings of the 1976 International Conference on Cybernetics and Society,* Institute of Electrical and Electronic Engineers, 1976, pp. 627-631.

[5]An illustration of this theme may be found in earlier works of the author. See D. Sahal, "Technological Systems: An Exploration in the Dynamical Aspects of the Theory of Hierarchical Strucures," *General Systems Yearbook,* Vol. XX, 1975, pp. 159-164; "System Complexity: Its Conception and Measurement in the Design of Engineering Systems," *IEEE Transactions on System, Man and Cybernetics,* Vol. 6, 1976, pp. 440-445; "Models of Evolutionary Processes in the Design of Engineering Systems" (footnote 4); and the references in these articles.

ISBN 0-201-04096-4

curves as the number of futurologists, it seems worthwhile to mention the fact that there is no shortage of tools to obtain as good a fit to *past* observations as one wants. To predict *future* events is, however, another matter. The point is simply that futures problems cannot be adequately conceptualized except in a future-oriented framework! Futures cannot be conceived in hindsight!

What is needed, then, is a theory that allows not just retrospective but evolutionary considerations in the conception of futures. And if *evolutionary futurology* is ever to be realized, then it is my belief that it will have to be necessarily based on truly system-theoretic (holistic) concepts.[6]

However, in its present form, the so-called mathematical general systems theory is of little help in understanding the nature of futures problems. According to the contemporary paradigm, everything is a system or a component of a system. While a variety of definitions of the concept of systems have been proposed, they all boil down to specifications of interactions between elements of a set. Such a formalism is grossly unsatisfactory. To begin with, it applies to all and sundry and is therefore logically empty.[7] It is no more enlightening than is the truism that all bachelors are males. What we have here, then, is a formal mathematical "general systems theory," which boils down to a theory of logically empty sets! Further, it reduces the specification of a system to interactions between its components and is therefore, in fact, reductionist. A holistic approach, as I have noted earlier in this paper, is necessarily an approach to the study *of* the whole *as* a whole. It is not merely an analysis of the parts of a whole. Despite their tall claims, however, the systems theorists have failed to operationalize the concept of a holistic approach.

The reductionism is more clearly seen in the so-called systems analysis techniques. Cross-impact analysis and the so-called systems dynamics techniques are good examples of a reductionist approach in the disguise of a holistic methodology. They are reductionist because they proceed to study the behavior of the system under consideration by studying the behavior of its parts. This does not necessarily reduce their usefulness, because analysis of parts is not without use. They may be capable of providing information about the wholistic aspects of the system being studied. It is erroneous to assume, however, that all by themselves these techniques also permit study of the holistic aspects of the system under consideration.

The implications for futures research are clear. We do have methodologies to build future scenarios of population change, growth of gross national product, increase in the number of graduates, etc. (characteristics of the aggregate). The existing intellectual technology is, however, woefully inadequate to permit conception, let alone prediction, of, say, education, societal stability, and human

---

[6]Cf. the discussion in the preceding section that evolution is inseparable from the whole. See also N. Georgescu-Roegen, *The Entropy Law and the Economic Processes,* Harvard University Press, Cambridge, Massachusetts, 1971, pp. 203ff.

[7]R. C. Buck, "On the Logic of General Behavior Systems Theory," in H. Feigle and M. Scriven (eds.), *Minnesota Studies in the Philosophy of Science,* Vol. I, University of Minnesota Press, Minneapolis, Minnesota, 1956, pp. 223-238.

ISBN 0-201-04096-4

well-being (characteristics of the whole). Counting is one thing. Measurement is, however, another matter.[8]

A systems framework for the conception of futures is nevertheless more than a mere academic necessity. It is just as important to be able to predict something about, say, the oceanic resilience (characteristic of the whole) as to predict, say, developments of a whale population (characteristic of the aggregate). And since the contemporary paradigm of systems theory has little to offer in this respect, it seems worthwhile to attend to future developments in systems theory, which is the theme of the following section.

Systems Theory in a Futures Framework

While a framework for the conception of futures is lacking at present, I believe that a theory of systems is emerging with potentially important implications. The developments in one such theory, that of *form,* raise much hope. The study of form is of considerable importance for understanding the law governing the behavior of the system under consideration. At any point in time, the form of, say, an organism is a result of the evolutionary process that has been at work: a mani-festation of the structure at that point in time. The significance of the study of form lies in the fact that, among other things, it may provide valuable insights into the otherwise unobservable aspects of the structure. The concept of form, like that of system, does not admit independent identity of the components – parts do not exist except as a *unitas multiplex.* The concept of form is that of holism and unity in diversity.

In recent years a number of studies have been made in the understanding of form and morphogenesis.[9-15] Of considerable significance is the work of René Thom and E. C. Zeeman in the structural stability of form.[13, 16] The behavior of

---

[8]It goes without saying that the growth of the gross national product and human well-being are likely to be positively correlated! The point nevertheless deserves some emphasis in view of the contemporary specification of the systems approach as an antireductionist approach. In my view, however, the two viewpoints are distinct but complementary. Like quality and quantity, one cannot exist without the other.

[9]R. E. Blacklith and R. A. Reyment, *Multivariate Morphometrics,* Academic Press, New York, 1971.

[10]D. Sahal, "Elements of an Emerging Theory of Complexity," *Cybernetica,* Vol. XIX, 1976, pp. 5-38.

[11]D. Sahal, "Towards a Theory of Systems," submitted for publication.

[12]W. H. C. Simmonds, "Industrial Behavior Patterns for Planners," *Futures,* Vol. 7, 1975, 284-292.

[13]R. Thom, *Structural Stability and Morphogenesis,* W. A. Benjamin, London, 1975.

[14]D'Arcy W. Thompson, *On Growth and Form,* 1917. Abridged edition, J. T. Bonner (ed.), Cambridge University Press, Cambridge, 1961.

[15]L. L. Whyte, *Aspects of Form,* Percy Lund Humphries & Co., London, 1961.

[16]E. C. Zeeman, "Differential Equations for the Heartbeat and Nerve Impulse," in C. H. Waddington (ed.), *Towards a Theoretical Biology,* Vol. 4, Edinburgh University Press, Edinburgh, 1972, pp. 8-67.

ISBN 0-201-04096-4

continuous processes can be understood by using calculus, but an equally effective form of mathematics for the prediction of abrupt processes has hitherto been lacking. The works of Thom and Zeeman represent an attempt to fill this lacuna.

Thom has christened this area of study "catastrophe theory" because of its emphasis on how a continuous cause can produce a discontinuous effect. A gradual change in control, that is to say, can cause a sudden catastrophic change in behavior. By its very nature, catastrophe theory can handle radical forms of behavior — e.g., sudden inflation explosion due to a gradual relaxation after a squeeze. Much remains to be done, however, before the potential of catastrophe theory can be fully realized.

Further developments in this area have led to yet other "noncatastrophic" approaches to structural stability and morphogenesis.[9, 17, 18] The limitations of space, however, preclude their discussion in this paper. Suffice here to say that the general theory of form may provide an appropriate systems framework for the conception of futures as well as a futures framework for the conception of systems.

A related area in which developments seem to offer considerable promise for both systems theory and futures research concerns the notion of "self." The whole knows no boundaries, and the only way it can be specified as a whole is with reference to itself — any other specification of the whole is necessarily reductionist. The study *of* the whole system *as* a whole system is studying the nature of its self.[17, 19]

Situations involving self-referential systems occur ubiquitously. In psychiatry, for example, the self-referential nature of the system is of considerable significance; in one context it may have destructive, but in another context constructive, consequences. As Bateson *et al.* note:[20] "Although in formal logic there is an attempt to maintain the discontinuity between a class and its members, in the psychology of real communications this discontinuity is inevitably breached." likewise, the physiological and cognitive regulation of mechanisms involved in memory and learning may be understood as arising from a circular and recursive neuronal network containing its own description as a source of further descriptions.[21-23]

[17] D. Sahal, "Homeorhetic Regulation and Structural Stability," *Cybernetica,* Vol. XIX, 1976, pp. 305-315.

[18] D. Sahal, "Principles of Regulation and Control," *Kybernetes,* in press.

[19] D. Sahal, "Cybernetics of Self-Referential Systems, A Research Proposal." Systems Science Ph.D. Program, Portland State University, Portland, Oregon, 1976.

[20] G. Bateson *et al.,* "Towards a Theory of Schizophrenia," *Behavioral Science,* Vol. 1, 1956, pp. 251-264.

[21] H. R. Maturana, "Biology of Cognition," Biological Computer Laboratory Report No. 9.0, University of Illinois, Urbana, Illinois, 1970.

[22] H. Von Foerster, "What Is Memory That May Have Hindsight and Foresight as Well?" in S. Bogoch (ed.), *The Future of the Brain Sciences,* Plenum Press, New York, 1969.

[23] H. Von Foerster, "Molecular Ethology," in G. Ungar (ed.), *Molecular Mechanisms in Memory and Learning,* Plenum Press, New York, 1970.

ISBN 0-201-04096-4

Another illustration of the self-referential nature of systems is found in the origin of cells:[24] only when a set of chemical reactions closes on to itself are stable systems attained.

Yet other illustrations of the self-referential nature of systems readily present themselves in the form of all such processes that are loosely termed "vicious circles": international armament races, interpersonal reactions which produce mental illness, the multiplier and the accelerator effects in economic development, and so on. Indeed, all systems involving (positive and/or negative) feedback share the characteristic of self-reference in their utilization of the results of the underlying process to change the process itself. Ultimately, self is the regulator.

In summary, a large proportion of the systems we observe in nature would seem to exhibit a self-referring structure.

One implication of this emerging theory of systems, based on the notion of "self" (and all such related concepts as self-reference, self-similarity, self-description, etc.), is that systems, and evolutionary systems in particular, cannot be studied *in vitro*. One has to explore them *in vivo*. A further discussion of self-referential systems analysis may be found in other works of the author.[19, 25] Suffice here to say that there is no escape (and there need not be an escape) from closed logical systems that include the referee in the reference, the observer in the description, and the axioms in the explanation.[26] The question really is one of congruence between the conceptual system and the conceived system.

Underlying the notion of self is the notion of a multiplicity which is governed by some unifying principle. The notion of self brings one closer to a realization of unity in diversity. I would like to illustrate this by means of one of my favorite examples.[27]

By extraneous standards, Dinkas of the White Nile have a mean height of about 6 feet and Congo Pygmies average about 4.5 feet. However, when every person is measured in terms of his own arm length, the two groups are virtually identical.

The above example, I hope, also illustrates one appropriate language of what I would like to characterize as an emerging Theory of Self. It is the mathematics of ratios — relative instead of absolute quantities. This I also view as an appropriate mathematics for systems theory, like that of futures research.

Reduction is inherent not in nature but in our method of conception.

---

[24]S. W. Fox and K. Dose, *Molecular Evolution and the Origin of Life,* W. H. Freeman, San Francisco, California, 1972.

[25]D. Sahal, "Self-Referential Systems Analysis," to be published.

[26]H. Von Foerster, "Computing in the Semantic Domain," *Annals of the New York Academy of Sciences,* Vol. 184, 1971, pp. 239-241.

[27]This example (from Thompson, *op. cit*) is essentially an illustration of my attempt to operationalize the notion of self and related concepts by means of the modern theory of dimensions (Sahal, footnotes 11 and 17).

ISBN 0-201-04096-4

IV. 4. Some Thoughts on the Mathematical Method and Futures Problems

WLADIMIR M. SACHS

Introduction

It is the aim of this essay to share with the reader some observations on the applicability of the *mathematical method* in the tackling of futures problems. This method is first evaluated in a rather impressionistic manner. Next, it is subject to a critical review in the light of two assumptions on the nature of futures problems. The essay ends with a brief outline of an alternative method for futures studies with an indication of a way in which it may integrate the mathematical method.

Note that it is not the object of this essay to provide a comprehensive review of all instances in which mathematical tools and techniques are or ought to be applied in planning. Rather, the focus is on the mathematical *method*,[1] which is understood here to denote the paradigm of inquiry derived from rationalistic philosophy.[2] Thus, for example, the discussion does not cover the use of extrapolative statistical techniques in forecasting.[3]

Note, also, that it is not my purpose to engage in a systematic review of the strengths and weaknesses of the use of the mathematical method in planning. Rather, the goal of this essay is to highlight a few important issues raised by the use of that method. The discussion is organized around an extreme or "pure" instance of applying the mathematical method to futures studies. This instance is largely hypothetical. I hope that the reader will excuse my polemical style, employed for the sake of sharpening the issues and for brevity and clarity.

---

[1]For the distinction between tools, techniques, and methods, see ref. [1]. A method is a procedure for the conduct of an inquiry, which may undertake different courses of action (techniques) for the achievement of its aims, and employ different instruments (tools).

[2]Rapoport [38] uses the term "physicalist paradigm" to denote what is herein called the mathematical method.

[3]In his classification of methods of inquiry, derived from the analysis of the traditional doctrines of Western philosophy, Churchman [16] distinguishes five basic inquiring paradigms: Leibnizian, Lockean, Kantian, Hegelian, and Singerian. In their review of applications of Delphi, Mitroff and Turoff [34] suggest that most planning is either Leibnizian (rationalist) or Lockean (empiricist). A similar point is made by Simmonds (Part I of this volume), when he suggests that the criteria for deciding whether future problems are well defined are either theoretical or based on the consensus of experts (the latter being typical of empiricist philosophy; see ref. [16]). It is important to note that the mathematical method, based on the construction of theoretical models, is rationalist, whereas statistical methods are empirical. Thus, although the techniques used by systems dynamics modeling and econometric modeling are often the same, the corresponding methods are based on diametrically opposed philosophies.

Futures Research: New Directions, Harold A. Linstone and W. H. Clive Simmonds (eds.)

ISBN 0-201-04096-4

The Mathematical Method: An Impressionistic Assessment

As a first approximation, the mathematical method may be described as consisting in two sequentially executed procedures. First, a mathematical *model* of the relevant reality is constructed. Then, and only then, the reality is replaced by the model in the conduct of the proper *inquiry*. That is to say, once the model is constructed, the inquirer cuts his contact with the reality — he disengages himself from it — and studies the model rather than the reality to answer whatever questions may be of interest to him.[4]

One may point out that there is nothing distinctive about the above characterization of the mathematical method. It is commonplace in epistemology that we reason with implicit or explicit representations of the reality rather than with the reality itself. In fact, some mathematical planners justify their model-building efforts on the grounds that what they do is merely to render explicit and more rigorous what every planner does ordinarily.[5]

In my opinion it is misleading to represent the mathematical method as simply being a rigorous version of *the* method applied in every form of future-oriented inquiry. The mathematical method imposes many restrictions on the way in which future problems may be represented and the way in which the inquiry may be conducted. Four of these restrictions will now be discussed.

1. *The mathematical method assumes that the model represents* all *the relevant aspects of the reality.*

In other words, the model is assumed to be complete in the sense that every relevant property of the reality corresponds unequivocally to some property of the model. This assumption is not tenable in most instances of future studies. Not only is our knowledge of many crucial aspects of the present usually incomplete, but also the future carries with itself an unknown, and, as it is argued below, it is an unknown of an unknowable nature. Past planning experience is witness to the dangers of the completeness assumption. For example, how many planners in the 1950's actually took into account the polluting effects of industrialization?

Most claims as to the completeness of mathematical planning models are based on the nonexistence or fuzziness of criteria for selection of real-world properties relevant to the planning exercise. Relevance is a function of the purposes of the inquiry.[6] These purposes are seldom specified in an operational manner.[7] The comprehensiveness of the model is often mistaken for its completeness. Needless

---

[4]See on that point ref. [19].

[5]See, for example, refs. [19, 28, 30]. All these authors justify their efforts in terms of the superiority of an explicit computerized model over an implicit or "mental" one.

[6]See on that point refs. [42, 43].

[7]The Club of Rome exercises [19, 28, 30] are prime examples of a situation in which the purposes of the inquiry are ill-specified. They are spelled out at such a general level that it is difficult to see how they allow one to determine what in our knowledge of the world is relevant and what is not.

ISBN 0-201-04096-4

to say that comprehensiveness has little to do with relevance. On the contrary, excessive comprehensiveness may reflect the lack of a well-specified purpose in the modeling exercise.

2. *The mathematical method assumes that all the properties of the model correspond unequivocally to the properties of the real world.*

Assumptions 1 and 2 express together what the general systems theorists call the structural isomorphism of the model with the relevant reality.[8] The second assumption implies not only that the nature of interactions among the properties of the real world is known, but also that these interactions are immutable, at least during the time period covered by the inquiry. This assumption is grounded in a mechanistic view of the world. It is assumed, whether explicitly or not, that the behavior of the real world is governed by laws corresponding to the mathematically specified rules transforming one state of the model into another. The dangers of the mechanistic *Weltanschauung* in future studies have been sufficiently emphasized in the literature, and it seems unnecessary to summarize them in this essay.[9]

3. *The mathematical method assumes that all relevant real-world properties may be expressed by means of the mathematical formalism.*

Even when all the relevant properties are known, it is seldom the case that they all be quantifiable. Indeed, many scientists argue that everything is in principle quantifiable.[10] This does not mean, however, that every relevant real property is quantifiable at the time of the inquiry. For example, "quality of life" is not satisfactorily quantifiable at the present time.[11] Too many mathematical planners choose to ignore the problems of quantification because of a dogmatic preference for bad numerical indicators rather than good qualitative judgments.

4. *The mathematical method establishes a well-specified sequence of operations in which the model is constructed prior to the conduct of the inquiry proper.*

Thus, the mathematical method precludes the inquirer from going back to the initial model to modify it in the light of his new experiences and increased understanding of the reality. That is, it assumes that the initial knowledge and understanding of the inquirer are not significantly altered in the course of the inquiry. The mathematical planner — so keen to use epistemological justification for his model-building effort — is surprisingly ignorant of another epistemological truth — namely, that the process of inquiry is adaptive and learning. He neglects to account for the fact that the reality and he himself undergo change during the inquiring

---

[8] See, for example, ref. [12]. For a definition of an isomorphic model, see ref. [43].
[9] See, for example, refs. [2, 15, 18, 36].
[10] See, for example, refs. [1, 3, 14].
[11] See on that point the discussion in ref. [3].

ISBN 0-201-04096-4

process. This is especially dangerous when one is planning in the context of a
rapidly changing reality.[12]

Sure enough, in practice many mathematical planners recognize, once their
inquiry is completed, the weaknesses of their models.[13] Usually, they set out to
construct a new modified version of their model which would be free of the
deficiencies identified in the old version.[14] However, since the unavoidability of
the model's deficiencies is not recognized at the outset of the inquiry, the organization of the work does not allow the inquirer to systematize the learning from
misfortunes. Paradoxically, those who claim to introduce rigor into planning are
particularly unrigorous in planning their own work. Furthermore, the time required to build a model and make inferences from it is usually too long to allow for
a meaningful learning and adaptive process to be implemented by a simple succession of revisions of the model.[15]

The above critique of the mathematical method deals with two types of restrictions which it imposes on future studies. First, the *definability* of future problems
in terms imposed by the mathematical method (i.e., through the mathematical
formalism) is questioned.[16] Second, the process of inquiry as specified by the
mathematical method is argued to be too restrictive. These arguments are sys-
tematized in the following section.

The Objects of Planning

The argument contained in the previous section is implicitly based on assumptions as to the nature of the objects with which planning deals — that is, on the
nature of planned entities. I now propose to spell out explicitly two of these
assumptions. It is then argued that the mathematical method or, more precisely,
the mathematical formalism used in constructing the mathematical model of the
planned reality is not adequate to capture the postulated nature of the latter. The
two postulates are that most objects of planning are *systems* and that they are
inductive. Consider these postulates in turn.

1. *The objects of planning are systems.*

The above postulate is commonly accepted, and it seems unnecessary to defend
it at length.[17] Most systems scientists emphasize the similarities of concepts of
"system" encountered in the literature. They are, of course, right in doing so,

---

[12]See ref. [46] for an argument in favor of an adaptive and learning based methodology of
inquiry.

[13]See, for example, refs. [19, 28, 30].

[14]See, for example, ref. [20].

[15]Once more, see ref. [46].

[16]For a discussion of the definability of future problems, see McHale, Simmonds, Teige *et
al.*, and others in this volume.

[17]Many authors consider the objects of planning as being "systems of problems" [2, 36,
41].

ISBN 0-201-04096-4

since all definitions of "system" are designed to convey the same essential idea
of an indivisible whole. Thus, at the most general level the concept of "system"
is sufficiently well understood and its implications for planning are quite clear.

However, a close look at the differences in definitions reveals that the meaning
of "system" is far from being clear. Furthermore, as it is argued below, these differences significantly affect the issue of whether complete mathematical models
of planned entities are desirable or altogether possible.

Most definitions of "system" are inspired by mathematical thinking or, more
directly, by the desire to build mathematical models of systems. They are usually
variations on the theme that "a system is a set with relations defined on its elements and on the attributes of those elements.[18]   Once such a definition of
"system" is accepted, there is no major problem in representing any system by
means of a mathematical model. For example, one can represent a system by
means of variables defining the state (attributes) of its elements at any moment of
time and equations relating the variables.

However, some authors argue that the mathematical notion of "system" is not
adequate to handle the concept of an indivisible whole (see the preceding paper by
Sahal). Already in 1941 Angyal [6] called for an effort to construct a new (nonmathematical) formalism designed to handle the notion of "system." Angyal's
argument is elaborated by Trist [48], who shows that the mathematical notion of
"system" is not holistic at all. On the contrary, it leads to a reductionist equation
in which a system is a simple aggregation of objects, relations, and attributes.
Trist's point is substantiated in detail in refs. [42, 43]. Bahm [8] and Phillips
[37] argue that the mathematical notion of relation is not adequate to handle the
concept of a whole. Bahm gives a satirical tone to his argument:

> To assume that one can start with parts which have no unity, and then build
> up entirely from them a system with unity, is to assume that you can get
> something from nothing, some unity from no unity. When primitive people
> claim to obtain something from nothing, we condemn their claims as hocus
> pocus. But when systems theory makes such claims, we praise it as the latest
> in scientific advancement [8, p. 175].

The essence of the criticism of the mathematical concept of "system" may be
summarized as follows. When it is used, the different elements and parts of the
system are combined together into a "whole" by specifying the nature of the
relationships between them or their attributes. However, in the truly holistic
concept of system the elements and parts are united into a whole not only by
virtue of their relationship with each other, but also and mainly by virtue of their

---

[18]For Hall and Fagen [22] "a system is a set of objects together with relationships between
the objects and between their attributes" (p. 18). In a more mathematical language, Mesarovic
[29] defines a system as "a relation defined on the Cartesian product" (pp. 6, 7). For related
definitions of "system," see refs. [7, 26, 45]. Surveys of different definitions of "system" may
be found in refs. [24, 50].

ISBN 0-201-04096-4

functional relationship to the whole [6]. The latter type of relationship has as yet not been expressed via mathematical formalism.

A nonmathematical notion of "system" is expressed through the following quote from Rapoport:

> A system is a portion of the world that is perceived as a unit and that is able to maintain its "identity" in spite of changes going on in it [39, p. 22].

Note that according to the above definition the relevant reality is a system because someone (i.e., the inquirer) perceives it as such. That is, the holistic notion of "system" is critically dependent on the nature of the inquirer's outlook and, in particular, on the purposes of his inquiry. That is why I have proposed elsewhere [42, 43] to call the above concept of "system" teleological. I have also shown that Ackoff and Emery's [4] formalism may be adapted to handle the teleological notion of "system."[19]

2. *The objects of planning are inductive.*

The notion of an inductive entity is explained in detail elsewhere [42, 43]. Here a brief explanation must suffice.

A mathematical model can be built in an axiomatic manner. It is always possible to specify a finite number of the model's properties (axioms), a vocabulary composed of a finite number of symbols (words), and a finite number of rules which allow one to infer all the properties of the model (expressed in the finite vocabulary) from the axioms. In other words, it is possible to specify a "logic" of the model such that within that logic a finite number of the model's properties are individually necessary and collectively sufficient for all the properties of the model. If the mathematical model of a system is assumed to be isomorphic with the relevant reality (in the sense discussed in the previous section), then the reality itself is assumed to be *deductive*. That is, it is assumed that it is possible to build a causal theory of that reality which allows every real property to be traced to a finite number of initial causes corresponding to the axioms of the model. It is postulated here that the objects of planning usually are not deductive — that is, that they are *inductive*.

In other words, it is postulated that no matter how many properties of the planned reality are specified, and no matter how powerful causal theories about that reality are built, there always exists a property of that reality which is relevant to the planning exercise and which cannot be inferred from the causal theory.

There are several reasons to postulate that objects of planning are inductive. Consider some of them. It has been known since Gödel that even some of the mathematical reality — namely, the totality of natural numbers and of their attributes — is too rich to be represented as a deductive system.[20] It may be argued

---

[19]The formalism of Ackoff and Emery [4] is not mathematical (syntactical), but teleological or pragmatic. See refs. [42, 43] on that point.

[20]For a discussion of Gödel's argument, see refs. [35, 47, 49].

ISBN 0-201-04096-4

[27] that human behavior, included in any object of planning, is still richer and thus is inductive. A simpler version of the same argument may be constructed using the fact that men are self-conscious animals [9, 27]. If it were known to a man what the rules governing his behavior were, then he could break those rules. That is, every deductive model of human behavior is in a way self-defeating, provoking by its very existence its own invalidity.

Many planners view the planned systems as being purposeful — that is, systems whose behavior is not completely determined by the environment and/or the ends at which that behavior is directed [4, 17, 18]. I have argued elsewhere [43] that the assumption of purposefulness is equivalent to the assumption that the system's behavior is inductive.

Finally, a methodological argument may be constructed in favor of viewing the planned system as inductive.[21] If nothing is known about the nature of the system under consideration, it is "safer" to consider it as being inductive rather than deductive. To assume that an inductive system is deductive may lead to the omission of properties crucial to the problem at hand.[22] To assume that a deductive system is inductive does not imply this type of danger. In other words, the methodology of inquiry implied by the assumption that the planned system is inductive subsumes the methodology which would be applied to a deductive system, whereas the contrary is not true.

That the mathematical method implies that the object of planning be viewed as a deductive system should be clear by now. This fact is well illustrated by the following summary of mathematical definitions of "system":

> It is a portion of the world which at a given time can be characterized by a given *state*, together with a set of rules that permit the deduction of the state from partial information. The state of the system . . . is a set of values of certain variable quantities at the moment of time in question [39, p. 17].

To summarize this section, it is argued that the objects of planning are not predictable. To be more precise, the future of planned systems can involve unknowns of unknowable nature — that is, unknowns that cannot be deduced from what is already known. The methodological implications of this postulate are briefly examined in the next section.

Methodological Implications

The function of planning is to make decisions about the planned system which would help it achieve some future ends.[23] Is planning at all possible if the future is

---

[21]See refs. [42, 43].

[22]It may lead to what Mitroff [32] and Mitroff and Featheringham [33] call the Error of the Third Type, consisting in solving the wrong problem.

[23] Similar concepts of planning may be found in the essays contained in ref. [23].

ISBN 0-201-04096-4

as unpredictable as I have argued in the previous section? How should one anticipate a future that is unknowable?

The answer to the last question lies in *adaptation*. Rather than on predicting the
future, the focus of future studies should be on designing systems capable of
adapting to changing conditions. "The concept of adaptation . . . focuses on
human actors who try to realize objectives, satisfy needs, or find peace while coping
with present conditions" [10, p. 847]. To render the planned system more
adaptive is a form of anticipating the future.

Of course, to predict threats facing the planned system in the future, and then to
design strategies for counteracting those threats, is a form of adaptation. However,
men can do better in their adaptive behavior than to passively adjust to detected
environmental changes. They are capable of modifying the environment to make it
more favorable for their purposes,[24] and of seizing opportunities for their better-
ment, or even of creating such opportunities.[25] Thus, planning should be devoted
to the design of systems capable of actively pursuing their objectives — that is,
capable of *active* adaptation.[26] In other words, planning should not be directed
at predicting the unpredictable, but at designing strategies for coping with the
unpredictable.

The above concept of planning does not preclude the use of the mathematical
method in future studies. It precludes the *exclusive* use of that method. Mathematical models can and ought to be used, whenever possible. Their simplicity and
the rigor of thought that they impose are unmatched.

However, the use of the mathematical method should be cautious and accompanied with an awareness of its limitations. It is necessary to immerse the mathematical method in a more general method which takes into account the unpredictability of the future and the impossibility of defining the totality of future problems
in mathematical terms.

Such a method cannot be too universalistic. The mathematical method attempts
to provide a procedure which could be used in each and every instance. The discussion above indicates that the nature of the planned reality is far too rich to allow
for such an approach. A planning method can at best be only a general scheme of
reference, providing the inquirer with initial guidelines and insights on how to
attack a problem. It has to be adapted in every instance of application to suit the
particular problem at hand.

A planning method cannot be static. The mathematical method is, in a way,
based on the prediction that all future problems are going to be of essentially the
same nature as past problems were. This prediction is generally unjustified. A
planning method has to be adaptive, changing as the nature of problems change.

---

[24]Adaptation by modifying the environment is discussed in refs. [4, 5, 25, 38, 40, 43, 45].
The discussion is summarized in ref. [44].

[25]Adaptation by seizing opportunities is discussed in refs. [5, 21, 38, 43] and is summarized in ref. [44].

[26]The distinction between passive adaptation (responding to contraventions) and active
adaptation (seizing opportunities) is formalized in refs. [43, 44].

ISBN 0-201-04096-4

To achieve the above requirements, a planning method has to be based on the inquirer's having a direct contact with the reality. In fact, the inquirer has to become part of the planned reality.[27] He cannot isolate himself from it by means of a rigid model. To study the model instead of the reality means excluding the possibility of perceiving the changes in the reality which are not reflected in the model's behavior, and these may be the most significant changes.

To accomplish his aims the planner may appeal to the mathematical method in several ways. He can use a mathematical model to analyze the current reality — that is, to build partial explanations of what he observes. He can also project the present behavior of the planned system (represented by a dynamic model) into the future in order to detect the breaking points of the system — that is, to predict what is not going to happen rather than to predict what is going to happen.[28] He can also use mathematics to model mechanistic subsystems of the planned reality — that is, systems, like machines, whose behavior is entirely predictable. Finally, the planner can simulate some aspects of the system in order to assess the sensitivity of the system's behavior to various policies or environmental changes.[29]

In lieu of a conclusion, consider the following quotation illustrating the dangers of separating the form from the content implied by the mathematical method in planning:

> The Piglet was sitting on the ground at the door of his house blowing happily at a dandelion, and wondering whether it would be this year, next year, sometime or never. He had just discovered that it would be never, and was trying to remember what "it" was, and hoping it wasn't anything nice [31, pp. 112-113].

References

[1] R. L. Ackoff, *Scientific Method*, John Wiley & Sons, New York, 1962.

[2] R. L. Ackoff, *Redesigning the Future*, John Wiley & Sons, New York, 1974.

[3] R. L. Ackoff, "Does Quality of Life Have To Be Quantified?" *General Systems*, Vol. 20, 1975, pp. 213-219.

[4] R. L. Ackoff and F. E. Emery, *On Purposeful Systems*, Aldine-Atherton, Chicago, Illinois, 1972.

[5] A. Angyal, *Foundations for a Science of Personality*, Harvard University Press, Cambridge, Massachusetts, 1941.

[6] A. Angyal, "A Logic of Systems," in F. E. Emery (ed.), *Systems Thinking*, Penguin Press, Harmondsworth (Middlesex), 1969, pp. 17-29. Also in ref. [5], pp. 243-261.

[7] W. R. Ashby, *Design for a Brain*, 2nd ed., Chapman and Hall, London, 1960.

[27]The term "action research" [11] is often used to denote the type of inquiry in which the researcher is in direct contact with the reality.

[28]A projection of the system's behavior into the future, called "reference projection" [2, 36], gives an image of a "logical future" [36] — that is, of a future that would occur if nothing changed in the system's patterns of behavior. Such a future is in general infeasible. The first Club of Rome exercise may be viewed as a sophisticated reference projection of the world's future [28].

[29]The second Club of Rome exercise [30] may be interpreted as consisting in the construction of a simulation model of the world.

ISBN 0-201-04096-4

[8]   A. J. Bahm, "Systems Theory: Hocus Pocus or Holistic Science," *General Systems,* Vol. 14, 1969, pp. 175-177.
[9]   G. Bateson, *Steps to an Ecology of Mind,* Ballantine Books, New York, 1972.
[10] J. W. Bennett, "Anticipation, Adaptation, and the Concept of Culture in Anthropology," *Science,* Vol. 192, No. 4242, May 28, 1976, pp. 847-853.
[11] W. G. Bennis, K. D. Benne, R. Chin, and K. E. Correy (eds.), *The Planning of Change,* Holt Rinehart Winston, New York, 1976.
[12] L. von Bertalanffy, *General Systems Theory,* Braziller, New York, 1968.
[13] W. Buckley (ed.), *Modern Systems Research for the Behavioral Scientist,* Aldine, Chicago, Illinois, 1968.
[14] C. W. Churchman, *Prediction and Optimal Decision,* Prentice-Hall, Englewood Cliffs, New Jersey, 1961.
[15] C. W. Churchman, *The Systems Approach,* Dell, New York, 1968.
[16] C. W. Churchman, *The Design of Inquiring Systems,* Basic Books, New York, 1971.
[17] C. W. Churchman and R. L. Ackoff, "Purposive Behavior and Cybernetics," *Social Forces,* Vol. 29, No. 7, 1950, pp. 32-39. Also in ref. [13], pp. 243-249.
[18] F. E. Emery and E. L. Trist, *Towards a Social Ecology,* Plenum Press, London, 1972.
[19] J. W. Forrester, *World Dynamics,* 2nd ed., Wright-Allen Press, Cambridge, Massachusetts, 1973.
[20] J. W. Forrester, "A National Model for Understanding Social and Economic Change," *Simulation Today,* Vol. 32, 1975, pp. 125-132.
[21] H. Gutman, "Structure and Function," *Genetic Psychology Monographs,* Vol. 70, 1969, pp. 3-56.
[22] A. D. Hall and R. E. Fagen, "Definition of System," *General Systems,* Vol. 1, 1956, pp. 18-28. Also in ref. [13], pp. 81-92.
[23] E. Jantsch (ed.), *Perspectives of Planning,* Organisation for Economic Co-operation and Development, Paris, 1969.
[24] G. J. Klir, *An Approach to General Systems Theory,* Van Nostrand, New York, 1969.
[25] A. Kuhn, *The Logic of Social Systems,* Jossey Bass, San Francisco, California, 1974.
[26] O. Lange, *Wholes and Parts,* Pergamon Press, London, 1965.
[27] J. Lucas, "Minds, Machines and Gödel," in K. M. Sayre and F. J. Crosson (eds.), *The Modeling of Mind,* University of Notre Dame Press, Notre Dame, Indiana, 1963, pp. 225-271.
[28] D. M. Meadows, D. Meadows, and J. Randers, *The Limits to Growth,* Universe Books, New York, 1972.
[29] M. D. Mesarovic (ed.), *Views on General Systems Theory,* John Wiley & Sons, New York, 1964.
[30] M. Mesarovic and E. Pestel, *Mankind at the Turning Point,* E. P. Dutton, New York, 1974.
[31] A. A. Milne, *Winnie-the-Pooh,* E. P. Dutton, New York, 1950.
[32] I. I. Mitroff, "On the Error of the Third Kind," in this volume.
[33] I. I. Mitroff and T. A. Featheringham, "On Systemic Problem Solving and the Error of the Third Kind," *Behavioral Science,* Vol. 19, 1974, pp. 383-393.
[34] I. I. Mitroff and M. Turoff, "Philosophical and Methodological Foundations of Delphi," in H. A. Linstone and M. Turoff (eds.), *The Delphi Method,* Addison-Wesley, Reading, Massachusetts, 1975, pp. 17-36.
[35] E. Nagel and J. R. Newman, *Gödel's Proof,* New York University Press, New York, 1968.
[36] H. Ozbekhan, "The Emerging Methodology of Planning," *Fields within Fields,* Vol. 10, 1973, pp. 63-80.
[37] D. C. Phillips, "Systems Theory – A Discredited Philosophy," *Abacus,* September 1969, pp. 3-15.
[38] A. Rapoport, "Methodology in the Physical, Biological and Social Sciences," *General Systems,* Vol. 14, 1969, pp. 179-186.
[39] A. Rapoport, "Modern Systems Theory," *General Systems,* Vol. 15, 1970, pp. 15-25.
[40] A. Rapoport, *Conflict in Man-Made Environment,* Penguin Books, Harmondsworth (Middlesex), 1974.
[41] M. W. J. Rittel and M. M. Webber, "Dilemmas in a General Theory of Planning," *Policy*

ISBN 0-201-04096-4

Sciences, Vol. 4, 1973, pp. 155-169.
[42] W. M. Sachs, "Toward Formal Foundations of Teleological Systems Science," *General Systems,* Vol. 21, 1976, pp. 145-153.
[43] W. M. Sachs, "Man, Design, Machine," Ph.D. Thesis, Busch Center, Wharton School, University of Pennsylvania, Philadelphia, 1976.
[44] W. M. Sachs and M. L. Meditz, "A Concept of Active Adaptation," Working Paper, Busch Center, Wharton School, University of Pennsylvania, Philadelphia, 1976. Submitted to *Management Science.*
[45] F. R. Sagasti, "A Conceptual and Taxonomic Framework for the Analysis of Adaptive Behavior," *General Systems,* Vol. 15, 1970, pp. 151-160.
[46] D. A. Schon, *Beyond the Stable State,* W. W. Norton, New York, 1971.
[47] R. M. Smullyan, *Theory of Formal Systems,* revised edition, Princeton University Press, Princeton, New Jersey, 1961.
[48] E. L. Trist, "Organization et systeme," *Revue Francaise de Sociologie,* Vol. 11, 1970, pp. 123-139.
[49] R. L. Wilder, *The Foundations of Mathematics,* 2nd ed., John Wiley & Sons, New York, 1967.
[50] O. R. Young, "A Survey of General Systems Theory," *General Systems,* Vol. 9, 1964, pp. 61-80.

ISBN 0-201-04096-4

IV. 5. Epistemological Aspects of Technology Assessment

HENRYK SKOLIMOWSKI

Technology assessment (TA) is a new mode of knowledge: it attempts to grasp the *impact* of large bodies of techniques and processes on large bodies of people and social institutions. We are not yet quite clear what exactly we mean by "impact," which is at the heart of TA judgments. Therefore it is of great importance that we look deeper into the epistemological foundations of TA, and attempt to learn where lie its strengths and pitfalls, under what circumstances it can be best practiced, and what kind of qualitites of mind it requires.

Knowledge and Action in Technology Assessment

I will not start with asking the perennial questions: "What is knowledge"? "What is action"? Instead, I shall assume that the context of our discourse sufficiently (or at least adequately) determines the meaning of the key terms we use. I shall first endeavor to analyze some peculiar dilemmas which are inherent in linking knowledge and action within the boundaries of technology assessment. The first dilemma is really the general dilemma of knowledge vis-à-vis action, which is purportedly *based* on this knowledge.

Human beings cannot help theorizing, cannot help trying to find "satisfactory" bases for their action. But how satisfactory are these bases? The fact that we link action with knowledge, practice with theory, does not mean that this link is a *necessary* one. Let us reflect on the peculiar epistemological status of this very link. Theories are a part of a certain cosmology, a certain world view – be it magical, theological, or scientific. But the *link* is of a quite different category. For the link belongs neither to theory nor to practice. The link is a bridge between the two. And if this is so, then it is at least theoretically possible that different theoretical foundations can be linked with the same body of practice, and, conversely, that different bodies of practice can be connected to (and justified by) the same theoretical basis.

What this argument attempts to convey is that the link between theory and practice (knowledge and action) is much more tenuous than we usually assume. It is a *contingent* link which is reinforced by a given society, culture, or paradigm of knowledge. By constantly linking a given theory with a given field of practice, we make this link firm. Let me illustrate this point. I have recently visited China, and while there I was constantly struck by *their* way of linking theory with practice (knowledge with action). Almost everything is related to the *Red Book* (of Chairman Mao). The book provides the basis, the knowledge for quite an extraordinary array of praxis: according to our way of thinking, it links quite a

Futures Research: New Directions, Harold A. Linstone and W. H. Clive Simmonds (eds.)

ISBN 0-201-04096-4

bizarre conglomeration of practices. That is to say "bizarre" when we look at it through our knowledge, through the way *we* link theory and practice. Yet it does not seem bizarre to *them.* To our mind the link between the theory (the body of knowledge contained in the *Red Book*) and a phenomenal variety of practices performed under its auspices simply does not exist. And yet they *act upon* this knowledge in good faith, and achieve good results, some might even say spectacular results. Their concept of knowledge justifies (but also directs and constrains) their praxis.

What follows from this examination for technology assessment? The Chinese technology assessment is indirectly spelled out by the way they link theory to practice. In a sense there is no need for technology assessment in present China. Their paradigm of knowledge-action, their canons of understanding and interacting with nature, spell out a frugal and ecologically sound way of behavior. (That is, as far as *natural ecologies* are concerned; urban ecologies are something else.)

Is this situation unique to present China? I believe not. Take ancient Greece, for example. The paradigm of knowledge that was held at the time (knowledge being predominantly the vehicle of man's enlightenment and man's perfectability) also served as a form of technology assessment and technology control. For witness in this context Plutarch's opinions about Archimedes and how disparagingly Plutarch talks about Archimedes' inventions:

> Archimedes possessed so high a spirit, so profound a soul, and such treasures of scientific knowledge, that though these inventions had now obtained him the renown of more than human sagacity, he yet would not deign to leave behind him any commentary or writing on such subjects; but *repudiating as sordid and ignoble the whole trade of engineering, and every sort of art that lends itself to mere use and profit,* he placed his whole affection and ambition in those purer speculations where there can be no reference to the vulgar needs of life.

In the intellectual and moral climate of Greece in which engineering and technology were deemed to be ignoble and sordid crafts, technology did not have a chance to flourish, let alone to devastate the environment. Hence there was no need for TA as a constraining influence. For knowledge (within the culture) itself was this constraining influence.

Even much later in our Western tradition (admittedly some centuries ago) we can still see that the concept of knowledge and that of action formed a kind of unity. St. Augustine, and later Thomas Aquinas, held that to behave well and to act well one must be properly enlightened. Action is the direct fruit of knowledge. To act well one has to know well. By this they did not merely mean that one must possess an appropriate body of know-how and then use it when the occasion comes, as if it were a chest of tools. But they rather meant that in order to act well one has to be in a privileged cognitive state; for only then action can bring desirable and beneficial fruit. Knowledge thus here appears to be not only and not so much an indifferent chest of tools, out of which we select first this piece then that piece

ISBN 0-201-04096-4

for the task at hand, but rather the state of enlightenment which (almost) of necessity enables us to embark on the course of action which is correct and right. Might it not be the case that we have lost the sense of this intimate connection: right knowledge/right action? And as a result we have been producing knowledge that is harmful. Technology assessment is a symptom of deeper causes of unrest in our world view and in our conception of knowledge. The appearance of technology assessment is an acknowledgment that we consider our present knowledge as potentially very dangerous. The appearance of TA is also an acknowledgment that we no longer think that in order to act well one has to think well (in the moral sense). Our thinking has been thoroughly instrumentalized, and deprived of the ethical dimension which it once possessed. If this is the case, then the resolution of TA problems lies not only in examining the fruits of our actions but also in examining the peculiarity of our knowledge — that is, in this larger scheme in which good knowledge should bear no harmful action. The perplexing dilemmas of knowledge and action are well expressed in *Bhagavad-Gita,* where Sri Krishna says:

> What is action? What is inaction? Even the wise are puzzled by this question. Therefore, I will tell you what action is. When you know that, you will be free from all impurity. You must learn what kind of work to do, what kind of work to avoid, and how to reach a state of calm detachment from your work. The real nature of action is hard to understand.[1]

The conclusion that emerges from these arguments is that the paradigm of accepted knowledge outlines for us the boundaries of accepted and favored action, and at the same time (in a subtle way) puts constraint on action. In our culture we put prices on instrumental knowledge and consider enlightenment "impractical": the paradigm of accepted knowledge favors action that aims at physical transformation of the world. This paradigm looks with disfavor on action that is directed toward the inner self. Hence an explosion of physical technologies and (until recently) lack of appreciation of the techniques of the soul — which might be considered as the major forms of technology in the Eastern world views, in India in particular.

In the link knowledge-action, knowledge is not only a body of cognitive statements but also a relentless vector: it sanctifies, justifies, and promotes certain forms of action — to be performed under its auspices. And here we come to a fundamental anomaly which TA is itself. For TA is a peculiar kind of theory which tries to *constrain* action. Technology assessment is anomalous (within our present paradigm of knowledge) from another point of view. Our conception of scientific-technological knowledge constantly pushes us to change and transform the world, pushes us to mechanize, manipulate, and control, whereas TA is attempting to put brakes — in a fundamental way — on this whole process. Hence, there is a friction between the general thrust of scientific-technological knowledge and TA, which is,

ISBN 0-201-04096-4

---

[1]*Bhagavad-Gita,* translated by Swami Prabhavananda and Christopher Isherwood, The Mentor Classics, Mentor Books, London, 1951, pp. 51, 52.

after all, a part of this knowledge, a part of theory in the broad sense.

What are the consequences of this state of affairs? Let me list some of them.

1. We may have to reassess the entire culture – its priorities, its direction, its worth – for culture ultimately sanctifies (by approving as *good, beneficial, worthy of pursuing*) forms of knowledge and forms of practice specific to a given society.

2. We may have to re-examine our way of *linking* knowledge with action and attempt to find another way of linking theory with practice.

3. We may have to look for another theory (knowledge) for our practice. Human action will go on. The scientific-technological basis may turn out to be of transitory significance.

4. We may need another conception and definition of practice or action. To sit still is no action for us. Zen philosophy finds it to be a very meaningful and different action.

Let us be aware that TA is not so much a magic wand that will mend all the defects of the technological society (although some people want to see it in such a role), but rather that TA is a *symptom* of deeper changes brewing beneath. In TA we indirectly acknowledge that there may be something wrong with the link between theory and practice (knowledge and action) which we accept; that there may be something not quite right with our knowledge; or that there may be something wrong with our way of acting; and finally that there may be some drastic disproportions in our cultural aspirations and priorities.

Let us also be aware that epistemology of our times – that is, professional, Western, analytically oriented epistemology – *assumes* the validity of one particular linkage between theory and practice, and this is the linkage that is the consequence of the world view of classical physics. Under a closer inspection, however, it can be seen that this linkage is perhaps more a consequence of specific semilogical categories of contemporary philosophy than one that reflects the realities of contemporary science, including its recent extensions. A very important and exciting task that is awaiting inspired epistemologists of our times is to look deeper into the ambiguity and versatility of the meaning of both concepts – "theory" and "practice" – in order to realize that actual reasons for our actions are fragile indeed; that epistemological complexities of our actions, as exemplified by TA, cannot be concealed by neat semilogical categories; that the process of understanding – of which epistemology must be a part – is an open-ended process with new problems, dilemmas, and phenomena appearing all the time; that the categories of empiricist epistemology are shown to be inadequate over and over again, even when propped up with the apparatus of twentieth-century semantics; for we are attempting to explore phenomena that go beyond the universe postulated by classical empiricism.

The Structure of Judgment in Technology Assessment

After having examined (ever so briefly) the nature of knowledge and action in

ISBN 0-201-04096-4

technology assessment — from above, as it were, and taking an Olympian point of view about the possibility of new paradigms of knowledge and action — let us now enter the present paradigm of TA (as fuzzy as its boundaries are) and examine it from within. In particular, let us try to identify the unique cognitive status of the operations that take place while we are doing the process called technology assessment. Let us examine then the structure of judgment in TA with its peculiar epistemological parameters and its unique characteristics. To begin with, I wish to argue that the most important outcome of TA, when it is taken in the strict sense as *assessment,* is judgment. And it is the structure of this judgment that we have to comprehend and learn to apply in specific circumstances.

The structure of judgment in TA is a peculiar *sui generis* epistemological category, which is neither entirely normative nor entirely descriptive, neither merely scientific nor solely based on values; but is a specific mesh of the descriptive and the normative, of the scientific and logical woven together with the visionary and axiological. In studying the peculiarity of this mesh in some depth — that is, in grasping the relationships that hold among its various components — we shall be reconstructing the structure of judgment in TA. From this reconstruction we should be able to draw some consequences regarding the development of technology per se; and also, if we go a step further (and we have to go this step further), some consequences regarding the development of society — for I see in the structure of judgment in TA a peculiar cognitive product of our times in which many of our perceptions (cognitive, social, and moral) find a focus.

Now, instead of describing the various components which form the structure of judgment in TA (and that would be a lengthy and tedious process), I shall use a diagram which, I hope, expresses the backbone of TA judgments; in particular, I hope, it expresses graphically some of the relationships between the descriptive and the normative.

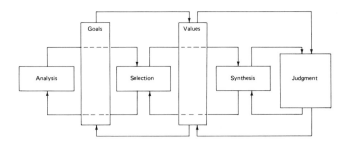

Diagram 1

ISBN 0-201-04096-4

The diagram represents the two layers of reasoning, or two different kinds of input that make up the process leading to the judgment which is the ultimate result of TA. The first is the layer of factual data and of scientific information; in the diagram it is represented by the horizontal boxes. The second is the normative layer of the goals and values, and it is represented by the vertical boxes.

The singularity of technology assessment from the epistemological point of view is that the factual layer is embedded in the normative layer (as the diagram shows). I am not saying that the factual layer is unimportant, or that it is dissolved in the normative layer, or annihilated by it. I am only saying that the descriptive layer is *embedded* in the normative one. Thus, ultimate judgment in TA is not only the result of the linear scientific progression of thought, based on hard data, but is profoundly influenced by those vertical inputs of values, which are more elusive and less tangible and not easily quantifiable, but which, nevertheless, shape the outcome of TA in an undeniable way.

In a nutshell, *the structure of judgment in TA is the dynamic matrix of epistemological dialectics between the descriptive and the normative which is resolved and expressed in social terms.* Thus, the structure of judgment in TA is a peculiar blend of epistemological reflection which is highly *integrative,* as it must constantly move between the descriptive and the normative, and it is also highly *interpretive,* as it must translate its integrative efforts into social terms which are economically and ecologically viable. The existing structure of education does not give us much opportunity to develop this kind of thinking. Present systems analysis, which is usually taught in colleges of engineering, is, *ipso facto,* a codification and sanctification of linear thinking, limited to hard data and factual information. This kind of systems analysis helps us to move only on the horizontal level. In so far as it usurps for itself the name of "systems thinking," it fundamentally distorts the nature of our complex problems, by reducing them to linear problems. Ninety-nine percent of our problems are nonlinear. Formal models (which I will discuss later) are an epitome of linear thinking, but they are often taken (or mistaken?) to be adequate for solving nonlinear problems.

Now in addition to the two layers, the horizontal (factual) and the vertical (normative), the structure of judgment in TA contains a number of loops. I am here, of course, concentrating on the mere backbone, on the ultimate conceptual spine, leaving the details for future elaboration. Even in outlining the two basic layers, I have already omitted a number of important points – for example, that in the very selection of data and in the initial analysis, judgment plays already an important part. So there is a cybernetic feedback loop between ultimate judgment and the very first act of "looking at data." This is important to remember, for your analytical mind works like a swift surgical scalpel, cutting across various layers and absorbing from them the underlying tissue of values; but the outcome of it all will be later seen as entirely homogeneous and factual in character. Let us be aware that the very act of "looking at data" is an enormously complex normative process.

Moreover, in postulating only one box for values, I have conflated at least two kinds of values: intrinsic human values and values specific to disciplines and specific to the methodology of research. Further elaborations will be needed to

ISBN 0-201-04096-4

make this structure of judgment a more adequate tool. But this will be a refinement, not a departure from the basic structure — namely, that the two respective layers are juxtaposed against each other and in a continuous dialectic relationship with each other.

As far as the loops are concerned, which are a part of the structure of judgment, there are at least two important ones. The first is the political-economic loop. It exerts its pressure from above with its political constraints, which are related to the political system that governs a given society. Needless to say, different kinds of political constraints are to be expected in the structure of judgment in TA in the Soviet Union as contrasted with that in the United States. But there are also "political constraints" in the second sense of the term, as related to "the politics of TA at present," with its configurations of power, sources of financing, and access to "influential" people. And of course, a very important part of this loop is the economic constraints. Technology assessment in the pre-Arab oil embargo era is one thing, and in the post-embargo era quite another. For witness in this context the blocking of the Alaska oil pipeline (for environmental reasons) and the swift unblocking of it (for economic reasons). It may be said that the economic structure of society is a form of technology assessment — not the most adequate form, one must add.

The second loop I call the cultural loop. It is much more subtle in character, and it acts from below. It has various components, some of which I have tried to express in Diagram 2.

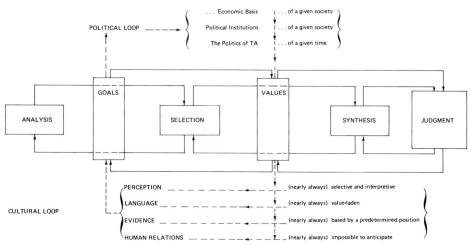

Diagram 2

ISBN 0-201-04096-4

Let me illustrate the existence of the cultural loop in the actual practice of TA by giving you an instance of what has actually happened. The instance involves two people with whom we are all familiar: on the one hand, a person who occupies an important governmental position in the area of TA in Washington, and, on the other, a person who is a free-lancer and a crusader for good causes, and who is not even connected officially with any university.

The subject is an assessment of a project. At work are (you might say) two different cultural paradigms. After a very lengthy discussion in which all sorts of social and moral considerations are discussed, the first person says, more or less, the following: "But look here. We do not give them any specific recommendations. What are the chaps going to *do* when they come to their offices on Monday morning? We must tell them in explicit terms what to *do*." The second person's reply was more or less the following: "But you are confusing your existential predicament with the process of assessment. Besides, you are confusing momentum with progress." If you look at their respective arguments, you can at once see the content of the cultural loop beautifully expressed: in terms of the perception of reality, which is selective and interpretive; in terms of the language, which is value-laden; in terms of evidence, which is bent once in this direction, once in the opposite direction.

The concept of "evidence" is actually very important for TA. One must be exceedingly alert whenever it is mentioned as an instrument of intimidation of the normative process. For so often the believers in "hard" evidence want to reduce all evidence to the evidence of science and of instrumental rationality. Such a strategy reduces, in one swift, subtle operation, the structure of judgment in TA to its factual layer. We must remember, to begin with, that the evidence of *social impact* of technologies in nearly always "soft," thus different from the sort that is required by hard science.

In constructing my model of the structure of judgment in TA, I followed some hints of M. L. J. Abercrombie as expressed in her book, *The Anatomy of Judgment*. Abercrombie analyzes the anatomy of scientific judgment. But clearly her analysis is also relevant to our larger task of reconstructing the scope of judgment in TA. Abercrombie suggests, and it would be hard to disagree with her, that "we may learn to make better judgments if we can become aware of some of the factors that influence their formation. We may then be in a position to consider alternative judgments and to choose from among many instead of blindly and automatically accepting the first that comes; in other words, we may become more receptive, or mentally more flexible."[2] In my opinion, we need both in TA: to become more receptive and mentally more flexible.

Let me very briefly draw some of the conclusions that follow from my examination of the structure of judgment in TA;

• Do not confuse mere deductions with genuine judgments.

[2]M. L. J. Abercrombie, *The Anatomy of Judgement,* Pelican Press, Penguin Books, Harmondsworth (Middlesex), 1960, p. 18.

ISBN 0-201-04096-4

- Do not confine the process of synthesis to the synthesis of factual information.
- Do not expect to find an algorithm for judgment in TA, for there is no algorithm for judgment in any sphere of human activity.
- Quantify your results if you can (and if you must), but always remember what you are doing — namely, that you are *assessing,* not quantifying.
- Be loyal to your profession, and be loyal to the integrity of a given technological project you are assessing. But don't be disloyal to society, which, in the final analysis, supports you as an intellectual; so remember that TA is a social service.
- Be knowledgeable and acquire as much expertise about a given technology or a given process as possible, but remember at the same time that the real assessment begins where expertise ends: there is no substitute for judgment. Judgment goes beyond expertise. And TA is about judgment.
- Be concerned with the future of technology, but also be concerned with the future of society. Do not "trade off" important social assets for bolstering a given technology. Always consider immediate technological (economic) gains vis-à-vis larger social perspectives.

Let me express at least one conclusion in positive terms. In studying the structure of judgment in TA, let us remember that the problem is complex but not entirely unique in human history. The ancient prophets were very good indeed in doing what we now call TA. Let us study, therefore, the structure of the judgments of the old prophets, for there is a great deal for us to learn from them. The art of technology assessment has been practiced not only by the biblical prophets. Spiritual leaders of so-called "primitive people," including medicine men and shamans, have always been consummate practitioners of TA. The practice of TA in their case, however, went hand in hand with judgments about life. The judgments of TA are a subclass of the judgments of life. Leaders of people, which almost invariably means spiritual leaders, were good at TA because they had wisdom, courage, and sagacity in coming to grips with the essential elements of life. We are living in a leaderless society. Managers are not leaders, but managers. We cannot trust their TA judgments, for they are (so often) divorced from "the essential elements of life" — from which ancient prophets and more recent spiritual leaders were not divorced. We are back to the problem of knowledge and action. Perhaps you *must* have "good" knowledge (based on some wisdom and not only on factual information) in order to act well, in order to act at all. The dilemmas of TA are therefore real. I have already suggested that TA is a symptom of deeper sources of unrest in our culture and in our world view. Our culture is good at concealing the causes. We prefer to preoccupy ourselves with symptoms. Let us try by all means to work out "the most efficacious schemes" for technology assessment. But let us not forget, at the same time, that technology assessment is not a thing in itself, not another technical discipline to be developed by experts. To have a "good" technology assessment requires more than technology assessment itself, for it requires a good society. The best TA is where there is no TA at all, where culture regulates the development and use of technology in an entirely

ISBN 0-201-04096-4

beneficial way, so that there is no need to harness and subdue technology a posteriori.

Formal Models: Esthetic Beauty and the Social Inadequacy

It would seem from the standpoint of technology assessment that the situation is clear: if the dialogue between the descriptive (analytical) and the normative (social, moral, esthetic, existential) aspects of TA is continuous and unavoidable, then it is illegitimate, and indeed *bad* methodology to limit TA to analytical and formal models and pretend that this is all there is to it. Yet these models seem to possess a relentless drive of their own, and they so often dominate our thinking. Let us examine some of the reasons why they still hold such a powerful influence over our minds. Let us take another look at the mystique of formal models.

The temptation of formal models is great, but it must be resisted. Formal models are elegant in themselves and therefore provide an esthetic satisfaction to deal with. Formal models are encouraged by the whole thrust of objective and analytical knowledge which has been the dominant mode during the last few decades, and dealing with these models gives us a feeling of doing the right thing according to the accepted canons. Formal models enable us to arrive at precise results (whatever simplifications we make in the process), and this again is hailed as a mark of good scholarship. In spite of all these advantages – and the temptations inherent in them – formal models must be resisted, for they are leading us astray from the realm where TA belongs – assessment.

Because formal models are so attractive, and because there is a danger that they may become a dominant tool of TA, something should be said about these models in an historical perspective. Formal models, as they are currently understood, were originated within the realm of mathematical logic. Undoubtedly their rudiments can be seen in Euclidean geometry, and in subsequent systems of mathematics. However, the explicit criteria of what the formal system is were worked out within mathematical logic, mainly through the work of Frege, Russell, and the Polish school of logic. These systems were regarded as a laboratory for the investigation of the properties of formal knowledge (J. Lukasiewicz);[3] moreover, they were conceived as an instrument enabling us to translate all mathematics into logic, and thereby securing the solid foundations for at least one branch of human knowledge – mathematics (Russell). The quest for reducing mathematics to logic alone proved to be abortive and was abandoned for other reasons, too, particularly after Gödel. However, the conceptual power of formal systems of logic was so great and so fascinating that they were soon used in other disciplines. The first instance is (probably) the Logical Atomism of Wittgenstein and Russell, which is a doctrine that attempts to reduce all physical reality to the matrix of the propositional

---

[3]See Henryk Skolimowski, *Polish Analytical Philosophy,* Humanities Press, Inc., Atlantic Highlands, New Jersey, 1967; and especially the chapter on J. Lukasiewicz.

ISBN 0-201-04096-4

calculus; and which invents in the process such oddities as negative facts, which are to correspond to the structure of negative propositions.

Further work in philosophy, inspired by the conceptual power of formal systems, was done in the Vienna Circle, where whole philosophical doctrines were conceived in the image of formal systems. This brought some very illuminating results, but also some drastic amputations of the body of knowledge traditionally known as philosophy. Rudolf Carnap's *The Logical Structure of the World,* originally published in 1928 (*Der Logische Aufbau der Welt*), is perhaps the culmination of this trend.

The quest for formal systems was more or less abandoned in philosophy in the late 1950's. But quite parallel to its fascination for philosophy, formal systems exerted a fascination on science. From the 1930's on, a great deal of work was done (Carnap, Hempel, Nagel, etc.) to translate the structure of science into the structure of formal systems, again with some illuminating results which are esthetically very pleasing, but which also do violence to science as it has been historically developed. Karl Popper (in *Conjectures and Refutations*) and Thomas Kuhn (in *The Structure of Scientific Revolutions*) have shown these glaring violations conclusively. Since the middle 1960's, the spell of formal systems no longer holds the minds of philosophers of science, with a few exceptions, of course.

The history of the last few decades in philosophy and in science shows that formal models have been tried and given a really ample chance to prove themselves, and that they proved themselves to be fundamentally inadequate — even for the reconstruction of the structure of science, and still more so for expressing the content of traditional philosophy. This story is amply documented in various books. And we must be able to learn a lesson from it all for TA. Intellectual competence and integrity require that, if we see a set of tools tried, found inadequate, and discarded in a discipline very similar to our own, it would be foolhardy, naive, and perhaps even arrogant to insist that these tools will be all right after all.

There is an extenuating circumstance, however. It seems that present social science places a great deal of hope in the formal models. Insofar as TA is partly in the domain of social science, the application of formal models (regarded highly in the social sciences) would seem justified. Indeed, social science does seem to have come under the spell of formal models. But it only shows its (methodologically speaking) derivative character. When formal models were quietly abandoned in philosophy and in natural science, social scientists suddenly "discovered" them in the 1950's and the 1960's. From the fact that social scientists do not seem to know any better does not follow that technology assessors should not know any better. And, by and large, social scientists, particularly those bent on quantitative methods, seem to be oblivious to the fact that there is a lesson to be learned from the application of formal models to philosophy and natural science. He who has gone through the rigors of formal systems knows well how splendid they are and how limited they are! He who has studied the application of formal systems to philosophy and science cannot but be convinced that these systems will prove

ISBN 0-201-04096-4

equally inadequate when applied to social science and technology assessment. After all, the people who tried to apply these systems earlier in the century were some of the greatest minds this century has produced: Russell, Whitehead, Carnap, Lukasiewicz. They did original work in formal logic, knew their disciplines inside out, but abandoned nevertheless the quest for remaking philosophy and science into the image of formal systems. Can we hope that lesser minds will succeed in a similar task and with regard to even more complex subject matters such as social science and technology assessment?

Now, I want to make it explicit that I am not against models and modeling. After all, provided here is a model for reconstructing the structure of judgment in TA. But I am against those extravagant cognitive and epistemological claims which modelers so often implicitly make, as if the formal perfection of a model, or its cybernetic intricacy, were the most important aspects of our intellectual activity. The trouble with our formal models is, as a friend of mine has put it: "We model nonlinear systems using linear techniques and hope that we will be 'approximately' correct in our analysis." We are modeling a reality (in a simplified way) which we do not really understand. Let us keep it very sharply in mind that *no model is a mind*.[4] We can do the modeling of the mind, but we must not presume that our models isomorphize the mind. Models are very primitive sets of boxes. We must not presume that we can force into them Nature, the human mind, or even knowledge, as evolved by the human species.

The number of scholars who take an increasingly critical view of the bequeathed tradition of objectivity is increasing. It is more and more universally accepted that the neutrality and objectivity of science and technology (hence of formal models) are a myth. Hazel Henderson has shown with consummate skill the value-laden elements in seemingly objective and factual structures.[5] Jack Shuman has shown the games bureaucrats play with mathematical model building in public policy making.[6] W. H. C. Simmonds and others in this volume have perceptively analyzed the nature of futures problems and the way they resist being forced into neat methodological boxes. Willis Harman has shown in his TA of the solar energy option that all the factual elements are deeply steeped in the magma of values.[7] And so on.

---

[4] For further discussion, see H. Skolimowski, "The Twilight of Physical Descriptions and the Ascent of Normative Models," in *The World System — Models, Norms, Variations,* Ervin Laszlo (ed.), International Library of Systems Theory and Philosophy, Braziller, New York, 1973.

[5] Hazel Henderson, "Ecologists versus Economists," *Harvard Business Review,* July-August 1973, pp. 28-36, 152-157; "The Entropy State," *Planning Review,* Vol. 2, No. 3, April-May 1974, pp. 1-4; "Philosophical Conflict: Reexamining the Goals of Knowledge," *Public Administration Review,* Vol. 35, No. 1, Jan.-Feb. 1975, pp. 77-80; "The Coming Economic Transition," *Technological Forecasting and Social Change,* Vol. 8, No. 4, 1976, pp. 337-351.

[6] Jack N. Shuman, "Mathematical Model Building and Public Policy: The Games Some Bureaucrats Play," *Technological Forecasting and Social Change,* Vol. 9, No. 3, 1976, pp. 309-334.

[7] Willis Harman, Energy Research & Administration, Scenario No. 49, Washington, D. C., 1976.

ISBN 0-201-04096-4

I should also make it clear that my intention is not to discredit the role of science and of the analytical process in TA, and in other forms of modeling reality. I have been taken to task on this point in a public debate, so let me put it on record: I consider the role of science in TA as very important. I really take its importance for granted. Though important it is, the role of science is also limited. *The actual TA begins when the factual and analytical part is completed.* This is why I have devoted most of my attention to this other part: normative and epistemological sui generis, for it is unique and specific to technology assessment.

Summary

Technology assessment is a sui generis discipline. It was created as a reaction against the pursuit of objectivity, as embodied in science and technology. It was created to be accountable in *social* terms. Therefore, it cannot and must not be reduced to the "objectivity components," as if it were another branch of objective knowledge, for (let us remember) it was created against the unchecked expansion of objective knowledge. In the context of our civilization, TA is that kind of knowledge that attempts to constrain certain forms of action. With the given socio-economic structure and the given thrust of technology, it is gratuitous, if not entirely betraying common sense, to call TA technology arrestment (as some do), for in the present context, TA *must* be a constraining influence. Of utmost importance in TA is the structure of its judgment, which is normative in character, both in terms of the processes of arriving at it and in terms of its product (assessment). The structure of judgment in TA is the dynamic matrix of epistemological dialectics between the descriptive and the normative which is resolved and expressed in social terms. The structure of judgment in TA is but a subtle and indirect articulation of the various epistemological assumptions concerning knowledge and action that are inherent in a given intellectual paradigm. The epistemological complexity of our present sociotechnological knowledge should make us aware that, in order to elicit the structure of judgment in TA in our present circumstances, we cannot rely on formal models, particularly if they are set to handle linear problems. Technology assessment is not a body of knowledge, even less so a body of techniques, but a guide to right action. Technology assessment, let us hope, will become this new knowledge which will guide our action in a positive and enhancing direction, so that it informs us "what kind of work to do, what kind of work to avoid, and how to reach a state of calm detachment from [our] work."

ISBN 0-201-04096-4

V. Recent Projects

V. 1. Introduction

HAROLD A. LINSTONE

> I have seen the future and it works.
> > Lincoln Steffens
>
> I saw the future and it didn't work.
> > Zero Mostel

In this Part we see a cross section of recent substantive futures activities — in the United States, England, and Sweden. The European work is done by governmental units, the American is done via contract by nongovernmental organizations (one not for profit, the other for profit). The two European groups operate on distinct lines. The English group performs a large number of studies, mostly quantitative and analytic, as input to a variety of governmental decision questions involving future technology-related policies. The Swedish group commissions studies and promotes public participation; it is less technology-specific and deals with far fewer studies.

Jones favors use of multiple techniques in parallel (as his countryman McLean recommends in his discussion on modeling in Part IV). Unlike many think-tank practitioners, Jones has no illusions about the tools: "There are no good 'techniques,' only techniques with varying degrees of inadequacy." The futility of improving models by adding variables and interactions is recognized, as is their subtle subjectivity.

Another interesting revelation is the trend toward use of scenarios — an inherently more holistic approach than that provided by other tools. A recent review of "good" technology assessments[1] led to the impression that the only "technique" common to them also was the use of scenarios. Jones echoes Sachs in sweeping into the discussion the essentially inductive nature of systems involving human beings, and Vickers, McHale, and Holling in focusing on the unique characteristics of societal systems (i.e., nonquantifiability, radical change, and instability behavior).

Backstrand describes an operation at once smaller and more holistic in its modus operandi. Its concern with avoiding both technocratic elitism and fringe-group narrow-mindedness or dilettantism makes it unusually significant. It is a serious effort to increase public awareness and widen the dialogue about future options. It assumes that "there is no problem that is too complex for public debate," a refreshing departure from the image of the simple-minded public reflected in

---

[1]Harold A. Linstone, George Lendaris, Christian Putz, Devendra Sahal, Wayne Wakeland, and Mark Williams, Report 77-6, *The Use of Structural Modeling in Technology Assessment, Progress Report – February 1977*, Systems Science Ph.D. Program, Portland State University, Portland, Oregon.

Futures Research: New Directions, Harold A. Linstone and W. H. Clive Simmonds (eds.)

ISBN 0-201-04096-4

political speeches, predilection for technical jargon, public relations efforts (e.g., annual corporation reports and institutional advertising), and schlock literature.

Cetron and Clayton apply the precursor event-train technique to probe potential value changes in the United States. The precursor country is Sweden. This work relates to earlier discussions in two significant ways:

1.   In Part I, Linstone discussed the discounting dilemma. It was pointed out that a temporally distant situation in our own physical setting could be brought within our limited planning horizon by substituting for it an analogous current situation which is physically far removed and then compressing the physical distance via telecommunications. The procedure is effective because technology enables us to shrink physical space far more readily than temporal space. The Cetron-Clayton procedure combines such a time-space shift with trend extrapolation to forge a societal forecasting tool.

2.   The use of a real-world system as a model is an excellent means to attain holism; it provides the *in vivo* setting which Sahal called for in Part IV. There are two obvious alternatives – current societal "models" and historical ones. Lynn White has shown us the invaluable insight obtained by historical study;[2] Cetron and Clayton use comparative modern societies, with Sweden serving as precursor to the United States in social legislation (e.g., consumer protection, paternity leave).

The second model discussed by Cetron and Clayton, Molitor's concept of multiple buildups of societal forces, is of a type also found useful in other futures research efforts. The project described by Teige *et al.* included an analysis by Linstone and McEachron of the development of large-scale technological projects (Parthenon, Apollo, SST). In each case there were four essential elements – technology, management, economic resources, and motivation – and each could be represented by a cumulative event curve similar to those shown in Cetron and Clayton's Fig. 10. Successful initiation requires the condition of simultaneity, i.e., the four element curves to be above a threshold level in the same time interval. The more one analyzes large scale projects in history,[3] the more evident it becomes that need and cost-benefit often are *not* decisive elements in their success. They may capture the national imagination, provide a unifying force, or a sense of group achievement – all not quantifiable. Nor does the technology need to be advanced or unusual. One key motivational component is the trigger or catalytic event or

---

[2] L. White, Jr., "Technology Assessment from the Stance of a Medieval Historian," *Technological Forecasting and Social Change,* Vol. 6, 1974, pp. 359-369.

[3] They appear to fall into a limited number of categories:
Survival – military defense (Chinese wall), water and food (aquaducts, irrigation systems)
Communications/transportation – railroads, road networks
Religious projects – temples, pyramids, cathedrals
Building projects – Forum Romanum, Colosseum, Piazza San Marco, Versailles
Scientific enterprises – Apollo, Stonehenge (?)

ISBN 0-201-04096-4

person (e.g., Pericles, Sputnik) integrating or fusing the separate elements into a single system.[4]

Teige *et al.* once more point us toward holistic perspectives. In fact, they suggest that the approach from below — i.e., a vast array of isolated component problems — may be far less productive than a direct holistic one: "The larger holistic pattern may indeed be more tractable than its individual component problems." They talk about problem solving as an "internal adjustment procedure in an ongoing, dynamic process."

This comment, like Molitor's statement about "dissonances" within the society that demand laws to "correct" the problem (p. 225), suggests a promising approach proposed by Christopher Alexander — the concept of misfit variables.[5] The solution to complex problems is assumed to consist not in optimization but in minimizing the misfits which occur in the process of change. The same direction has been taken by Fried and Molnar[6] as well as by Sharma.[7]

The effort to identify critical future problem areas which are not obvious and are relevant to the kinds of decisions made by the United States Office of Science and Technology Policy was fraught with precisely those problems raised in Parts I, II, and III (for example, by Linstone, McHale, Loveridge, Mitroff, and Michael).

Teige *et al.* conclude that a paradigm shift in science and technology is essential and see some evidence of its emergence. The presently dominant paradigm is replaced by one that balances the attributes of a dichotomy strikingly similar to that presented in Table 1 of the Part II Introduction. Thus, the paper provides a most appropriate closure to the collection.

---

[4]Such a mechanism was clearly lacking in the case of the SST.

[5]C. Alexander, "Notes on the Synthesis of Form," Harvard University Press, Cambridge, Massachusetts, 1964. (Also see Part I, p. 8.)

[6]J. Fried and P. Molnar, "A General Model for Culture and Technology," *Technological Forecasting and Social Change*, Vol. 8, 1975, pp. 175-188.

[7]K. J. Sharma, "Misfit Variable — A Useful and Efficient Concept for Technology Assessment Methodology," *IEEE Proceedings of the 1975 International Conference on Cybernetics and Society*, September 1975, pp. 8-10.

ISBN 0-201-04096-4

V. 2. One Organization's Experience

PETER M. S. JONES

Introduction

The art of prediction has a long and undistinguished history. The pseudo-science of forecasting has a relatively short history, distinguished, perhaps, by the lack of *worthwhile* progress and improvement in techniques – at least if futures prediction is the goal. This dialogue is particularly welcome in that it rejects the alchemist-like search for the philosophers' stone and seeks to establish a rational basis for understanding what we are about and what we can hope to achieve.

This paper seeks to condense into a short space the thinking that has developed during ten years of active practice of futures studies in the Programmers Analysis Unit (PAU), a small unit faced with the task of advising on specific decisions or general policy formulation within the government sector. These decisions or policies relate particularly to the allocation of resources to research and development, to industrial technology, and to the social, economic, and environmental impacts of technical change.

The vast majority of the two hundred or so studies undertaken by the unit have noticeably influenced thinking and, where appropriate, decisions. In less than 10% of the cases would the analysts involved feel that their work had been inadequately considered, and in these the cause has been, almost invariably, a change in personnel within the sponsoring organization. This is not to say that all recommendations are accepted and implemented to the full or that all studies meet the sponsors' needs. About 10% fail to add significantly to the sponsors' knowledge, though even these may give added confidence to decisions, coming as they do from a detached objective source.

This paper is divided into three sections: the first, a brief and very incomplete catalogue of case studies; the second, a series of assertions about applied futures studies; and the third, a presentation of conclusions and speculation on the way forward in the futures field.

Case Studies

UK Space Launcher and Satellite Development

Studies undertaken in 1967-1968 sought to establish the economic value of development programs. Likely upper limits were set to nonmilitary satellite markets to the year 2000 by expert opinion and scenario approaches. Likely United Kingdom and European market shares were estimated similarly. The European and export demand for satellite launchers was thus derived, and the unit

Futures Research: New Directions, Harold A. Linstone and W. H. Clive Simmonds (eds.)

ISBN 0-201-04096-4

costs of launchers, including spread development costs, were computed on the basis of expert opinion and analogy with data from the United States, including success/failure rates in development launchings.

The conclusion was that the costs of large European-developed launchers, on the basis of plans then current, would be prohibitively high (an order of magnitude) and a decade behind, technologically, the state of the art in the United States in the 1980's (Fig. 1). On economic grounds, which were not the sole determinant, it was expected that it would be preferable to buy rather than develop large launchers. Markets for satellites were expected to be sufficiently large to justify specific development programs. A subsequent study in 1971 expanded on the latter conclusion and applied limiting probability analysis[1] to quantitative market estimation in parallel with scenario and expert opinion methods.

The studies were accepted, and the recommendations have so far been justified by events.

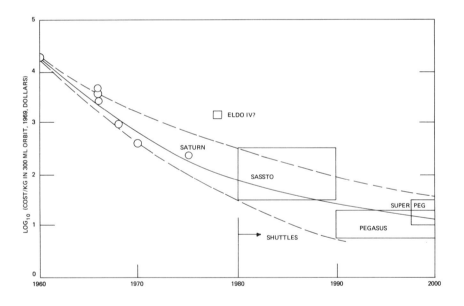

Fig. 1. Satellite launching costs.

Desalination

A study mounted in 1967 looked at the direction and balance of research and development programs in the United Kingdom. Through expert opinion and a

ISBN 0-201-04096-4

[1]"Collected Essays by PAU Authors – Part II, Uncertainty and Risk," PAU Report M25B, HMSO, London, 1974.

conventional study of overseas market needs, based essentially on extrapolation techniques, an estimate of the market open to United Kingdom industry into the 1990's was produced. Political links were identified as being a crucial factor in marketing strategy. The prospects for alternative technologies and the change in the unit cost of water over time were examined through expert opinion and techno-economic assessment (Fig. 2). Recommended changes in the balance and size of the programs were implemented. Views on markets have proved correct.

A second study in 1971 looked at potential United Kingdom needs. In the intervening years public opposition to reservoirs, a factor not considered in 1967, had hardened. The "insurance" value of having an available desalination technology was therefore highlighted, and social costs of alternatives, trends in social attitude (qualitative), and water demand (quantitative) were projected to the year 2000. The views formed part of the debate on United Kingdom policy.[2]

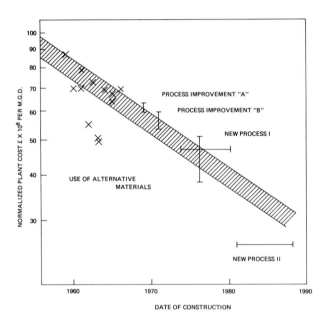

Fig. 2. Anticipated capital costs of desalination plants. Cost normalized to 2 million Imperial gallon per day units with P.R. 8 : 1. Crosses indicate actual plants (normalized). Bars indicate range of cost improvements from research and development program.

———————
[2]"Desalination 1972," Water Resources Board, HMSO, London, 1972.

ISBN 0-201-04096-4

Carbon Fibers

A series of studies have been made on carbon fiber research and development programs covering the period from 1967 to 1971. These examined the potential markets for carbon fiber composites on the basis of technoeconomic estimates of (1) manufacturing costs, scaled from laboratory studies and crude plant design studies, and (2) value to users based on comparative advantages of lightweight composites vis-à-vis metals, glass-fiber-reinforced resins, etc. Speculative and reasonably assured markets up to the mid-1980's could thus be derived. They justified scaled-up expenditures for research and development, though not immediate investment in the large-scale manufacturing plant being recommended elsewhere.[3] Views on technical improvement, competing manufacturing techniques, and competing materials were derived from a survey of expert opinion.

Reality fell short of median expectation with the nonadoption of carbon fiber for the Rolls Royce RB211 engine fan blades, but this risk had been recognized in the study and had tempered the conclusions.

Applied Radiation Technologies

Studies in 1968-1969 reviewed United Kingdom Atomic Energy Authority (UKAEA) applied radiation programs related to food sterilization and pasteurization, chemical synthesis, and paint curing. Comparative economic and technical assessment, taking account of likely technical development, made it seem unlikely that radiation would be a preferred route for food sterilization or chemical synthesis. Paint curing offered marginal advantages in some specific circumstances, and pasteurization could be economic. In the case of the latter in particular, adoption of the process would be dependent on public acceptability and the attitudes of statutory committees. Limited funding only was justified and should be directed primarily toward gaining international acceptance rather than technical aspects. The findings were accepted, and the programs changed.

Ion Implantation

The medium-term commercial prospects for the United Kingdom were reviewed in 1969, in 1971, and again in 1974. The approach was one of identifying technological opportunities of potential relevance to the sponsor and the benefits that might flow from their exploitation. The structure and interests of the manufacturing industry were such that rapid exploitation of the technique could not be forecast in the United Kingdom even though specific applications were attractive. This finding led to a realignment of the program and the establishment of a successful implantation service calculated to speed the adoption of the technique. The techniques employed were based on expert opinion surveys and technoeconomic appraisal.

---

[3]"Carbon Fibers," Report from the Select Committee on Science and Technology, HMSO, London, 1969.

ISBN 0-201-04096-4

Computers and Television Markets

Surveys of the markets for computers in the United Kingdom and Europe, and for television sets in the United Kingdom, were undertaken to assist government policy formulation for these industries. The former was conducted in 1968-1969 and relied on a statistical approach based on historic sales by category and trend extrapolation over a decade for disaggregated user categories, taking account of likely technical advance. A second-order polynomial gave the "best fit," and allowance was made for model replacement. Other models involving parametric linking to gross domestic product, etc., were tried, as was analogy with growth in the United States, allowing a five-year (empirical data fit) lag. The extrapolative models seriously underestimated growth, and this became apparent within four years. The analogy-based model was vastly superior as a forecasting tool, though not identified as such at the time.

Television receiver sales forecasts were similarly analyzed on the basis of historic trends. The model took account of average set life and a rising population in the United Kingdom. The important outcome was the identification of major natural demand fluctuations independent of fiscal policies. This aspect has been confirmed by time. The forecast sales levels have been greatly exceeded, owing partly to changes in fiscal policy, and partly to a much more rapid penetration of color sets at a time of comparative affluence. Again, had United States experience been translated to the United Kingdom scene, the steep rise in sales would have been anticipated (Fig. 3).

Despite overconservatism, both forecasts gave correct indications for policy.

Transport

Several land-based transport studies have been undertaken. The first (1972) involved a review of the likely global market for personal rapid-transport systems and was based on a Delphi review of long-range planners in 151 cities in 22 countries backed by a system dynamics model exploring the impact of technological transport alternatives within an urban environment. The latter compared the efficacy of alternative transport policies in attracting travelers to public transport and took into account social and environmental acceptability. The likely world market open to United Kingdom industry was estimated, using limiting probability analysis.[4] The findings were accepted and used as a basis for decisions on development programs.

A more recent study (1975) has examined alternative land transport scenarios for the United Kingdom in the 1990's. The impact and relevance of alternative

---

[4]"Collected Essays by PAU Authors – Part I, Project Appraisal and Needs Research," PAU Report M25A, HMSO, London, 1974; P. E. Love, F. J. Walford, and D. Atkinson, "The Likely Export Market for PRTS," PAU Report R15/72A, 1972, available on request.

ISBN 0-201-04096-4

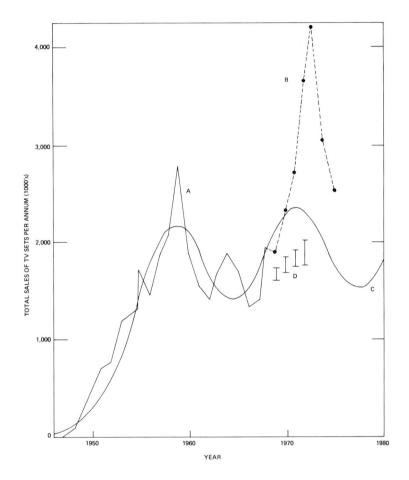

Fig. 3. Television sales forecasts (1969). A, historic data; B, outcome; C, PAU 1969 model; D, National Economic Development Council 1969 forecast.

technological development programs has been examined against these scenarios, using an extended signed digraph technique.[5] The objective in this case was to test method feasibility and back up inputs into a review of the usefulness of technology assessment by the Organisation for Economic Co-operation and Development (OECD).

A third, narrower study has examined various aspects of linear motor development including future transport applications using the limiting probability

---

[5]J. I. Gershunny, "Towards a Social Assessment to Technology," PAU Report M27, HMSO, London, 1976.

ISBN 0-201-04096-4

technique and expert opinion. The studies were used as a basis for decisions on development and, coincidentally, research expenditure.[6]

Marine Transport

High-speed marine craft (1969) and the nuclear merchant ship (1971, 1974, 1976) have been examined. The basic approach has been technoeconomic comparison of performance and cost between alternatives. In those areas where economic advantage could be expected, the markets were estimated by a variety of techniques ranging from dynamic models (hovercraft) to trend extrapolation and parametric correlation. Due account was taken of social and environmental acceptability, market structure (building and operating), and operational parameters as they seemed likely to develop.[7]

The pessimistic market indications for large hovercraft led to reductions in development expenditure, while the nuclear ship studies have supported a cautious approach.[8] The 1971 study failed to anticipate the rapid escalation in oil fuel prices, though it was pointed out that a major rise in the relative cost of oil would change the then unfavorable nuclear ship economics. The 1974 limited update suggested that the situation could indeed have reversed and led directly to a more thorough and critical review, taking into account the infrastructural, safety, and other factors.

Energy

Through its UKAEA sponsorship the unit has been closely concerned with studies of energy-demand forecasting and environmental impact assessment. Forecasts of electricity demand have been made in association with the UKAEA,[9] employing a range of techniques — socioeconomic and demographic scenarios, trend extrapolation with logistic curve fitting, parametric correlation (GDP — useful energy consumption) and technoeconomic assessment.[10] Currently, linked iterative models, allowing fuel switching and relating energy usage to a multisector input-output model of the economy, are being used to test the internal consistency of scenarios such as those developed in "Energy R&D in the United Kingdom,"[11] to which the unit contributed.

[6]"Advanced Ground Transport," Select Committee on Science and Technology, Appendix 1, HMSO, London, 1976.

[7]K. M. Hill, "A Note on Some Considerations for Government Policy," *Hovering Craft and Hydrofoil*, Vol. 10, No. 3, 1970, pp. 14, 15.

[8]Department of Trade and Industry, "First and Second Reports on the Nuclear Ship Study," HMSO, London, 1971 and 1975.

[9]L. G. Brookes, "An S-Curve to Forecast Electricity Demand," *Atom*, No. 144, October 1968, pp. 277-282.

[10]K. Main and N. J. D. Lucas, "A Feasibility Study of the Supply of Industrial Process Steam from Nuclear Reactors in the U.K.," *British Nuclear Energy Society Journal*, Vol. 16, No. 1, 1977, pp. 63-70.

[11]Department of Energy, "Energy R&D in the United Kingdom," London, June, 1976.

ISBN 0-201-04096-4

Forecasts of energy growth made eight years ago now seem optimistic in the light of the upheaval in the world economy, and the accent in the unit has moved away from "forecasts" to alternative scenarios and the evolution of rugged strategies preserving options into the future.

A 1972 study examined the prospects for synthetic transportable fuels in the 1990-2030 era[12] and employed demand-supply projection to establish need and technoeconomic analysis to review alternative manufacturing routes for a range of fuels. Large-scale use of synthetics was forecast post 2000 A.D., and the cost of synthetics was argued to provide a barrier (in the long term) to rises in the relative price of mineral oil.

Mineral Resource Availability

Mathematical modeling techniques have been employed to examine the likely long-term availability of some nonrenewable resources.[13] Statistical distribution models have been developed to extrapolate known reserves and resources to likely global totals. Models of exploitation behavior have been produced in consultation with industrial mining experts, and market demands estimated as a function of price, using extrapolative methods. All extrapolations take account of techno-logical developments. If the underlying assumptions were right, then the model could predict supply, demand, discovery rates, and prices. However, the approach is not yet at the stage of a predictive device and probably never will be. It is a valuable aid to logical thinking and can link the sensitivity of the "system" to alternative policy assumptions and technical developments. Perhaps the major lessons are the sensitivity of the future to nontechnical factors and the undue pessimism of commonly quoted resource lifetimes. The studies have been used by the United Kingdom Cabinet Office and the UKAEA.[13]

Environmental Impacts

Impact analysis necessarily involves taking a look into the future. Several PAU studies have done this. Global marine oil pollution and its impacts on marine life and humans were reviewed (1972) using trend extrapolation on shipping and shipping accidents and the best available data on oil destruction and dispersal, set against different avoidance and control strategies.[14] The significance of social impacts was set in perspective by a field survey in Europe. The study was a basis for international discussion at the International Maritime Consultative Organisation.

---

[12]G. V. Day, "The Prospects for Synthetic Fuels Futures," Vol. 4, 1972, p. 331; and Institute of Electrical Engineers Publication No. 112, IEE, London, 1974, p. 139.

[13]H. Inston, "Modelling the Materials Production, Consumption and Recycling System," Proceedings of the Conference on Conservation of Materials, AERE, Harwell, 1974; "Future World Trends," Cabinet Office, HMSO, London, 1976.

[14]"The Environmental and Financial Consequences of Oil Pollution from Ships," PAU Report M24 for International Maritime Consultative Organisation, 1973, available on request.

ISBN 0-201-04096-4

A subsequent study (1975) has examined the likely level of future accidents to personnel and structures in the course of North Sea oil exploitation. It has employed statistical analysis of existing international experience and analogy, and served as an input to discussions on research and development programs and a study on pollution in the North Sea.[15]

Other studies based on trends in fuel utilization, trends in antipollution technology, and trends in legislation and social acceptability, partly quantitative and partly qualitative scenarios, have looked at air pollution and its social and economic costs in the United Kingdom up to 1980,[16] nitrogen oxide pollution in Europe to 1985,[17] and the implications of noise legislation for manufacturing industry. These studies have also been inputs to debates on general policy and research and development expenditure.

Industrial Futures

Published studies have embraced the technological future of the textile industry[18] and all aspects of the garment industry.[19] In the latter, a wide range of independent approaches examined past, current, and likely future patterns of demand by product, labor availability and turnover, technology, productivity, structure, management, international competition, etc., using trend extrapolation, scenario, technoeconomic comparison, simple quantitative models, Delphi reviews of social need, etc. The whole, when brought together, presents a single coherent scenario qualified by views on the potential impacts of alternative policies. These studies were used as the basis for industry-government discussions (some through the National Economic Development Office) and continue to act as reference documents.[20]

Similar studies have dealt with other industries, some in connection with the current industrial strategy debate in the United Kingdom, but have not been published.

Social Futures

Current interests include such themes as the likely development of manufacturing processes in the light of social pressures and health and safety legislation. Inevitably, future social scenarios are linked to political developments and must be

---

[15]"Accidental Oil Pollution of the Sea," Department of Environment Central Unit on Environmental Pollution, Paper No. 8, HMSO, London, 1976.

[16]P. M. S. Jones, K. Taylor, M. Clifon, and D. Storey, "An Economic and Technical Appraisal of Air Pollution in the U. K.," PAU Report M20, HMSO, London, 1972.

[17]K. Taylor, "Environment and the Quality of Life: Nitrogen Oxide Emissions 1970-1985," EUR 5136e, Commission of the European Communities, Brussels, 1974.

[18]A. G. Hamlin, R. G. Collier, and M. W. Drew, "A Technological Forecast for the U. K. Textile Industry, 1972-1990," PAU Report R5/73, available on request.

[19]P. M. S. Jones, A. G. Hamlin, and G. I. W. Llewellyn, "Technology and the Garment Industry," National Economic Development Office, HMSO, London, 1971.

[20]"The Anatomy of a Multinational," General Federation of Trade Unions, London, 1975.

ISBN 0-201-04096-4

looked at as a series of alternatives on which choices can be based. Thus one set of scenarios, based on postulated trends toward a technocratic society, offers a series of alternative futures depending on the nature of society's goals (equality of opportunities or results) and the nature of government itself (Fig. 4). Some might be stable societies, and some unstable.[21] Clearly a range of other and more attractive alternatives could be spelt out.

It is expected that studies in this area will figure increasingly in inputs to decision and policy formulation.

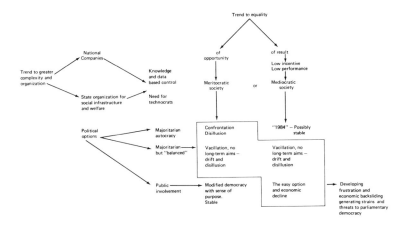

Fig. 4. Illustrative national futures — social and political trends.

Lessons to Be Learned

The above brief cases and others described elsewhere[22] give a representative picture of the nature of futures studies in one organization and their application. The factors considered and the techniques deployed are summarized, nonexhaustively, in Table 1. The following conclusions can be drawn:

1. If futures studies are to be of value to decision and policy makers, they need to be centered on the specific issues under review. Random speculative studies will almost invariably fail to identify all the critical factors.

2. The sponsor of a study must be closely involved with its definition and its progress if willing acceptance is sought.

---

[21]P. M. S. Jones, "Industry and Society, Outlook for the Future," *Chemistry and Industry,* November, 1975, pp. 939-941.

[22]"The Programmes Analysis Unit, 1967-71," "The Second Five Years, 1971-76," PAU publications, available on request.

ISBN 0-201-04096-4

Table 1

Partial Summary of Futures Studies by PAU

GENERIC TITLE (Number of related studies in parenthesis)	Factors Considered						"Techniques" Used									Application		
	Techno-logical	Economic	Social	Ecological and Environ-mental	Health and Safety	Insti-tutional	Expert Evidence	Delphi	Trend	Analogy	Scenario	Morphology Relevance	Math. Models	Techno-economic	Limiting Prob-ability	Decision	Policy	Other
Computer markets (2)	x	x	x				x		x	x	x		x				x	
TV markets		x	x			x	x		x	x	x		x				x	
Launcher development (2)	x	x				x	x		x	x	x			x		x	x	
Satellite development (2)	x	x		x		x	x		x		x		x	x	x	x	x	
Desalination development (3)	x	x	x	x	x	x	x		x		x		x	x	x	x	x	
Carbon fiber and composites (3)	x	x			x	x	x		x	x	x	x	x	x		x		
Hydrostatic extrusion (2)	x	x			x	x	x		x		x		x	x	x	x	x	
Ion implantation R&D (2)	x	x	x			x	x				x		x	x		x	x	
High-speed marine craft	x	x					x	x						x		x		
Metal-working techniques (4)	x	x					x	x			x		x	x		x		
Fuel cells and batteries (2)	x	x	x				x		x		x		x	x	x	x	x	
Linear motor development	x	x					x		x			x	x	x	x	x	x	
Nuclear steelmaking	x	x				x	x	x	x									
Micro electronics application (2)	x	x	x		x	x	x	x	x				x		x		x	
Fishing systems	x	x				x	x		x				x				x	
Marine mining	x	x	x	x			x					x		x	x	x	x	
Ceramic applications (3)	x	x	x				x		x		x			x			x	
Peaceful nuclear explosion markets	x	x		x	x		x			x	x			x	x		x	
Nuclear process heat	x	x		x		x	x		x		x		x	x			x	
Electricity needs	x	x	x			x	x		x	x	x		x	x			x	
Synthetic fuels	x	x	x			x	x		x	x	x		x	x		x	x	
Radiation applications	x	x	x		x	x	x				x	x	x	x		x	x	
Computer-based learning systems	x	x	x			x	x				x							x
Use of DDT (2)	x	x			x	x	x				x	x	x	x		x		
Superconductor applications	x	x	x		x		x	x			x	x		x		x	x	
Marine R&D opportunities (3)	x	x	x		x	x	x	x	x		x	x		x		x	x	
Basic research areas (3)	x	x	x			x	x	x	x	x	x		x			x	x	x
Garment industry future	x	x	x			x	x		x		x		x	x			x	x
Textile industry future	x	x	x			x	x		x		x		x				x	
Printing industry future	x	x	x			x	x		x		x						x	
Aluminum foundries	x	x	x			x	x		x		x					x	x	
Minor industrial sectors (6)	x	x	x		x	x	x		x	x	x	x	x	x		x	x	x
Air pollution in UK	x	x	x	x	x	x	x		x		x		x	x		x	x	
Marine oil pollution	x	x	x	x	x	x	x		x		x			x		x	x	
Noise legislation	x	x	x	x	x	x	x		x		x		x				x	
Impacts of energy systems	x	x	x	x	x	x	x		x	x	x		x				x	
Offshore accidents	x	x	x		x	x	x		x	x	x		x				x	
Mineral resources (2)	x	x	x	x		x	x		x		x		x	x		x	x	
Nuclear merchant ships (3)	x	x	x	x	x	x	x		x		x		x	x		x	x	
Urban transportation (2)	x	x	x		x	x	x		x		x		x	x	x	x	x	
Automation (2)	x	x	x	x		x	x		x		x			x		x	x	x
Vehicle pollution	x	x	x	x	x	x	x		x		x			x		x	x	x

ISBN 0-201-04096-4

3.   There are no good "techniques," only techniques with varying degrees of inadequacy.

4.   In any real study several techniques are deployed in parallel, the selection being dependent on the nature of the problem, the availability of data, and, to some extent, the analyst.

5.   In applied futures studies, two "techniques" have been of particular value to the author and his colleagues:

   (a) Establishing the practical barriers to change, whether technical, economic, social, or institutional;

   (b) Establishing the incentive to change through technoeconomic or socio-economic appraisal.

6.   Major changes have occurred during the past fifteen years in the significance attached to factors affecting decision. In the 1950's technology was believed by many to have its own momentum. The 1960's saw the growth of more critical economics-based approaches to resource allocation. The late 1960's then saw the switch by affluent society to environmental concern, followed rapidly by concern for global resources and health, safety, and the humanization of working conditions. Developing nations, employment, and social stability are expected to become more dominant factors over the next five-year period. Not all studies need to embrace explicitly all factors, since the impacts may be minor.

7.   Most policy-oriented futures studies and some decision-oriented studies would now be presented as a series of alternative futures scenarios with indications of their likelihood and the factors that may favor movement to one or another alternative. Those using the studies will seek to manipulate the course of events to their advantage. Forecasts therefore become normative and potentially self-fulfilling or self-defeating. Some argue cogently[23, 24] that this is the only proper procedure for social forecasting.

8.   Many decision-oriented futures studies, however, take the form of forecasts. The professional forecaster will make his assumptions and believed degree of confidence clear to those employing his conclusions, though not always in his publications! Fully defined forecasts such as "the *world* market for *fractional horsepower* linear motors in 1985 will exceed £xM *(January 1975£s) with 90% confidence*" would be meaningless and untestable without the italicized qualifications.

9.   Any attempt to judge the reliability of a forecast or forecaster must:[25]

   (a) Recognize that it should measure whether the forecaster's confidence in his forecasts is substantiated by events; i.e., do the expected propor-

[23]I. Miles *The Poverty of Prediction,* Saxon House, Farnborough, U. K., 1975.

[24]S. Encel, P. K. Marstrand, and W. Page, *The Art of Anticipation,* M. Robertson & Co. Ltd, London, 1975.

[25]P. M. S. Jones, "The Credibility of Forecasts and Forecasters," *R & D Management Journal,* Vol. 7, No. 2, 1977, pp. 97-98.

ISBN 0-201-04096-4

tions of outcomes lie within his forecast confidence limits. Probabilistic statements cannot be said to be right or wrong.

(b) Recognize that conformity or nonconformity with expectation has meaning only when the forecast is explicit in its time frame, its spatial location, and its confidence limits.

(c) Recognize that unforeseen events are more a function of the definition of the original forecasting framework than the forecaster or his methods — a man looking for diamonds may fail to record stray pearls even if he sees them.

(d) Recognize that policy- or decision-related forecasts may be self-fulfilling or self-defeating if they are acted upon.

10.   A high proportion of our work has involved the estimation of existing or likely markets or the benefits attached to alternative options in welfare economic terms.   This is inevitable if studies are to be linked to practical decisions and policies in the industrial and economic sector.   It is not possible to go this far in broad studies related to the major infrastructure or shape of future society, and it may not be necessary to involve economic factors if the remit is narrowly constrained — e.g., to future technical performance parameters, etc.

Development of Futures Studies

What Are We Trying To Achieve?

I will start from the basic assumption that policies developed, or decisions made, against a properly researched background assessment of likely future developments, and which have been objectively appraised by disinterested groups to minimize the risks of unanticipated side effects, are generally likely to be better than those developed in the absence of such aids. This may seem to be a truism, but it is far from universally accepted.

One can only approach certainty in relation to things or events that are here within sight or reach now, and even glossing over metaphysical arguments, the limitations of our senses preclude complete certainty. Relaxation of the spatial constraint, time constraint, or event definition leads to a rapidly expanding spectrum of alternative possibilities. Knowledge of things past or expectation of future events is necessarily uncertain. The principal aim of futures studies is to define the range of credible alternatives as clearly as possible. This is why stress is laid in our studies on alternative scenario generation (Table 1) and methods of identifying constraints or incentives that inhibit or favor certain outcomes (item 5 above). If, for convenience, we reduce our space (s), time (t), and event (e) alternatives to a three-dimensional representation (Fig. 5), with "event" signifying a state of nature embracing social, technical, economic, and other aspects, then futures studies consist in tracing the expanding funnel of (s, t, e) or defining the range of alternative values of any one or two parameters with the others fixed (time in Fig. 5).

ISBN 0-201-04096-4

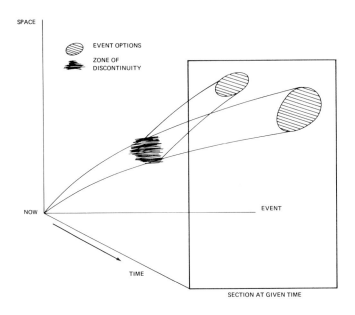

Fig. 5. The nature of forecasts. Ovals indicate event options. Shaded area indicates zone of discontinuity.

Two or more distinct alternatives may arise as a result of endogenous or exogenous choices or unknown states of nature. For example, we may or may not choose to develop fusion power; it may or may not prove to be a feasible technology. The attempted identification and evaluation of such discontinuities and their implications is an integral part of any futures study.

What Can Be Done?

The futures analyst is effectively an observer situated within and interacting with a complex dynamic system whose boundaries stretch beyond his ken. Small parts of the system show temporary order, only to be shattered when a new component, which has lain outside the observer's vision, enters the scene (Rachel Carson's *Silent Spring,* the Yom Kippur war, stagflation, etc.). Provided a problem is, or can be, constrained and isolated from the main system, more or less precise forecasts can be made, for a time at least. Efforts to improve the reliability of forecasts have involved the introduction of ever more factors in complex dynamic interaction,[26] but no model can ever be exhaustive, and the philosophical basis under-

---

[26]D. Meadows, D. Meadows, and J. Randers, *The Limits to Growth,* Universe Books, New York, 1972.

ISBN 0-201-04096-4

pinning such forecasts is in dispute.[23, 24]

It may be that an omniscient observer outside the system could see overall order: if so it may be possible, in principle, to gradually deduce the natural and sociological laws and work towards better forecasts. On the other hand, if individuals are entirely free and unpredictable in their actions, then no amount of effort will eliminate anything more than minor uncertainties. Is international conflict caused by the arrival of a Hitler, or is the man (or another just like him) a product of preceding history and social environment? A plausible argument can be developed relating civil disorder, promiscuity, and other social manifestations to the liberal philosophies which evolve in affluent societies; or regional nationalism to reaction against the centralization inherent in complex, large technology-based societies.

This is perhaps the fundamental question facing the futures analyst. The answer either defines the practical constraint beyond which he can never go, or exposes new vistas. The outcome will probably be neither the stark rejection of historicism nor the universal acceptance of social engineering favored by Popper.[27]

However, forecasters continue to adopt an essentially deterministic approach with a clear element of historicism. Scant attention has been paid to the identification of singularities and discontinuities, and the whole basis of social reaction and political development is still largely unquantifiable. Our understanding of social phenomena parallels that of the Greek philosophers of 500 B.C. in their attempts to understand the physical world. We can observe and we can measure a few superficial parameters, but radically new concepts may be needed to give us the greater understanding necessary to predict with high confidence national or global developments over periods of weeks, let alone decades.

For this reason the practice of forecasting has to be a continuing exploratory exercise which may indicate the boundaries and constraints and problems and pitfalls, but no more. Within this framework certain policies or actions will appear more likely to nudge events in a desired direction than others.

Even with this recognized limitation a further complication exists in that "models" are almost inevitably egocentric and reflect the disciplinary and cultural background and ideals of their progenitors. Thus there would be grave dangers in overcentralizing or overcoordinating futures studies within a country or relying on work done by overseas groups. Diversity of approach and exposure of ideas to peer groups for criticism is the only credible safeguard that a decision-maker can have at the present state of the art.

If new concepts are needed, where should they be sought? The biggest barrier we face is our cultural straightjacket which determines modes of thought. In our materialistic age the health of nations is frequently judged solely in terms of gross national product per capita, which is about as sensible as measuring a horse's health by its consumption of hay or the work it can do. Society is a complex organism,

---

[27]K. Popper, *The Poverty of Historicism,* Routledge and Kegan Paul, London, 1957.

ISBN 0-201-04096-4

and to measure its condition by a simple, possibly ill-chosen parameter can only divert its development into "suboptimal" paths as weighed against other better-selected criteria. This is the force behind the search for social indicators, which itself may be misleading if it seeks additive combinations of symptoms rather than new ways of seeing the whole.

Conclusion

Scepticism about the practicability of worthwhile futures studies is still wide-spread. This is not altogether surprising when one views the development of management aids over the past two decades, with the exaggerated claims of successive purveyors of universal elixirs — the misplaced application of operational research optimization models, the claims for and abuses of Delphi forecasting, the overreaction to experimental systems dynamics models, and the rapid changes that have taken place in the criteria against which policies are developed and decisions made.

Nevertheless, practical experience has shown that properly conducted applied futures studies are helpful to decision-makers and policy makers. The futures analyst is still practicing an inexact art involving judgment, however, and not a science. His tools are weak and largely unproved, and his own way forward is unclear. Such progress as has been made has been largely in developing a better understanding of the constraints and an appreciation of more useful ways of harnessing what is feasible to management needs.

Radical improvements on the present situation may require as great a change in cultural outlook as that brought about by Charles Darwin in the nineteenth century or by Keynes and Rachel Carson in the twentieth century.

ISBN 0-201-04096-4

V. 3. The Public and the Future

GORAN BACKSTRAND

So far, the most clearly discernible scenarios in the debate on long-term trends and development have been commissioned by private institutions and independent research organizations. Future studies directly organized by governments are more rare. Those few initiatives that do exist have as a point of departure most commonly a rather elaborate short-term and medium-term planning system — e.g., in the Netherlands or in France.

The conditions under which the Secretariat for Future Studies was established as a government commission in Sweden in February 1973 were different from those in the countries just mentioned. Sweden does not possess the corresponding planning tradition. The activity in future studies in Sweden cannot, therefore, be organized as an extension of already established planning over broad societal sectors.

The Special Profile of Projects Initiated by the Swedish Secretariat for Future Studies

The fact that future studies have *not* been based on formalized national planning has given future studies in Sweden a different perspective. It is more correct to see these studies as a supplement, a new style, for government investigations. The special profile of these future studies can thus be expressed in the following headings:

- A freer search for alternatives
- A tool for deepening the democratic process
- Testing the position of the small state in the global society

The characteristics of the Secretariat for Future Studies can also be summarized as follows. In the quest for achieving a more balanced view between long-term and short-term interests within society, the Secretariat has two main goals:

- To commission future studies in order to provide a more accurate and broad documentation — i.e., elaborated alternatives for political decision-making.
- To promote the public interest — i.e., the very process of making public participation more common in the debate about possible futures.

The Parliament allocated funds in May 1974, and topics were chosen for the first projects:

- Working life in the future
- Sweden in the world society
- Resources and raw materials
- Energy and society

Futures Research: New Directions, Harold A. Linstone and W. H. Clive Simmonds (eds.)

ISBN 0-201-04096-4

In the beginning of 1975 these four projects were in operation, and the studies are due for successive completion during the course of 1977.

Although the experiment of introducing the concept of future studies within the Swedish government machinery has been in existence only a few years, and still another year will be needed before any final results of the projects will appear, it is already possible to make some comments about the popular interest in the search for alternatives and the ways in which the Secretariat has tried to promote and develop this interest.

Future Studies and Democracy

The practice of democracy in a modern, industrialized, mixed-economy and complex society creates significant problems. First of all, many important and guiding decisions, mainly economic ones, are taken in centers which not at all, or indirectly in a very limited sense, are under democratic control or open to the public eye. Second, several questions are technically very difficult. Democracy demands responsibility, but responsibility demands that one understand for which purpose this very responsibility shall be exercised. The problems with bureaucrats and experts are real ones and are a mirror of the dilemmas of a specialized society.

It is quite clear that a new organized activity under the heading of "future studies" carries a pre-eminent risk that the technostructure (to use Galbraith's terminology) gets another powerful tool. Genuine democratic functions within the society may lose more ground.

On many occasions this risk has been voiced very consciously. However, expressing dismay with governmental future studies has also created a tendency to "throw the baby out with the bath water." If 100% of all future studies should be free and autonomous in relation to the existing societal machinery, these studies would be characterized by a more exclusive criticizing function, very similar to the role of the press and other media. Political and commercial administrations with their shortsighted routines and procedures would be left more or less untouched.

To avoid some of the risks of adding itself to the technocracy, the Secretariat has tried to establish a framework wherein it is possible:

- To keep the projects free from routine, shortsighted, political tactics; it has thus been firmly stated that project members are as independent in their work as any other researchers.
- To produce reports on problems that are of political relevance and of direct concern to the government administration.
- To publish regularly — i.e., openly show the steps that preceded the final future study.
- To write the reports in a language that can be widely read and enjoyed.

ISBN 0-201-04096-4

How We Tried To Organize the Dialogue

In organizational terms, the Secretariat for Future Studies has been built up with the intention of combining the alternative aspects with a commitment to the decision-making bodies. The following chart illustrates this idea.

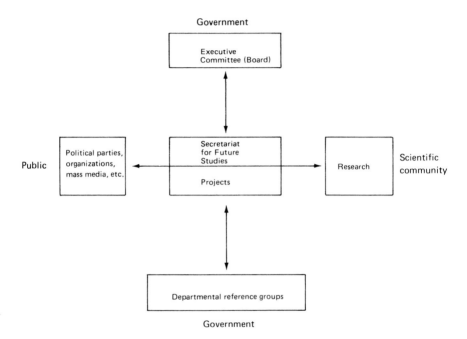

Under the direction of the executive committee, the Secretariat commissions study projects. These are carried out in project groups which, if possible, are directly linked to an existing research institution. The project groups are *not* part of the Secretariat, but independent units that have agreed to study a certain problem area and to follow a certain mode of work — i.e., time limits, "readable" reports, etc. The Secretariat performs a coordinating and supporting role in the work of the project groups.

For each project group there is a reference group with representatives for the ministries whose work areas come within the scope of the projects. The reference group has no responsibility with respect to publications issued from the projects. These groups are created to bridge the gap between research and administration and to try to involve the administration in the problem areas *before* a final report is ready for distribution.

ISBN 0-201-04096-4

Deepening the Awareness of the Future

It is difficult to indicate any limits to the contacts the Secretariat is to maintain: the Parliament, ministries, and government committees make up the first group. Political parties, interest organizations, educational associations, and popular movements are also supplied with information about the projects. A subscription service enables groups and private persons to follow the various projects on a continuing basis through interim reports. (In August 1976 we had about 6000 subscribers.) Among the subscribers are private firms (800), libraries (200), schools (800), municipalities, county councils, etc. Mass media are, of course, a further point of contact. Newspapers, journals, and other publications (700) are supplied with material from the projects.

The first series of publications in 1976 were given a rather broad attention in the Swedish daily press. This has, of course, been of great help in developing the contacts with associations and individuals. It has particularly been encouraging to see the number of individual subscriptions rise substantially.

At this stage of the work the Secretariat has especially promoted the links with the educational system. Interest from the public high schools has been expressed on several occasions. During recent months more regular contacts have begun with groups of teachers from all levels in the school. These discussions are developing favorably.

Interest and support has also been increasingly expressed by different popular movements which play an important role in organizing study courses, now also introducing the theme of "future studies" in connection with the projects organized by the Secretariat.

Conclusions

Half-way through the first phase of the experiment with future studies initiated by a government body, it seems that the Secretariat has been able to establish a certain degree of respect and integrity. It is well known that the projects do not take political orders from the ministries concerned, and the publications seem by and large to receive some credit — i.e., the content having an acceptable qualitative standard in view of the different subject matters discussed. In 1974 the government asked for public participation in order to get a clearer view on which course to follow with respect to energy policy. Study groups mushroomed all over Sweden within the framework of educational associations and other popular movements with different ideological perspectives. We hope that the discussion around the projects that the Secretariat has initiated may be a further step in a direction in which future development no longer is assumed to consist of such complex solutions of our problems that public participation is excluded. In any country — poor or rich alike — real development demands the active participation of all people. In such a perspective there is no problem that is too complex for public debate.

ISBN 0-201-04096-4

V. 4. Investigating Potential Value Changes

MARVIN J. CETRON and AUDREY CLAYTON

One of the major weaknesses of futures studies is the inability to account for changing attitudes and values which together establish the social context in which specific technological and economic forecasts must be evaluated. Accepted forecasting techniques do very poorly when applied to societal factors, but, pending a major theoretical breakthrough, we have recently had considerable success with an empirical approach to the problem, which exploits the phenomenon of the diffusion of such developments internationally, without analyzing the cultural factors that affect the flow.

There are two principal approaches to forecasting:

- Linear projection from present events, which fails to place the events into the societal framework of the future, or to allow for novel events,
- Use of a prototype, which involves the use of correlations between events in various societies that have basic similarities, but where there are time differences in the adoption of the technology or occurrence of the event.

It is this latter technique which offers us a tool for exploring changes in public attitudes and social values.

It is widely recognized that in many areas, and certainly in terms of experimentation with, and implementation of, public policy, there exist certain "bellwether" jurisdictions consistently years ahead of all others. These leading jurisdictions vary with different times in history, and for different issues. Some of them are domestic, but in the domain of attitudinal and value changes it is of greater value to explore the experience of other nations, some of whom have proved to be decades ahead of the United States. Figure 1 shows typical examples of innovative diffusion both domestically and internationally, where the vertical axis is some measure of activity in a given area — such as number of acts passed per year relating to that topic; the horizontal axis is elapsed time. Sweden is a particularly consistent and striking example of such a "precursor" nation.

Others have been aware of this phenomenon: throughout de Gaulle's period in office, the French five-year plan was built on the recognition of Sweden as a precursor. The practice was discontinued on his death, but this appears to have been a political decision rather than any breakdown of the theory. A recent study in Scandinavia[1] dealing with the food distribution system revealed that Norway, Finland, and Denmark also tend to use Sweden as an indicator of change and to

---

[1] Solveig Wikstrom, "A Comparative Study of Food Retailing and Wholesaling in the Scandinavian Countries with an Outlook over the Seventies," Department of Business Administration, Stockholm University, Stockholm 1971.

Futures Research: New Directions, Harold A. Linstone and W. H. Clive Simmonds (eds.)

ISBN 0-201-04096-4

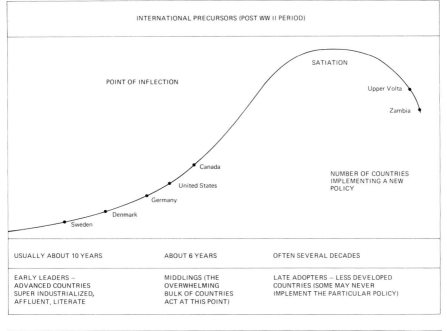

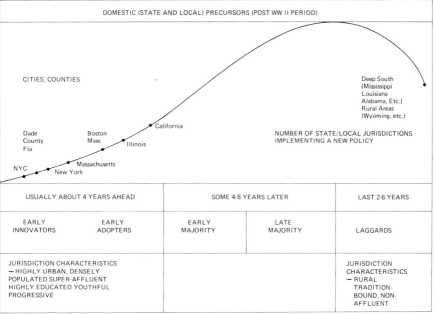

Fig. 1. Domestic and international precursors.

ISBN 0-201-04096-4

follow her example. (This is relevant to the present discussion because the study incorporated such considerations as the consumer's desire for "freedom from confusion" as contrasted to "freedom of choice" — that is, an incipient rebellion against the uncontrolled proliferation of brands, of package and can sizes, etc.)

As we stated[2] when first proposing this approach, however, this does not imply that any one country can be taken as an absolute precursor to the United States or to any other nation: each is composed of a different population, with different needs and motivations. However, nations that have evolved to a comparable productive economy — the "advanced" or "postindustrial" countries such as the United States, England, Japan, France, Sweden, Canada, and West Germany, — are very likely to encounter similar problems, to accommodate to such strains in recognizably similar ways, and to react with similar changes in attitude or values. This does not imply any deterministic theory of development: because it is essentially impossible to "go back and start all over," a group of nations with similar cultural background, which remain in social and economic contact, are very likely to come to share common features. Such nations exhibit close similarity in the pattern of development of typical issues. We do not say that these parallels are inevitable: we *do* contend that they must be considered in any future planning, by evaluating each trend within the United States context to determine its potential impacts. Moreover, by observing Swedish response to these developments, we can identify effects that we could not predict by intuition alone, and we can weigh the success or failure of courses of Swedish action based on various responsive policy decisions. It is important to emphasize at this point that we are *not* assuming that the same development in both countries will have the same or similar impacts. However, we *can* obtain in this manner a "check list" to assist our assessment process, and a "test-bed" to enable us to observe the Swedish consequences of policies which might be analogous to those considered in the United States.

Random and unstructured observations which indicate a correlation between Swedish and United States experience are totally inadequate as evidence to *prove* such an assertion. However, we are now in the second phase of a study, sponsored by the National Science Foundation,[3] designed to investigate the existence of such a precursor relationship in the social area, and to explore its nature and extent. This project focuses particularly on various aspects of consumerism, an area in which Sweden has a long history of innovative accomplishment, having initiated the "modern" concept of a people's representative with the establishment of a King's Ombudsman in 1713, followed a century later by the appointment of a People's Tribune. This example was followed by Denmark, New Zealand, and various individual states in this country, and can now be found all over the world.

---

[2]M. J. Cetron and Audrey Clayton, "Social Forecasting: A Practical Approach," *Technological Forecasting and Social Change,* Vol. 7, No. 4, 1975, pp. 339-355.

[3]M. J. Cetron, N. Nisenoff, A. Clayton, C. Lane, E. Huggare and G. T. T. Molitor, *Forecasting the Effects of Events on Consumer Affairs* NSF/RA 77-002, National Science Foundation, Washington, D. C., October 1976.

ISBN 0-201-04096-4

In order to validate our contention that attitudinal changes can be detected early in Sweden which are later likely to occur in the United States, the first task was to collect and examine an enormous amount of data concerning "events" which would serve as indicators of change in the general area of consumerism in both countries. We employ the term "event-train" to describe a series of events, in time sequence, which relate to a single coordinating topic, or which appear as milestones marking progress toward a perceived common goal. For instance, we have developed event-trains for both Sweden and the United States which depict the evolution of the consumer movement as a whole, showing the gradual shift of emphasis from the early, informative phases to the protection and regulatory aspects. Similar evolutionary trends can be detected in the area of environmental concern, validation of advertising claims, eradication of sex discrimination (Sweden now has a mandatory policy of *paternity* leave following the birth of a child), etc.

Most of these event-trains include hundreds of relevant entries and are too lengthy to include here. For purposes of illustration, however, Fig. 2 shows a partial listing of events relating to the regulation of advertising practices.

When event-trains with the same common theme have been developed for both countries, a set of "matched pairs" of comparable events is selected – that is, an event in the United States is paired to its partner in Sweden. It should be noted that considerable intensive research is involved in each area to derive an appropriate interpretation of comparability specific to that topic. Such a set cannot always be identified: there are many instances where lines of development have been parallel rather than identical. However, in the simplest case, we will consider those areas for which comparable pairs of events can be extracted from the national event-trains, and time lags computed.

In practice, we have found that the most useful method of portraying these data, based upon actual event-trains, is to plot the lag time between a pair of matched events, against the year in which the event occurred in Sweden. In all cases examined so far, the points for any one topic fall roughly in a straight line, representing a decreasing time lag between Sweden and United States experience. This provides us with a predictive tool to estimate the approximate date of occurrence of other related events in the United States, which have thus far occurred only in Sweden. There will also be events in the total set which are unique to one country or the other. However, we are not concerned here with the prediction of individual events, but rather in confirming the establishment of a *trend*, and the identification of *potential* developments in public concern and attitudes. Our findings so far indicate that either we *do*, as a whole, follow the same evolutionary change of attitude and response in a given area as does Sweden, or we do not, and the distinction can be made fairly early on. If we do, then the time lag appears to exhibit no statistically significant dependence upon topic.

So far we have completed case studies for six discrete subject areas. Three of these provide us with hard quantitative data in the form of about ten event-pairs for each topic.

ISBN 0-201-04096-4

HISTORICAL PERSPECTIVE OF REGULATIONS ON COMMUNICATIONS/ADVERTISING

Year	
1940	FM, on commercial basis, authorized — Adv. as % GNP: 2.0%
1940	
1941	TV, on commercial basis, authorized (X2XBS, later renamed WNDT)
1950	Adv. as % GNP: 2.0%
1951	Color TV, on commercial basis, authorized
1957	Hidden Persuaders (motivational manipulation of consumers) published by Vance Packard
1957-1959	TV quiz scandals ("primed" contestants)
1960	Adv. as % GNP: 2.4%
1962	Communications Satellite Corporation established
1969	Adv. as % GNP: 2.1%

HISTORICAL DEVELOPMENT OF ADVERTISING/VOLUNTARY (PRIVATE) AND MANDATORY (PUBLIC) PROMOTION

Year	
1952 ▼	TV code established by National Association of Broadcasters
1954 ▼	Advertising and Editorial Code established by Comics Magazine Association of America
1958	Automobile Information Disclosure Act (auto price posting required)
1958	Federal Aid Highway Act — outdoor advertising bans on rights-of-way rewarded by 1/2% Federal funds bonus
1960	"Anti-payola" amendments to Communications Act of 1934 (provided criminal penalties for not disclosing product "plugs")
1960 ▼	Magazine Publisher's Association established copy advisory committee to screen questionable ads
1962	All-channel set law (TV sets manufactured after 1964 must be capable of receiving both UHF and VHF)
1965	Highway Beautification Act (barred billboard placement within 600 ft of interstate and primary road systems — as of 1969, 34 states/territories had enacted legislation to comply
1965	Federal Cigarette Labeling and Advertising Act (health warning labels)
1967	John Banzhof's FCC petition allows first anti-smoke ads (counter-advertising)
1968	FTC votes to ban cigarette advertising
1969	FTC bans cigarette advertising
1969 ▼	Ads for products containing DDT or five other insecticides banned from Sunset magazine
1970	Public Health Cigarette Smoking Act — restricted advertising of cigarettes required stronger health warning; granted FTC power (after 1971) to require warning in advertising
1971	TV ad ban imposed on cigarettes
1971	FTC rules stores must have advertised "specials"
1971	FTC requires ad substantiation with back-up data
1971 ▼	National Advertising Review Board established
1974 ▼	Children's Advertising Review unit established within BBB's National Ads Division

(▼ - Signifies and highlights *voluntary* regulation)

Fig. 2. Section of advertising event-train.

ISBN 0-201-04096-4

The top portion of Fig. 3 shows a national comparison of hypothetical event-trains. The top line represents a series of related events in Sweden, arranged in time sequence, which have been labeled e_1 through e_n. The bottom line is a comparable series, occurring at different times, for the United States. Events marked with a prime – for example, e_a' for Sweden, e_b' for the United States – clearly belong in the event-train but are unique to each country, with no identifiable counterpart in the other's experience. In the case shown here, it is clear that there is at least a basis for investigation of the consequences if event e_n should occur at time x in the United States.

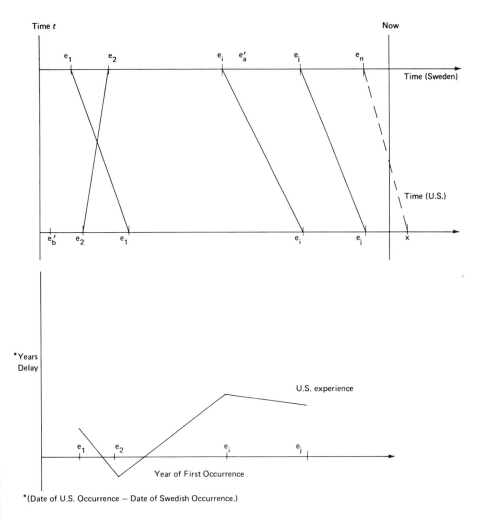

Fig. 3. Comparison of national experience.

ISBN 0-201-04096-4

In practice, as we have said, such consistency of slope and correlation of "exact matches" cannot always be achieved. Nevertheless, significant patterns do emerge in many cases, particularly if the data are presented in somewhat different fashion, as shown in the lower portion of the exhibit. This plots the lag time against the year of Swedish occurrence, so that points above the axis indicate a positive lag — that is, we are behind Sweden for these events. For this example, as you can see, there is one event, e_2, where the United States was ahead, and there is no particular pattern that we can observe.

When we actually carry out this process, constructing the national event-trains and plotting the lag time against the date of Swedish occurrence, we fit a least-squares curve to the various points corresponding to events in the United States. So far, a straight line has provided an adequate fit. In theory there are just three possibilities then: this line is parallel to the time axis, or it converges or diverges as time advances. This corresponds to a constant, decreasing, or increasing time lag.

Three such plots will be discussed here, based upon event-trains constructed from actual data gathered in many different areas. Figure 4 shows the increase in the establishment of standards for automobile construction and indicates the growth in concern for passenger safety. Again, the vertical axis represents the

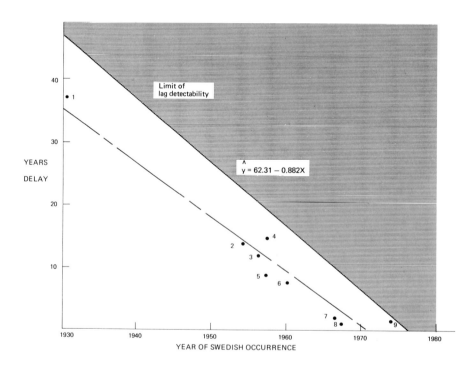

Fig. 4. Lag times for auto safety compared with computed curve.

ISBN 0-201-04096-4

United States lag, and the horizontal axis is the year of Swedish occurrence. Thus for example, event number 4 took place in Sweden in 1957, and the corresponding lag was 15 years — that is, the comparable event occurred in this country in 1971. Similarly, event number 1 occurred in 1930 in Sweden, but the United States event lagged by 38 years. The line represents the "least-squares" fit computed for these data points. (This may seem a confusing way to represent the data, but it makes pattern detection extremely easy. To demonstrate the difference, Fig. 5 shows the same data plotted in a straightforward manner, by date of occurrence in the two countries. It may be easier to comprehend, but it is harder to draw conclusions.)

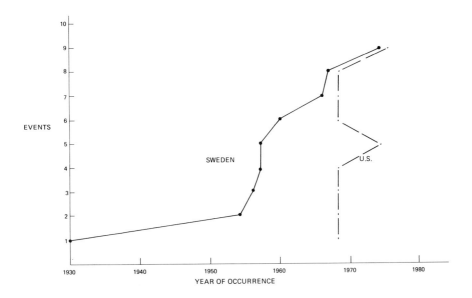

Fig. 5. Events in the area of auto safety, by year of occurrence.

The events that were used in constructing these plots were as follows:

Auto Safety Items

Laminated windshield (shatterproof)
Windshield defrosting/defogging
Padded dashboard
Establishment of maximum allowable noise level
Two-point safety belt (lap belt)
Windshield washers associated with wiper system
Split brake system
Three-point safety belt (shoulder harness)
Provision of fuel consumption information

ISBN 0-201-04096-4

We have similar results in the areas of environmental contaminant control (Fig. 6) and alcohol policy (Fig. 7). The former shows eleven points corresponding to the various events which were found to be strictly comparable. The lag time varies from 10 years to zero, in this case. This field of environmentalism did not become active until about 1963. The dispersion of the points around the computed line is rather greater here than for auto safety.

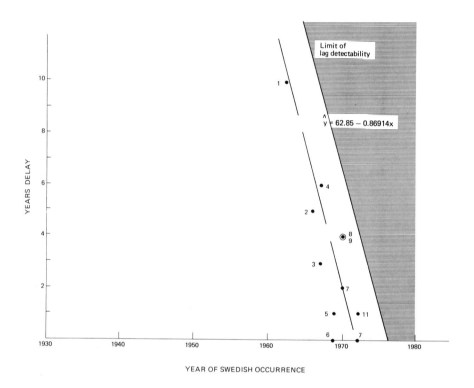

Fig. 6. Lag times for environment/contaminants compared with computed curve.

The third example relates to alcohol policy. In Fig. 7, there is one point, event number 6, where the Unites States was ahead by about 2 years. Again, we have a considerable variation in lag time, from 23 years to minus 2, but the points are pretty well distributed about the line. However, in 1968 Sweden passed a single bill which incorporated five items dealt with individually and at various times in this country; this shows up in the vertical group of points.

ISBN 0-201-04096-4

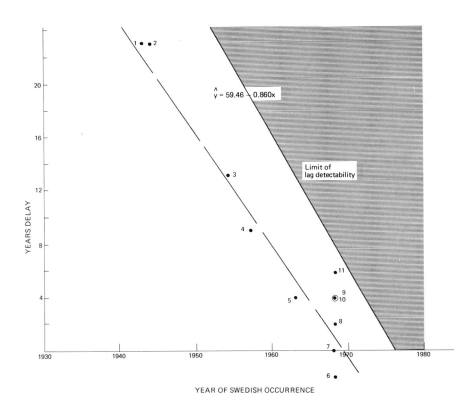

Fig. 7. Lag times for alcohol policy compared with computed curve.

The most remarkable similarity between these separate examples is not immediately obvious from these exhibits, owing to the difference in scale. However, the table given here shows the coefficients for the equation of the straight line which expresses the lead-lag relationship in the three areas. Both the intercept and the slope show minimal variation. The mean intercept is about 61½ years, with a standard deviation of less than 2. The mean slope is .87, with a standard deviation of one hundredth.

Lead-Lag Equation Coefficients

$$y = a - bx$$

Topic	a	b
Auto safety	62.31	.882
Environment	62.85	.869
Alcohol policy	59.46	.860
Mean	61.54	.870

ISBN 0-201-04096-4

In all strictly comparable cases examined so far, the time lag is decreasing, at roughly the same rate. To what extent the decrease is due to faster diffusion rates because of such externalities as modern communications, for example, was not ascertained in this phase. Whatever the reason, we can take advantage of the consistency it imposes on our empirical findings, while still checking out newly acquired data for the appearance of counter-examples.

It should be borne in mind that the direction of the plot is also influenced by the choice of coordinates — for example, a hypothetical 20-year time lag is no longer detectable once we approach closer to the present than 20 years (along the elapsed-time axis).

There are many areas, as we have mentioned earlier, where strictly comparable events cannot be identified in the event-trains, despite an overall similarity of national experience. For instance, in the case of furniture labeling (as an indicator of the trend toward provision of consumer information, followed by concern for consumer satisfaction), there has been considerable activity in both countries, although it started some 30 years earlier in Sweden. However, the approach has been slightly different, and there are no specific events which can be said to be "comparable." Swedish standardization and testing procedures apply over the whole furniture industry, while in the United States there are three distinct and almost independent segments, depending on intended use (home/business/institution). Nevertheless, there are parallels; the concern with safety, information, and regulation can be seen to be expanding in comparable fashion, and general conclusions can be drawn about future United States experience, based on developments in Sweden.

This is true also in the total field of consumerism, where four discrete phases can be identified: agrarian, household, informative, and protective. Even without the identification of strictly comparable events, we can examine the national event-trains and perceive that Sweden is consistently ahead, and is now well into the fourth phase, while the United States appears to be nearing the end of the third.

In these areas, we can also utilize a model developed by one of our consultants,[4] which is based on a study of legislative change, and the way it relates to public attitudes. New laws emerge out of an evolutionary process: the actual appearance of an event is preceded by long trains of activity. In examining almost any field of enquiry, and specifically in the area of consumerism, one can observe a cyclic distribution of activity levels, measured in terms of number of related events, or number of government actions taken, per year. When the cumulation of such events over time is examined, we end up with the ubiquitous "S-curve" growth pattern, characterized by a slow inception period, a steep slope implying massive concentration on the problem area, followed by a tapering off or "saturation"

---

[4]Graham T. T. Molitor, "Choosing Our Environment: Can We Anticipate the Future," presented to the Panel on Environmental Science and Technology, Senate Committee on Public Works: Subcommittee on Environmental Pollution, February 27, 1976.

ISBN 0-201-04096-4

when the goal is achieved, or for some other reason (e.g., international crises) attention is directed to other areas.

If we consider the life cycle associated with one specific area, we can trace the development of six major forces. As Mr. Molitor has described it,

> The process of change invariably starts with aberrant and unique events which, when aggregated, reveal meaningful patterns. Scientific/technical/ professional authorities undertake to comment on and analyze such phenomena. Shortly thereafter the observations of leading authorities are reduced to writing and begin appearing in leading literature. The written data base provides widespread dissemination of the ideas, increases the level of activity, and gives rise to various kinds of organizations which institutionalize the cause and provide a sustained base for advocating change. Politicians . . . pick up such trends, and leading jurisdictions, both domestic and international, begin to implement them.

> These six forces follow sequential patterns, at some point swelling toward a convergence, thereby creating a "dissonance" within the society that demands laws to "correct" the problems. As events flow along over time, authorities/advocates pick up on them; next, the number of published articles builds up to provide a permanent written analysis and wider-spread dissemination; at about this stage, a number of organizations begin to emerge around an issue; bringing the cycle to a close, political jurisdictions finally are pressured to respond.

> Once a new law is implemented by a number of jurisdictions, either internationally or at state and local levels, other jurisdictions follow suit, provided the policy proves effective. The process of other jurisdictions following the lead of early adopters results in what I call "diffusion patterns." For different periods of history particular countries or groups of nations have been "early adopters." Sweden is now such a leader, and has been an early implementer for at least 10-20 years.

Figure 8 shows typical growth curves for the initial set of catalytic events in a specific area; the printed material generated on this topic, in consequence of the events; the accretion of individuals joining in support of the cause; and the increasing institutionalization. It also indicates the interrelationship between these various forces, and the governmental response to the increasing pressure of the public attitude.

The contribution this relationship can make to the present problem is significant: once sufficient data have been gathered and analyzed to define component curves for a specific application in Sweden, it is possible to examine any of the early indicators which portend increasing activity on an increasingly formal level, indicative of changing public attitudes. Extreme care must be exercised, of course, in the selection of appropriate parameters, and generalizations cannot be transferred from one field of application to another without explicit justification.

ISBN 0-201-04096-4

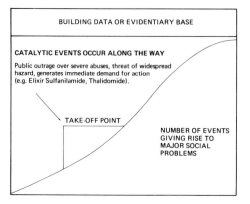

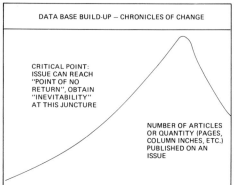

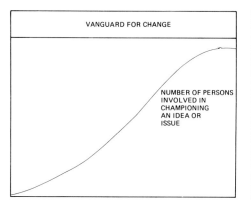

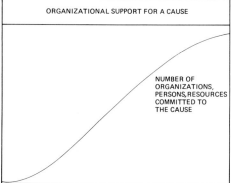

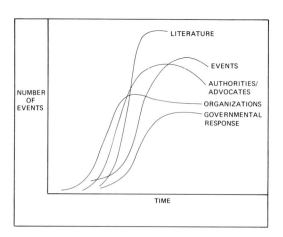

Fig. 8. Typical pattern and interrelation of evolutionary waves of change.

ISBN 0-201-04096-4

To conclude with a specific prediction, based upon our studies so far, we must concur with those[5] who foresee an increasing emphasis on quality of work life. Recent events in Northern Europe have shown Sweden to be a leader in areas of increased productivity and economic growth, and it has recently emerged (given present exchange rates) as having one of the highest gross national products per capita among the Western industrial nations. While the United States witnessed decreases in productivity during the years 1973 and 1974, Sweden has experienced a decade of marked industrial growth and continuous and self-perpetuating productivity increases. In view of the economic recession, our national concern with economic growth and productivity is particularly acute at the present time, and we foresee that American corporations will adopt many of Sweden's programs. Quality of work life may well be a key issue in the late 1970's in the United States, and corporate interest in Swedish experiments is already apparent. The drastic increase in unemployment in this country over the past three years is an additional inducement to examine Swedish experience, where the social goals to minimize unemployment and underemployment have been dominant for many years. We can profit from detailed examination of their policies — in terms of both successes and failures.

Productivity is traditionally defined as the ratio of goods and services produced (output) to factors of production consumed in manufacture (input); it measures the efficiency of use of economic resources. This is a prime concern of industrial and governmental interests, and should be also for the consumer, because economic resources are limited, and to the extent that they are used at less than maximum efficiency, our economy will produce less than maximum wealth for its members. Thus, in the area of quality of work life, for example, the individual's direct and expressed interest will relate to his personal job satisfaction; it is also indirectly to his benefit that improved working conditions have been demonstrated to increase productivity.

While the earliest theories in this field were developed in the United States,[6] Scandinavia has rapidly taken the lead in experimental innovations[7] designed to improve both productivity and quality of work life, many of which have proved highly successful and have contributed in large measure to the country's economic growth. Factors that have undoubtedly been important to this success include:

- Swedish corporations tax policy, which encourages increased application of

---

[5]See, for example, Arthur S. Weinberg, "Work Experiments and Improving the Quality of Work Life in the United States," in *European Industrial Relations Review,* October 1974, No. 10.

[6]For example, the work of Elton Mayo, and what has become known as the Hawthorne experiments, sponsored by Harvard University, and begun in 1924 at the Hawthorne Works of the Western Electric Company in Chicago.

[7]See Einar Thorsrud and Fred E. Emery, *Form and Content in Industrial Democracy,* Tavistock Publications, London, 1967. This effort originated in Oslo, but was adopted and expanded, both quantitatively and qualitatively, in Sweden.

ISBN 0-201-04096-4

technology; innovative managerial methods; maintained and/or increased level of employment.

- The Agreement of Rationalization of 1971, which commits both the Swedish Employers Confederation (SAF) and the Swedish Confederation of Trade Unions (LO) to increasing both productivity and job satisfaction.
- Swedish manpower policy, which encourages early phased-out retirement (assisting young workers into the labor market); government subsidies to encourage corporations to locate in areas of high unemployment; government assistance to individuals to relocate in seeking new employment; social and psychological counseling to immigrant workers and their families; and an efficient national employment service to assist in the location of job vacancies.
- Job design and job enrichment programs to facilitate greater job satisfaction and thus promote increased productivity. The planning of urban housing and mass transportation to facilitate a more satisfying "off-the-job" environment and to increase and facilitate occupational mobility.
- Corporation efforts to improve work environment by providing maximum conditions for industrial safety and on-the-job amenities — e.g., luxurious dining facilities and personnel facilities which include sauna baths, swimming pools, lockers, company-provided work clothing, etc.
- Provisions for occupational safety and health in most companies are among the finest in the world with respect to control of toxic substances, safety equipment, and reduction of noise and pollution level within factory.

It is not feasible in the space of a single article to explore the various attitudinal and value changes implicit in such areas of activity as these, nor in other general trends which are apparent, such as the shift of the onus of responsibility to proving the need for and safety of each ingredient in a food product, rather than allowing its inclusion until evidence of related hazard is disclosed. We mention these in passing, only to indicate the potential benefits which may be derived by a structured examination of Swedish experience, and a monitoring of significant indicators of change.

To summarize, then, the project discussed here had two major objectives: to determine whether a precursor relationship did in fact, exist between Sweden and United States experience in the areas with which we were dealing; and, if so, to define how best to use this relationship to assist our program planning on both governmental and corporate levels.

The first objective has been achieved: So long as we keep continually in mind the fact that we are dealing with two distinct nations, each composed of a different population, with different needs and motivations, and that each event must be evaluated in its unique context to establish the validity of its implications, then the precursor nation can function as a trail-breaker for those considering a similar route. This means that we can be alert for indications of attitudinal and value changes that can influence our long-term planning; we can have time to consider disadvantageous consequences of potential innovations, and redesign the experi-

ISBN 0-201-04096-4

ments accordingly; we can make the best use of limited funds, manpower, and national resources, if we have a clearer picture of what lies ahead. We are not able to watch *all* developments over *all* the nations of the world simultaneously — but knowing where to look, we *can* gain information, and time in which to put that information to work.

ISBN 0-201-04096-4

V. 5. The Problem of Critical Problem Selection

PETER TEIGE, WILLIS HARMAN, and PETER SCHWARTZ

Introduction

Multiple crises are a recurring feature of the past few decades. Energy shortages, urban decay, pesticide contamination, drug abuse, etc., received national attention only when they reached crisis proportions. Crisis-oriented planning is the rule rather than the exception. Typically, immediate needs get a higher priority for attention than do longer-term needs. Thus, until a situation becomes a crisis demanding immediate attention, we tend to leave it on the back burner simmering slowly. The disadvantages of this approach are multifold. Constructive responses often require long lead times, especially where new knowledge is required. Complex crises are often closely coupled to other problems (e.g., the linkage of energy to employment and environmental issues); in the heat of crisis this is harder to take into account. Politization of issues in crisis situations often forces undesirable trade-offs in linked areas.

Part of the process of changing this undesirable situation lies in providing credible early warning. Most of our current crises were anticipated in some way or another. What was missing was a systematic way of searching out and assessing those early warnings. As part of the legislative mandate of the newly created Office of Science and Technology Policy (OSTP), the White House Science Advisor, who directs OSTP, was given an early-warning function. This paper reports on a project supported by the National Science Foundation (NSF) intended to be a step toward fulfilling the need for early warning.

The study had two objectives: (1) to develop and test systematic approaches to problem identification, selection, and analysis, and (2) to identify a set of critical problems and to provide initial analysis on a subset of the more important problems.

Our approach was dictated by the characteristics of the problems we were searching for. First of all they should be *critical* problems — i.e., they should have a serious effect on large numbers of people. They should be largely *unattended to*; i.e., they should not be receiving significant attention (e.g., not food or energy). They should be *future* problems; though the situation may already be problematic, the crisis looms somewhere ahead. The problems should have some significant connection to *science and technology policy*. That is, they should be researchable and/or they should be solvable by technological means and/or they should result from the advance of science and technology.

Futures Research: New Directions, Harold A. Linstone and W. H. Clive Simmonds (eds.)

ISBN 0-201-04096-4

The Problem of Problem Selection

One of the basic goals of futures research has been to increase awareness of long-term, large-scale societal problems. Over the past decade a number of important contributions have been made to the identification and classification of major problems, including John Platt's seminal article in *Science*, "What We Must Do";[1] the DEMATEL project of the Battelle Institute;[2] and a study by our own group called "Contemporary Societal Problems."[3] The focus of these studies was on problems that are likely to cause great difficulty in the future, but that also tend to be ignored or discounted because they lack the immediacy of current problems. Many of these problems are commonly acknowledged, and certain effects of them are being experienced already. These studies attempt to set this type of problem in a context which reveals more sharply their interrelationships and suggests the urgency with which they should be regarded if they are not to get beyond control. These efforts have awakened a new awareness of problem development and the necessity of taking early action.

Our study is an extension of this earlier research. Whereas the identification and classification of many of the more obvious future problems has been fairly comprehensive, there is another class of less apparent problems that, rather than simply being discounted or ignored, are for the most part unknown. A few of these have surfaced into more general awareness from time to time, but no systematic attempt to detect such problems as a distinct class has been previously made. This is not because they are not important or threatening problems, but simply because they are often the subtle consequences of highly complex societal activity and are noticed by few observers, if any. These problems are especially troublesome because they could emerge rapidly and unexpectedly as full-blown crises for which we might be totally unprepared.

Our approach to the problem of problem selection had two basic sequential elements. First was the development of problem identification techniques designed to surface information on the class of problems of interest. Second, having compiled a set of these problems, we devised a systematic means by which the set could be internally differentiated and prioritized.

Problem Identification

In order to search for something, one must first define it. The conventional definitions of the word "problem" are not particularly helpful, a "problem" commonly being defined as something like "the gap between what is expected and what is desired." Clearly, the subjective nature of what one calls a problem is

---

[1] John Platt, "What We Must Do," *Science*, November 28, 1969, pp. 1115-1121.

[2] A. Gabus and E. Fontella, "DEMATEL — Report No. 3 — Perceptions of the World Problematique," Battelle Institute, Geneva Research Center, Geneva, Switzerland, 1975.

[3] O. W. Markley, D. A. Curry, and D. L. Rink, "Contemporary Societal Problems," Report EPRC 6747-2. Educational Policy Research Center, Stanford Research Institute, Menlo Park, California, June 1971.

ISBN 0-201-04096-4

revealed by such a definition. Failing to produce a less ambiguous definition, however, we settled pragmatically on defining a problem (for the initial listing) simply as "a condition which someone or some group labels as a problem," thereby hoping to reduce any particular bias and increase the inclusivity of our search.

The other criteria which defined our problem search (i.e., future, unattended, critical, and science- and technology-relevant) were much more explicit, but did little to make our task easier. We were, by definition, in fact, looking for information which was either very scarce, very difficult to recognize, or both. Besides being low-frequency, low-amplitude information embedded in a vastly larger domain, information on hidden future problems is dispersed almost randomly, cutting across virtually every major discipline and conventional scheme of information classification. We determined, therefore, that a varied set of search strategies would be superior to any single approach in extracting our desired "needles" from this large and diverse informational "haystack." We devised eight search strategies, listed in Table 1, which we felt would span a considerable range of information sources and filter out a variety of problems.

Research on future problems is premised on the notion that, rather than springing forth suddenly upon us, full-blown, problems generally develop somewhat more gradually over time. This development, though usually unnoticed until its more critical stages, is occurring around us all the time, almost subliminally, in its more primal form. It is most easily perceived through the observation of various trends, noting their growth, reversal, or interactive effects. Our search strategies were conceived to help us do this in an organized manner. We either observed these trends first-hand, or relied on the observations of others. In addition, we projected these trends through various possible future social conditions and value perspectives, as well as examining possible new and unexpected twists in more widely recognized trends.

All these strategies met with some success, though some were more productive than others. In surveying a group of scientists and engineers, both at Stanford Research Institute (SRI) and at a national meeting of the American Association for the Advancement of Science (AAAS), relatively few truly unrecognized problems were identified. On the other hand, the literature survey produced over 1000 candidate problems. Science fiction literature proved to be less productive, tending to be either too far-flung or too conventional. The quantity of problems produced by a given strategy did not necessarily correlate with their quality. The search for critical trend discontinuities produced relatively fewer problems, but nearly all of them turned out to be more important and critical than most.

Problem Selection

Once the problem identification procedure had yielded a large set of problems, it was necessary to discriminate internally among them to determine which were most worthy of further consideration and possible action. For this purpose we devised a rating scheme by which each individual problem was evaluated on the

ISBN 0-201-04096-4

Table 1

Problem Search Strategies

Problem lists – Compile and review a list of problems from the literature and screen using the following two criteria: (1) potential seriousness of the problem and (2) indications that it may not receive adequate and prompt attention.

Alternative futures – Conduct a brief overview of futures research literature to identify problems that arise in the context of specific alternative futures.

Science fiction – Conduct a brief overview of science fiction to identify problems that have been identified by this form of subjective anticipation.

Opinion surveys – Survey key persons from the Stanford Research Institute staff and attendees at a major scientific conference to identify future problems that might be anticipated from the perspective of specialized discipline areas.

Cross-paradigm analysis – Survey alternative societal paradigms to identify problems that might appear clearly in one paradigm and be overlooked in another.

Trend discontinuities – Examine key societal trends to find trend discontinuities forced by absurdities that would appear if the trends were to continue.

Problem "level" analysis – Compare alternative interpretations at different "levels" of societal structure for problems that have been identified as serious and possibly persistent, with the purpose of identifying new manifestations of the problem area that might emerge in the future.

Missed opportunities – Search for significant opportunities for technological or social innovation that, because of characteristics of the current political or social climate, might be exploited.

basis of its relative criticality and appropriateness for additional attention by the Science Advisor. The rationale for this comparison of problems was based on the practical reality that only a very limited number of problems can be taken on within the resource constraints of any agency. Therefore, those problems should be the most appropriate and crucial problems which that agency is capable of dealing with. Our selection process was thus geared to setting aside problems that were less urgent, and those for which scientific or technological responses are either not possible or desirable.

In order to efficiently and effectively sort through the sizable number of problems we had accumulated, a system was devised whereby the problems could be evaluated in a series of iterative screenings. Each successive screening reduced the number of problems as those of less apparent criticality and appropriateness were set aside. The initial screenings were fairly crude, in part because the information available on the problems varied greatly in quality, some amounting to little more

ISBN 0-201-04096-4

than a simple statement. Even at this point it was obvious that a great many of the problems could be dropped from further consideration. With each additional screening, the reduced quantity of problems permitted further research to enhance our knowledge of those that remained. At the same time each problem was evaluated with increasing scrutiny at each step. This selection process is diagrammed in Fig. 1.

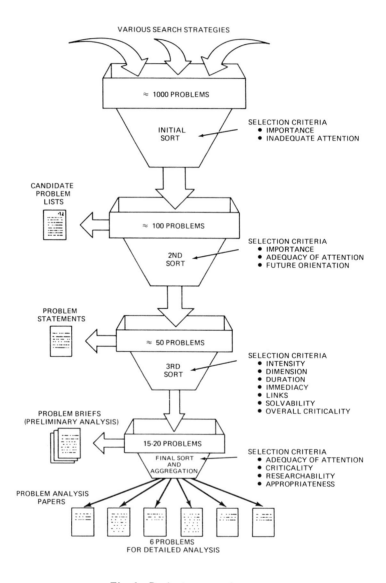

Fig. 1. Project approach.

The criteria for assessing problem criticality were relatively well-defined and easy to apply, since all the problems had been initially included, partly on the basis of potential criticality. The specific criteria of criticality are given in Table 2. We found it necessary to rely on these more distinct measures of criticality only in the later stages of problem evaluation when finer distinctions had to be drawn among the problems of clearly greater criticality.

Table 2

Rating Criteria

Intensity of impact – The perceived severity of impact that the problem would be expected to exert on those affected, should it occur.

Dimension of impacts – The number of people that could be expected to experience the impacts of the problem.

Duration of effects – The length of time over which the significant, direct impacts of the problem might be felt.

Immediacy of criticality – The relative length of time until the problem becomes critical, if ever.

Links to other problems – The degree of interaction with, or isolation from, other problems.

Solvability – The likeliness of the problem's being solved before it has major impacts, based on the will or ability of the society to find and implement a solution.

Overall criticality – The intuitive evaluation of the problem as a whole, independent of individual criticality measures.

The measure of appropriateness was somewhat more difficult to determine. Essentially, we wanted to establish the relevance of each of the most critical sets of problems to our client, the OSTP. Here we had to judge whether or not a given problem would be of direct concern to the Science Advisor. This included dealing with such questions as the following:

- Is it within the well-established domain of science and technology? (What are the frontiers of the domain of science and technology?)
- Is the problem researchable?
- Is the problem politically very sensitive?
- Is the government already dealing with this and related problems?
- Is there reason to believe that calling attention to the problem might eventually produce a solution?

ISBN 0-201-04096-4

Obviously, these questions did not lead to clear-cut distinctions. They did, how-ever, enable us to discern more clearly the subtleties of problem relevance.

Preliminary selection narrowed the original set of over one thousand problems to a set of approximately one hundred. Because of commonalities among members of that set, we were able to aggregate or recast many of the problems so that a set of forty-one remained. Applying more rigorous selection criteria to this set left fifteen that were clearly more potentially critical and at least provisionally appro-priate. Briefs were prepared to further elaborate each of these fifteen. We were then able to select a final six problems that stood out more distinctly in all respects. These six were analyzed in yet greater detail so that the client might have ample information on which to base any further action.

In going through the process of problem selection we found it impractical and unnecessary to adhere rigidly to the established selection procedure. Instead, it was useful as a guiding framework within which more flexible judgments could be made quickly and reliably. In some instances, problems were included that scored exceptionally high in a particular dimension, while others were eliminated if they scored exceptionally low in a single dimension, despite their aggregate score. The actual selection of the problems took place in a series of project staff meetings in which problems were subjected to group rating along the various criteria. The entire selection process was also periodically reviewed, and the selections were occasionally modified, by an independent panel of experts in problem identifica-tion.

The Problems

The list of forty-one future problems is included at the end of this paper. It might be helpful to use a few of the problems from this list to illustrate the process by which they were selected and the rationale for their inclusion in the list.

The problem of "malnutrition-induced mental deficiencies leading to social instability" (the first problem on the list) is a good example of how careful examination of some current facts can suggest a future problem.

It has only recently been established that there is a direct link between malnutri-tion in the early stages of life and permanent mental retardation.[4] There has as yet been little speculation into the implications of this on the structure of societies in the developing world where large segments of the population face malnutrition. The problem therefore met the basic criteria of being currently unattended. Because severe famines may lie ahead, and because the greatest mass of victims are now only children, whose greatest burden on their societies will occur later in adulthood, the problem has definite future aspects. Its criticality is clear in terms of the undermining of social and economic development that would result if large numbers of people were unable to contribute to development, instead requiring

---

[4]Roger Lewin, D. A. Curry, and D. L. Rink, "Starved Brains: A Generation of Clumsy, Feeble Minded Millions," *Psychology Today,* September 1975.

ISBN 0-201-04096-4

special care and attention. The problem is also one which could be dealt with, in its earlier stages, by science and technology in the form of special medical or nutritional treatments, and, of course, in a larger sense by food research.

A somewhat different problem was No. 27, "catastrophic experiments." This problem arises out of scientific research, particularly in such fields as nuclear physics and genetics, that could get out of control with widespread, severe consequences. Although these occurrences are generally of low probability, the risks are extremely high and knowledge of possible consequences is only speculative.

While some awareness exists of the dangers of certain types of highly hazardous research, particularly that involving recombinant DNA, there is currently little recognition of the whole class of such research. That there is at present no means for controlling this class of research suggests that it is not being adequately addressed and could become a matter of heightened concern in the future. Its potential criticality is overwhelmingly apparent, particularly if the odds for experimental catastrophe are raised by a proliferation of such research. Clearly, too, this is a matter appropriately addressed in the context of national science policy.

On the surface, the problem of "chronic unemployment" (No. 36) may seem out of place in a list of future problems. It is, however, an excellent example of a future problem that is the outgrowth of a more widely acknowledged current problem. While the actual condition of unemployment may be the same, it is the underlying causes, the severity, and the duration of unemployment in the future which make this problem distinct. This is a problem that became perceptible through the examination of growing trends, trend discontinuities, and the probable interaction of trends. There are few who perceive the future of the unemployment problem in this way currently. Demographic, environmental, and economic trends indicate that the problem could be quite severe. Whether this is an appropriate problem for the President's Science Advisor's consideration was not so easy to determine. However, advances in technology certainly play a role in the employment situation, and matters beyond the scope of the "hard sciences" have been dealt with by top-level science advisory groups in the past.

The Final Six Problems

The group of six problems which emerged at the end of the screening process were:

- Chronic Unemployment and Underemployment
- The Growing Conflict between Central Control and Individual Freedom
- Barriers to Large-Scale Technological Projects
- Limits to the Management of Large, Complex Systems
- The Effects of Stress on Individuals and Society
- Potential Uses and Misuses of Consciousness Technology

ISBN 0-201-04096-4

It should be noted that these six are not all reflected in the earlier list of forty-one problems because of restatement, retitling, and aggregation of some problems.

Virtually every problem on the list of forty-one could be recommended as deserving additional investigation. There was, however, an important, if subtle, distinction that set the final six problems apart from the rest. This distinction is most clearly indicated by the fact that these problems were all more closely linked to a greater number of other problems. This pattern of multiple linkages is characteristic of problems that are more fundamental to basic system functions. These are problems that frequently must be dealt with before effective solutions to more peripheral problems can be effectively attempted. At the same time, they are more likely to become increasingly intractable as they develop. As such, these are problems for which national-level initiative and early response are often required.

Let us briefly consider two of the final six problems as examples. The problem of "central control" illustrates this quality of interlinked centrality. It is concerned with much more than obvious manifestations, such as growing government regulation. It is in a sense a problem of how to deal with problems, and as such is a factor that could have immense and far-reaching effects.

"Barriers to Large-Scale Technological Projects" also exhibits this fundamental quality. Many of the proposed solutions to other societal problems involve the application of large-scale technologies. If we do not deal with this problem effectively, a series of other failures may result. This problem is also one that is clearly within the purview of the President's Science Advisor.

Conclusions

A New Type of Problem

Out of this process of gathering and organizing information on future problems there emerged an additional insight that was, we feel, quite significant, though not altogether unexpected. In examining the close linkage among these little-recognized problems, and between these and more widely acknowledged problems, we were afforded a first-hand glimpse of that larger pattern of problems sometimes referred to as the "problematique." This concept derives from the heavily interdependent nature of modern societies and specifically from the interrelation of various problems such that dealing with them successfully in isolation is impossible. Often this means that the solution to one problem has the effect of making others worse.

While this observation bore out our intuitive expectations of interproblem synergy, of greater interest was the additional insight that, somewhat paradoxically, the larger holistic pattern may indeed be more tractable than its individual component problems. Whereas the individual problems may seem overwhelming when regarded independently, when viewed as an integrated pattern they appear to be more amenable to the kind of understanding that could lead to eventual resolution.

ISBN 0-201-04096-4

Changes in the Characteristics of Science and Technology

Science and technology have been geared, and with great success, to the solution of problems in isolation. It is in part this overwhelming success in many areas which has given rise to a whole new class of problems. These problems are systemic in nature. They arise out of continuing trends interacting in new ways, or approaching some kind of inherent limits, or both. Typically they involve diverse social institutions, sectors, and strata, and impinge on various stakeholder groups in a widespread and pervasive manner. This, in turn, means that these problems confront a dispersed and largely uncoordinated set of decision-makers who approach them with varied emphases and objectives. Finally, the problems significantly involve attitudes, values, and beliefs, and are typically viewed from a wide range of quite different perspectives. From this we conclude that, if the problems uncovered in our study are at all typical of future problems, a different order of response is required if they are to be dealt with effectively.

Generally, in responding to this new type of problem there is a need to regard problem solving as an internal adjustment procedure in an ongoing, dynamic process. This would presumably entail monitoring of components of the problem pattern in a holistic fashion, generating and implementing appropriate interventions, and assessing the results in a continuous cycle. Central to this kind of approach in a democratic society would be the provision of opportunities for participation by all interested groups, preferably in an exploratory (rather than adversary) mode.

Establishing such an overall approach to problem resolution would also require a shift in the basic orientation of science and technology. There is some evidence that such a shift is beginning to occur, though its exact direction is as yet not entirely clear. Existing evidence suggests that it would probably involve a balancing of the now-dominant attributes given below on the left, with those emergent attributes listed on the right:

Reductionistic	Integrative
Objective	Subjective
Prediction and control emphasis	Emphasis on guiding human and social development
Deterministic models	Teleological models
Value-free	Value-focused
Exploitative ethic	Ecological ethic
Efficient technology	Appropriate technology

Such an integration of problem-solving capability would help to assure a more adequate response to synergetic clusters of problems.

The Future of Problem Monitoring

As we reflect upon our entire effort, we can see that the questions of perspective and interpretation lay at the heart of most of the difficulties we encountered. What

ISBN 0-201-04096-4

is admitted as a problem in the first place is a function of perspective. A reductionist view of science, for example, might not see systemic problems as meaningful ones. Similarly, it requires multiple perspectives to allow for meaningful, multiple interpretations of a problem. Even with identical overt objectives the interpretation of the nature of the problem can be dramatically different. To comprehend the full nature of the problem then requires accepting the validity of a significantly different interpretation seen from multiple perspectives.

We have learned that it is indeed possible to devise means to detect problems in their precritical stage of development. Having proved the feasibility and, we hope, the desirability of consciously and systematically uncovering hidden problems, we feel strongly that this work should be continued. If this experiment is to have any lasting value, it is imperative that these problem identification and selection techniques be expanded and improved. Early warning is not a one-time venture. To be effective it should be explicitly integrated into the functioning of existing institutions on a permanent ongoing basis. We would hope that our study is only an early step in this direction.

APPENDIX

A Survey of Future National and International Problems

1. *Malnutrition-Induced Mental Deficiencies Leading to Social Instability:* Malnutrition during the prenatal period and infancy seems to result in permanent mental and emotional damage. The social and political results of mentally deficient and possibly emotionally unstable populations, especially in the Third World where malnutrition is endemic, will be serious for an increasingly complex and interdependent world.

2. *The Cultural Exclusion of the Aged:* In all developed countries the absolute and proportional growth of the aging population is straining social and economic institutions. Growth occurs through a combination of demographics, lengthening life span, and earlier retirement. The economic problem is that of an increasing economic load per worker to support the aging, which may intensify the political conflict between young and old. The sociocultural problem is that of wasted lives – citizens without participating roles. The breakdown of extended family structures in many nations is making the time of growing old one of enforced idleness and loss of meaning in life. Structural change in society may be required for the eventual resolution of the problem of the aging.

3. *Global Firewood Shortage:* About one-third of the world's population relies on wood as its principal fuel. Rising population has created overwhelming demands on forest reserves, particularly in Africa, the Indian subcontinent, and Latin America. The major consequence has been massive deforestation, with resultant flooding, erosion, climate change, and loss of land suitable for farming. The substitution of animal dung for wood fuel has further damaged

ISBN 0-201-04096-4

the soil by denying it natural humus and fertilizer. High prices for fossil fuels discourage wood-dependent peoples from abandoning destructive use of wood and animal wastes.

4. *Critical Advances in Biomedical Technology*

(a) *Access to Life Extension:* The development of life-extending medical techniques raises important questions about access. Experience with renal dialysis machines indicates that the supply of surgeons and of natural organ or machine replacements will probably not meet demand.

(b) *Genetic Engineering:* Developments in bioscience, particularly in what is called genetic engineering, pose unprecedented social and ethical problems. The ability to control the sex of human beings and their physical, mental, and emotional characteristics (using techniques modeled on animal husbandry) threatens the moral basis of human social organization. These forms of population shaping and control are more direct than even drug or mass psychological manipulation.

(c) *Euthanasia:* Strong movements are developing for the adoption of euthanasia to dispose of the aged and unfit. Supporters of this movement promote the concept of voluntary death for those lacking a place in society.

5. *The Growing Conflict between Central Control and Individual Freedom:* The advance of science has produced technologies of enormous power, scale, and sophistication. The size and scope of both public and private organizations have grown enormously in the past 200 years. Many of society's ills, especially crime, the economy, and energy, seem to be demanding immediate and effective solution. The growth of giant urban complexes, with highly mobile populations, contributes to the decline of social cohesion and binding institutions, such as the community and the family.
The power of our technology seems to require equally powerful regulation. The scale of our organizations increasingly makes them remote from and dominant over the citizenry. The urgency of problems often seems to demand the sacrifice (albeit willing) of individual freedoms and sometimes civil liberties (the threat of airplane hijacking led to warrantless search at airports). The decline of social cohesion places ever greater demands on the formal institutions of society. The net result is a reduction in the accountability of institutions, in the efficacy of individual choice, and in the preservation of civil liberties – in short, producing the conditions for a progressively authoritarian society.

6. *The Conflict between Low Growth and Rising Expectations:* Worldwide expansion of communications and transportation networks is leading to rising material expectations and a growing sense of inequity among those in the lower economic spectrum. The gap between rich and poor nations grew rapidly from only $100 to $200 (per capita product) in 1850 to over $2000 in 1970. Until recently, world industrial growth was seen as the chief means of closing the gap. However, if the world is, indeed, facing fundamental limits to growth, or if, for other reasons, nations are unable to achieve growth,

ISBN 0-201-04096-4

expectations will be frustrated. Widening the gap will increase the likelihood of political instability and violence.

7. *Police Alienation from the Populace:* New technology is having an unanticipated effect on the nature of law enforcement activities in the United States. The demand has been for technological augmentation and extension of each officer's capabilities. The economic pressures that necessitate increasing the area of his coverage, the speed of his response, and the level of force he employs has increased the social distance between the officer and the citizens he serves. Alienation of police officers from all segments of our society is such that police forces are regarded in some places as an army of occupation.

8. *Loss of Cultural Diversity:* The emergence of one interdependent world economy linked by rapid communications and transportation is leading to homogenization of world culture. The resulting standardization would allow greater economic efficiency and greater political and social stability. However, a culturally unified world might be less adaptable and less creative than a culturally heterogeneous one. It is well known that a complex ecology (e.g., a tropical rain forest) has greater potential for survival and is more stable than a simple ecology (e.g., monoculture). Moreover, our rich mix of cultural systems is worth preserving because such systems have intrinsic worth and may also contribute understandings essential to the solution of human problems.

9. *Potential for New Urban Violence:* The deterioration of older American cities and the decline of their economies threaten to trap urban populations in a situation not unlike that of Appalachia. The situation of these depressed and despairing agglomerations − particularly already impoverished minority groups − portends widespread and persistent violence. Quasi-guerilla warfare in the inner cities with raids against outlying, more affluent areas and assaults against police and public service facilities may reach intolerable levels.

10. *The "Invisible" Famine:* Even slight variations in world climate can have significant impacts on food and hunger problems. Because this effect is widespread, an "invisible famine" blankets many of the poor nations rather than being focused in a particular geographical area. The victims are likely to be in less visible rural areas because city populations are fed first to ease the threat of disruption there.

11. *Persistent Malnutrition Despite Affluence:* Serious lack of nutrition as a result of the composition of the diet imperils even affluent Americans. New deficiencies are continually being discovered as nutritional knowledge improves. Well-known problems such as obesity, overconsumption of sugar, and nutrient removal in cereal processing persist owing to public taste and the influence of technology and advertising (e.g., cost and efficiency pressures in over-the-counter and other food services, and total exposure to advertising influences through television and other sophisticated motivational methods).

12. *Teenage Alcoholism:* Heavy consumption of alcohol among adolescents (13 to 18 years of age) is now at about 25%. This extension of adult drinking patterns into youth groups indicates that the present serious problem of high

ISBN 0-201-04096-4

alcohol consumption endemic in the United States may grow worse. Further, teenage alcoholism contributes to the problem of juvenile crime.

13. *Lack of Functional Life Skills in Adults:* Recent U. S. Office of Education tests indicate that less than half the nation's adults possess the basic skills to function well in today's society. More than 20% are barely able to read want ads or to do the arithmetic necessary to use a checkbook. These results raise severe questions about the efficacy of American education and suggest that as our society becomes increasingly complex many more people will be unable to master the skills necessary to function well.

14. *A Growing Subculture of the Information-Poor:* A postindustrial society places high value on possessing and effectively using information. However, the gap is widening between those who are information-rich and those who are information-poor. Economic, educational, social, and motivational factors create an uneven distribution of ability to make use of our sophisticated new communications technology. More equal access to such technology is an in-effective solution because ability to use the technology depends on the information already held by the user. Thus, those who possess the information can use the new technology to increase their existing advantage over those who have not.

15. *Barriers to Large-Scale Technological Innovations:* All industrial nations find it increasingly difficult to carry out large-scale technological projects in critical fields such as transportation, energy, food production, environmental protec-tion, and housing. Huge public, private, or mixed investment schemes either fail to achieve the promised results technically (BART, the Bay Area Rapid Transit) or prove far more costly than originally estimated (the Concorde SST project). Such failures – contrasted with earlier successes (railroads, airlines, television) – contribute to growing disbelief in promised benefits and dis-courage both private and public willingness to invest. There is a consequent loss of faith in technology and a growing disinterest in taking bold innovative risks.

16. *The Social Impact of the Changing Role of Women:* Increasingly, women are entering the work force. Equal opportunity laws and changing mores suggest that many will eventually assume senior positions in government and business. Moreover, they will do so without having to adapt to male behavioral norms. As the number of women in these positions increases dramatically, the nature of the institutions will probably change in response. In the long term, the change should prove productive and beneficial. During the transition, however, internal problems, resembling those of a clash of cultures, can be anticipated. Institutional effectiveness may suffer a short-term decline while the problems are resolved.

17. *The Sociocultural Impact of Media:* Rather than direct experiences in the real world, an increasing proportion of people's life experiences are vicarious through the media. Consequently, their perception of social reality may be distorted, and their judgment may be more susceptible to intentional and un-intentional manipulation. They may also tend to withdraw from direct

ISBN 0-201-04096-4

political and social participation.

18. *The Social Implications of Changing Family Forms:* During the past decade
the United States has seen a drastic increase in the divorce rate and in the
number of single-parent families. Traditionally, we have expected the products
of broken homes to exhibit undesirable social behavior. If this is true, society
can expect increased delinquency, alienation, and mental illness. Perhaps as
significant is a growing acceptance of the nonpermanent marriage and non-
related family groups, which undercut older expectations of permanence and
family stability. This will have impact on the whole range of social, economic,
and legal institutions designed for the nuclear family (parents and children).

19. *The Effects of Stress on Individuals and Society:* The negative effects of stress
may cost the United States more than $100 billion annually. Although much
is being done to treat the symptoms of stress through such remedies as drugs,
there are significant aspects of the problem that are barely recognized, let alone
studied. There are, for example, different types of stress — some of them
potentially beneficial. Our treatment approaches tend to be monolithic,
perhaps worsening some kinds of stress. Similarly, we know little about
societal stress resulting from individual stresses. Because stress-producing
situations such as job and family insecurities seem on the rise, stress-related
pathologies will also likely increase. At the same time, with growing demand
for some form of national health care, the costs for medical treatment of stress-
related symptoms could be expected to increase substantially. If the apparent
correlation between the rate of social change and social stress are real, it can be
expected that stress on the social level will rise as well.

20. *The Potential Use and Misuse of "Consciousness Technologies":* Various
"consciousness technologies" constitute an applied science that draws upon
medicine, physics, psychology, neurophysiology, and parapsychology.
Research is revealing the potential impacts of these technologies upon human
beings — both for good and for ill. Whether they present a considerable opportunity or a considerable problem depends on their diffusion and application
as illustrated below:

- Alternative medicine — A growing body of research indicates that many
  diseases involve psychosomatic mind—body interaction. If so, integrating
  the psychological/mind-body component into the treatment would be a
  potent aid in reducing disease. Serious questions about the fiscal depend-
  ability of national health care insurance and the rapid inflation of medical
  costs indicate that we badly need supplements to expensive traditional
  medicine.
- Capacity-enhancing technologies — Evidence exists that the human potential
  for rapid learning, creativity, healing, and the like exceeds customary
  assumptions. Consciousness research suggests that sociocultural barriers and
  professional taboos may be restricting application of new techniques in
  problem solving, health care, education, and criminal rehabilitation.
- Psychic abilities — There is growing evidence that psychic abilities may exist
  and that they may have considerable potential for misuse, principally in two

ISBN 0-201-04096-4

forms: acquisition of confidential information, and generation of long-distance effects that could be psychologically disorienting and physically harmful.   At present we have insufficient information to evaluate with confidence the existence of such abilities or the threat presented by this technology of mind — a technology that may be rapidly developed, given current scientific investigations.

21. *Decreasing Capital Productivity of New Technology:* New technology seems to offer increasingly small return on capital investments. Investors fear that prevailing commodity prices in many industries are too low to support the risk and that necessary increases would not be supported in the market. The alternative is to seek government subsidy or tax incentives. However, to do this is to invite government regulation or intervention in business decision-making. Rather than risking an uncertain market or sharing control with the government, industrialists may increasingly elect to restrict their investments and live on past earnings while the general economy stagnates.

22. *Regulatory Restraints and Economic Growth:* Demand for stricter regulation of the economy appears to be rising as a result of more universal appreciation of needs (to contain pollution, conserve resources, reduce hazards), better organization of special-interest groups, higher levels of public support, and distrust of large institutions. Regulation could be restrictive enough to reduce productivity, discourage free enterprise, eliminate development of significant resources, such as oil shale, and increase costs in domains such as coal mining. There may be a problem of increasingly onerous trade-offs between the need for regulation and the requirements of a healthy economy.

23. *Weapons Technology and the Right To Bear Arms:* In the past, certain weapons (explosives and machine guns) have been excluded by law from inclusion in the constitutional right to bear arms. However, new weapons technology, resulting from military research and the public's demand for better anticriminal weapons, is already beginning to strain existing laws. Weapons such as electric-shock Tasers and tranquilizer guns are already widely available. Controlling this proliferation of new weapons is difficult because of a perceived growing gap between the arms allowed the private citizen and the arms used by the police and military.

24. *Cumulative Effects of Pollution:* As new industrial processes are developed and new products are manufactured, the number and quantity of new chemical compounds released into the environment have increased dramatically. The effects of these compounds on human health and personality and on the stability of the ecosystem may be unknowable for years or even generations. The large number of such new compounds (estimated at about 5000 per year) makes it almost impossible to establish an acceptable testing program, which is the necessary first step in determining potential deleterious effects. Monitoring of pollutants, understanding how they reach man and his environment, characterizing their interactions with other chemicals, and assessing their potential for inducing low-level, long-term effects are beyond our present capabilities.

ISBN 0-201-04096-4

25. *Limits to the Management of Large, Complex Systems:* The power to create large, complex systems (economic, political, social) does not automatically confer the power to effectively control such systems. There is growing evidence that we have aggregated small, comprehensible systems into super-systems that are very difficult to manage at all, let alone in a democratic, participatory fashion. Further, large, complex systems tend toward conditions of relatively low performance as they become more incomprehensible and less amenable to democratic control. There is a trade-off between reduced efficiency and increased capacity for survival through many levels of back-up systems. Large, complex systems also tend to become increasingly vulnerable to disruption at key points as a consequence of increasing levels of inter-dependence. They also demand an ever higher level of self-discipline on the part of individuals.

26. *The Apparent Conflict between World Peace and World Justice:* The success of efforts to preserve world peace and a tendency to replace peace with stability and the absence of conflict may result in the preservation of existing inequities within and between nations. This poses the danger of the defense of injustice in the name of peace and the danger of far more serious and un-controllable eruptions in the future.

27. *Catastrophic Experiments:* The destructive potential of some new and emerg-ing technologies has raised questions about whether some experimentation might have catastrophic results and, hence, should not be permitted. However, the traditional ethic and practice of science and the potential benefit foreseen from the successful development of such technologies seem to demand that the experimentation go forward in spite of the risk. Examples can be drawn from physics (especially the nuclear field) and from the biological sciences (e.g., test-tube creation of new strains of bacteria). No mechanism exists for identi-fying potentially catastrophic experiments.

28. *Vulnerability of Water Supplies:* The development of highly toxic chemicals and bacteriological substances and the increasing availability of powerful radiological materials pose a clear and present danger. Their accidental or deliberate introduction into public water-supply systems would have disastrous results. The complexity of modern water-supply systems and the vast popula-tion they serve exacerbate the problem.

29. *The Dangers of Computer Dependency:* Increasing reliance on computers and a lag in supporting functions that make computer technology safe are becom-ing a national and an international problem. Legislative attention is being given to the loss of personal privacy relative to computer data banks. However, even more serious losses are increasingly associated with the use of computers and data telecommunications. Innovations such as electronic fund transfer (EFT), point transaction automation, and process control (such as rapid transit scheduling) entailing the safety of human life are accelerating the number and seriousness of risks due to accidental or intentional disruptions or loss of information.

ISBN 0-201-04096-4

30. *Decreasing Utility of Higher Education:* The formal educational system may be increasingly inefficient in training people to perform needed tasks, especially those of coping with a technologically advanced society. The universalization of access to colleges and universities may be diluting the quality of curricula designed for individual personal development. Thus, higher education may be contributing less to individual and social needs and may no longer ensure the greater personal and societal rewards traditionally expected.

31. *Effects of Technology on the Individual Psyche:* Constant exposure to technological devices may be having a serious impact on the human psyche. Examples are numerous: media-presented violence with its concomitant effect on the human approach to life; high mobility, which leads to rootlessness and weakening of family ties; excessive television viewing, which blurs the distinction between reality and fantasy; an overload of stimuli, which leads to ever higher needs for sensation. Few systematic attempts have been made, however, to observe or measure such changes or to determine their effects.

32. *Loss of Political and Social Cohesion:* There seems to be a decline in political and social cohesion — the sense of shared purpose that provides the balance between individual desires and the general well-being. This decline seems to result from a number of forces, including high mobility; erosion of communities; the replacement of the extended family with the nuclear family; an inward turning of personal goals resulting from a sense of individual powerlessness in a mass society; and the growth in effectiveness of interest group politics. The consequence of this loss is the undermining of the efficacy and legitimacy of society's basic institutions.

33. *Institutional Boundaries as Impediments to Societal Problem Solving:* As the scope, scale, and concentration of human activities have increased, our societal institutions have become more tightly interconnected. Institutional boundaries created for a less tightly coupled society tend to compartmentalize aspects of problems and to resist more comprehensive attempts at solutions. The resulting frustration and conflicts call into question the legitimacy of the entire institutional fabric of the society and to generate demands and violent actions aimed at its destruction.

34. *The Need for Better Socioeconomic Models:* At a time when the managers of both corporate business and government have developed powerful tools for systems management, it is important that their models be accurate for the system they propose to manage. Unfortunately, management technology appears to have grown faster than design capabilities for social science systems. There is danger that management tools will be ineffective because the social systems model is insufficient for assessing the problem and defining the remedy.

35. *Advanced Microcomputers and Rights to Privacy:* The development of powerful microcomputers, combined with improved semiconductor memories, will make possible inexpensive and highly sophisticated individual surveillance and the maintenance of vast numbers of data banks. Individuals will find it impossible to know who is keeping dossiers on them and what information is in those

ISBN 0-201-04096-4

dossiers. Privacy and other personal rights will be threatened as this technology develops.

36. *Chronic Unemployment:* Contrary to many predictions, fundamental changes in the economic situation (e.g., environmental and other constraints to economic growth, and basic long-term capital shortage) present the possibility of chronic unemployment. Various analyses indicate high degrees of hidden unemployment at present, and more in the future. Various societal full-employment bills in Congress betray awareness of the problem. Inaccurate identification of the long-term nature of the new unemployment could result in expensive attempts to resolve the problem with the wrong approaches.

37. *Social Response to Energy Disappointments:* Delays and uncertainties will almost certainly occur in obtaining new energy sources over the next decade. In the interim, economic uncertainties will make private investors reluctant to invest heavily in older technologies. Inevitably strong pressures will be exerted for control of consumption through rationing and for nationalization of utilities and of the coal, oil, and gas industries. These delays and associated conflicts could result in a number of negative social consequences.

38. *A Growing Need for "Appropriate Technology":* There is a growing array of "appropriate" or "intermediate" technology that could provide practical support for a much simplified way of living. Examples of these technologies include solar power, wind power, intensive gardening, biological means of pest control and fertilization, and composting toilets. In general, these technologies tend to be ecologically more sound, energy-conserving, comprehensible, and efficient when used on a small scale.
As we confront apparent limits to growth — whether induced by economic or by political forces — we may have to simplify our level and patterns of consumption. Failure to nurture, in appropriate ways, the development of intermediate technology and supportive social forms will make it more difficult to solve the practical and pressing problem of finding new ways to live healthily in a world of increasing scarcity. Failure to develop appropriate technology would also result in a missed opportunity for creative social and technical learning during a time of stress and transition.

39. *The Societal Changes Required To Adapt to New Energy Sources:* Even though new sources of energy from advanced technologies may produce abundant cheap energy, the form in which the energy is available could be quite different from fossil fuels. Thus, when diminishing fossil fuel supplies have become prohibitively costly, we may find ourselves with a system whose structure and behavior are inappropriate for the new forms of energy. If required changes could be anticipated, we might more effectively plan long-term investments and prevent undesirable consequences.

40. *Emerging Nations and the End of Oil:* Over the next twenty-five years, as the developed nations invent and install new energy sources, they will deplete most of the world's oil reserves. As they do so, they will deprive much of the Third World of access to cheap fuel at a time crucial to development. Because the new alternative energy sources may be too complex and costly for these

ISBN 0-201-04096-4

poorer nations, they may be relegated to permanent poverty.

41. *Social Effects of Redefining Legal Liability:*   Increasing complexity, interdependence, and scale of action in society have increased the potential liability
for decisions of individuals and organizations, while permitting lines of responsibility to blur.   Legal devices to avoid responsibility tend to reduce the
legitimacy of existing institutions and to reinforce loss of trust and confidence
in institutions and the professions. Loss of trust and confidence, in turn, has
been reflected in increasing resort to the courts to seek redress for real or
imagined grievances.   Consequently, entrepreneurial and professional risk-
taking has become far more hazardous.*

ISBN 0-201-04096-4

*Editor's Note: Kenneth Boulding has called attention to a pervasive, albeit subtle, move-
ment of responsibility: from the individual to the society, from "me" to "them". This trend is
reflected in medical malpractice suits, in placing blame for an individual's crimes on society and
for a child's ignorance on the school system, etc. (HAL)

VI. Epilogue

VI. Epilogue

HAROLD A. LINSTONE and W. H. CLIVE SIMMONDS

> Not in the lifetime of most men has there been so much grave and deep apprehension . . . The domestic economic situation is in chaos. Our dollar is weak throughout the world. Prices are so high as to be utterly impossible. Of our troubles man can see no end.
>
> *Harper's Weekly,* October 1857

> At the moment I don't think we have any serious big problems. People aren't used to not having problems. They can't stand it. So they ask — 'What's the problem?'
>
> Herman Kahn in "The New Class,"
> *The Co-Evolution Quarterly,* Spring 1977, p. 32.

The first quotation is 120 years old and makes us feel curiously comfortable; the second is only a few months old (at this writing) and makes us feel strangely uncomfortable.[1] Why? The prevalent view among intellectuals today is that problems are difficult to isolate or to identify, that they are converging to a single "megacrisis," and that our time is spent "rearranging the deck chairs on the Titanic." Ominous new words are introduced: problematique, triage, entropy state. The pessimism-is-in group has its counterpart at the other end of the spectrum. Buckminster Fuller, Herman Kahn, and their disciples are technological optimists. These extremes are actually useful just as lighthouse beacons are to navigators: they aid self-regulating systems to adjust their courses and avoid hazards.

Kahn's comment reminds us that, as products of an achievement-oriented society, we need the challenge of problem solving. Since each solution creates new problems we might say, with Linstone (Part I), that we are in effect shifting, rather than solving, problems. No matter — motivation is provided in either case and there is a sense of resultant forward movement. Only rarely do we empathize with the Meeting of the Council on Cybernetic Stability, a scenario developed by Turoff.[2] In 2011, 1% of the population has the responsibility to create work (i.e., games) for the work force. One critical task of the supervisory staff is to minimize chances of discovery on the part of the work force of the gaming nature of the "work" (e.g., recognition that a "new" problem was already solved years

---

[1] It should be noted that Kahn is referring to the United States, Canada, and Australia. He admits that these countries can get into serious trouble in the future — if they work hard enough at it.

[2] M. Turoff, "Meeting of the Council on Cybernetic Stability: A Scenario," in H. A. Linstone and M. Turoff (eds.), *The Delphi Method,* Addison Wesley Publishing Company, Advanced Book Program, Reading, Massachusetts, 1975, pp. 563-569.

Futures Research: New Directions, Harold A. Linstone and W. H. Clive Simmonds (eds.)

ISBN 0-201-04096-4

earlier). In such a society Herman Kahn would represent a subversive threat in the eyes of the controllers.

Simmonds has noted elsewhere that "the future will not be easy but it can be manageable."[3] Churchman has reminded us not to disdain faith, hope, and love (p. 90). They may ease the task of *homo ludens* in managing the transmutation of *homo sapiens* into *homo humanus* (p. 257).

In these final pages we briefly merge form and substance of change in futures research.

Changes in Concepts of Growth

The Pearl, logistic, or *S* curve (Fig. 1*a*) has replaced the exponential curve as the focus of forecasts. It serves both optimists and pessimists. In fact, they even agree that the United States is at the transition point on the curve; i.e., in the process of moving from accelerating to decelerating growth.[4] The principal difference between them is the time to reach a steady state and the level of socio-economic product at such time. Dennis Meadows, for example, sees the leveling off within fifty years, while Herman Kahn reaches the plateau in two hundred years.

Kahn's 2176 world is characterized by 15 billion people, $300 trillion gross world product (GWP), or $20000 per capita GWP. Comparing these figures to the 1976 levels — 4.1 billion people, $5.5 trillion GWP, or $1300 per capita — the extraordinary optimism is vividly displayed.[4a] The beguilingly simple calculations of global energy, food, and raw material needs vs. resources potentially available suggest to Kahn little apparent cause for serious concern. The real dangers which he recognizes are three: (a) a nuclear blunder setting off a global holocaust, (b) large scale adverse biological/ecological effects caused by technological goofs, and (c) rotten images of the future involving loss of faith, will, or self-discipline.

---

[3] W. H. Clive Simmonds, "The Alternative Society," Speech in Series, *Nature, Science, and Man,* April 6, 1977, at Queen's University.

[4] For Kahn this point conveniently falls in America's Bicentennial Year, 1976, "the year the Messiah came back" ("The New Class," *The Co-Evolution Quarterly,* Spring 1977, p. 9). In its survey of America's prospects for its Third Century, *The Economist* expressed the fear that 1975 might mark a turning point from dynamic entrepreneurial growth to a risk-avoiding, comfort-seeking, guilt-ridden era; i.e., a loss of nerve and panache as England experienced a century earlier:

"The British upper class was strengthening its gut feeling that new sorts of commerce were surely rather vulgar, while the British business-decision-making class had itself become bureaucratic and protectionist rather than entrepreneurial . . . These same reasons can be cited in 1975 to suggest that old America may be about to give up [entrepreneurial] leadership to somebody else." (Norman Macrae in *The Economist,* October 25, 1975, Survey, p. 4.)

[4a] Note that dollar figures are given in constant 1976 dollars. Source: H. Kahn, W. Brown, and L. Martel, "The Next 200 Years: A Scenario for America and the World," W. Morrow, New York, 1976.

ISBN 0-201-04096-4

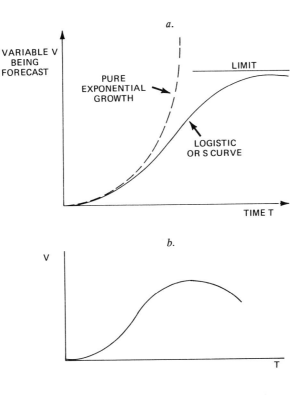

Fig. 1. Examples of growth curves.

There are, of course, variations on the S curve theme. For example, one modification includes a declining stage representing diseconomies and system crises subsequent to the attainment of the peak (Fig. 1b).[5]

This corresponds to the well known rise-and-fall theory of civilizations. Salk speculates on an evolutionary growth concept[6] reminiscent of technological forecasts; i.e., a sequence of logistic curves (Fig. 2). Linstone suggests that such two-dimensional representations are an example of unwarranted reductionism: they assume one variable; e.g., GNP per capita, changing over time. History suggests that there was "growth" long before GNP per capita even became a meaningful measure. This variable may be appropriate for an industrial society but it clearly does not fit either a pre- or post-industrial society. In a hunting society the animal population may have been a meaningful variable; in an agricultural society farm production is reasonable. A post-industrial society will undoubtedly need another

_____

[5]"Assessment of Future National and International Problem Areas," Vol. I, Stanford Research Institute, Res. Report CSSP 4676-14, February, 1977, p. 39.

[6]J. Salk, *The Survival of the Wisest,* Harper & Row, New York, 1973, p. 26.

ISBN 0-201-04096-4

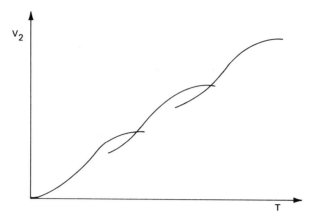

Fig. 2. An evolutionary sequence of growth curves.

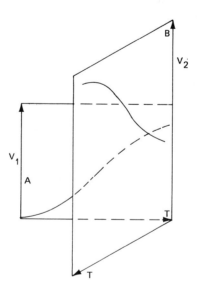

Fig. 3. Three-dimensional presentation of growth curves.

ISBN 0-201-04096-4

descriptor (information?). This tells us that each logistic curve should lie in a different plane (Fig. 3).[7]

We note that many other socioeconomic and cultural schema have been proposed.[8] For example, there are the cyclical economic theories of Levy-Pascal, Kuznets, and Kondratieff (recently revisited by Forrester[9]).

One interesting schema is the combination-separation concept of Bryan Bergson.[10] He proposes a spiral growth pattern for atoms, biological evolution, and human societies (Fig. 4).

It should be apparent at this point that the popular debate of growth vs. no growth is misdirected. The concept of limits to growth, concretized in the steady-state society, is in a real sense immoral. If evolution is to proceed, human beings must continue to develop and grow. The proper question is: what kind of growth?

Willis Harman thinks of human (intellectual, spiritual) rather than material growth,[11] Robert Hutchins talks about a learning society,[12] Daniel Bell suggests an information or knowledge society.[13] Geoffrey Vickers proposes limited decentralization or uncoupling to facilitate human development (Part II). Magoroh Maruyama sees extraterrestrial communities as a new direction of human evolution (incorporating many aspects of his heterogenistic society sketched earlier in this chapter).

Aurelio Peccei[13a] envisions a thrust in the direction of a new humanism: man's further development is dependent on a profound change in his behavior, a "human revolution." He believes this to be essential now to steer, and control the effects of, the other revolutions — industrial, scientific, technological, and socio-political.

---

[7]H. Linstone and D. Sahal (eds.), *Technological Substitution,* American Elsevier Publishing Co., New York, 1976, p. 276.

[8]The concept of cycles is ancient indeed. The final statement on the human situation in the I Ching attests to its durability:
The over-all judgment: order and prosperity in a confused world are being realized. The chaos, which has been turned into order following deliberation and caution, is merely dormant. In its turn, the order is now entering the incipient stages of chaos. The yin-yang cycle begins anew, as it has always been and will be repeated for ever and ever.

[9]J. W. Forrester, N. J. Mass, and C. J. Ryan, "The System Dynamics National Model: Understanding Socio-Economic Behavior and Policy Alternatives," *Technological Forecasting and Social Change,* Vol. 9, 1976, pp. 51-68.

[10]B. P. Bergson, "The Combination-Separation Principle," Lockheed Missiles & Space Company, Sunnyvale, California (unpublished).

[11]W. Harman, "An Incomplete Guide to the Future," San Francisco Book Company, San Francisco, California, 1976, p. 48.

[12]R. Hutchins, "The Learning Society," Praeger, New York, 1968.

[13]D. Bell, "The Coming of Post-Industrial Society," Basic Books, New York, 1973.

[13a]A. Peccei, "The Human Quality," Pergamon Press, Oxford, 1977, Chapter 7.

ISBN 0-201-04096-4

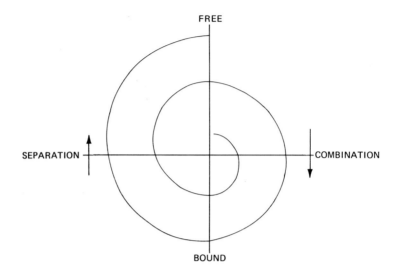

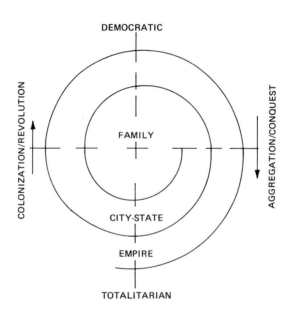

Fig. 4. Spiral growth patterns.

ISBN 0-201-04096-4

The aspects of the new humanism of most concern to Peccei are (1) sense of globality, (2) love of justice, and (3) abhorrence of violence.[13b]

It is remarkable to find considerable similarity in several key thinkers' perceptions of the "human revolution." We find this idea reflected not only in the writings of Harman (p. 260) and Vickers (Part II), but note that it makes strange bedfellows of Western industrialist Peccei and Eastern communist Mao.[13c] All are convinced that man himself must change if the current cognitive dissonance between his behavior and environment is to be eliminated. It is interesting to speculate whether telecommunications technology, facilitating both global unity and global diversity, can serve as a catalyst in transforming *homo sapiens* to *homo humanus*.[13c]

Jean Houston suggests that the human psyche is the new frontier:

We use but a fraction of our capacities — perhaps 10% of our physical capacity and 5% of our mental potential . . . It is my belief, based on many kinds of evidence and 16 years of research in the field, that we can definitely give human beings the capacity to use much more of their potential than all but a few can use presently . . . Among the capacities contributing to such unblocking and unfolding are all of the sensory imageries, but also the uses of subjective time and the acceleration of thought processes, cross-sensing, self regulation of pleasure and pain, and the establishment of voluntary control over some of the autonomic functions by means of biofeedback and autogenic training . . . To do these things . . . is to extend the frontier of inner space, which, unlike outer space, has inexhaustible resources.[14]

Harman notes that the scientific community is altering its previously rigid stand of opposition to both consciousness and psychic research and speculates that "the transition from rejection to acceptance may be at hand."[15]

[13b]Peccei sees six critical subjects which must be urgently addressed to advance the "human revolution":
- knowledge of the outer limits (physical/biological/environmental)
- knowledge of the inner limits (psychological/mental)
- means to maintain cultural pluralism
- models of world organization (the future of nations and the world community)
- the human habitat — for twice the present population
- the future economic or production system

The reader may wish to compare these six future challenges with the six problems crystallized in the Stanford Research Institute project (p. 237).

[13c]L. S. Stavrianos, "The Promise of the Coming Dark Age," W. H. Freeman and Co., San Francisco, 1976, 154-155, 190-191.

[14]J. Houston, "Prometheus Rebound: An Inquiry into Technological Growth and Psychological Change," *Technological Forecasting and Social Change*, Vol. 9, 1976, pp. 254-257.

[15]W. Harman, op. cit., p. 98.

ISBN 0-201-04096-4

We next sample several holistic societal images which augment the ideas brought forth by Vickers, Von Foerster, and others in the preceding Parts of this volume. They provide the seeds for "myths" (in Michael's sense, Part III); i.e., for created "social realities."

Magoroh Maruyama presents a concise description of an emerging society, comparing it to the traditional one:[16]

Traditional	Emerging
Uniformistic	Heterogenistic
Unidirectional	Mutualistic
Hierarchical	Interactionist
Quantitative	Qualitative
Classificational	Relational
Competitive	Symbiotic
Atomistic	Contextual
Object-based	Process-based
Self-perpetuating	Self-transcending

Scheele sees a different transformation − toward an idiomergent society (*idio* is derived from the Greek meaning uniqueness, separateness, distinctness; *mergere* is of Latin origin denoting to immerse, combine, lose identity).[17]

Industrial	Idiomergent
Reality external and knowable	Reality constructed and negotiable
Hypotheses are general and are applied for validation	Hypotheses are context-specific and serve to redirect the ongoing discovery process
Future extrapolated from past (exploratory)	Future invented out of creative integrations of reality (normative Gestalt)
Organizations and roles are structures defining possible actions	Actions and need for their explication define roles and organizations
Management predicated on adherence to comprehensive plans developed to reach selected goals and objectives defined in limited dimensions and periodically revised	Management incorporating participation of those directly affected in the selection of means to respond to short range opportunities identified by multidimensional plans produced by continuing review

[16]M. Maruyama, "Commentaries on the 'Quality of Life' Concept," unpublished.

[17]D. Sam Scheele, "Reality Construction as a Product of Delphi Interaction," in H. A. Linstone and M. Turoff (eds.), *The Delphi Method,* Addison-Wesley Publishing Company, Advanced Book Program, Reading, Massachusetts, 1975, pp. 37-71.

ISBN 0-201-04096-4

Harman sees five fundamental dilemmas — growth, work roles, distribution, control, and a cultural crisis.[18]   Their resolution is achieved through a trans-industrial paradigm involving:

- Recognition of inadequacy of value postulates of industrial society and movement toward a frugal society
- Science aimed at evolutionary development of man and society, placing more emphasis on understanding and less on generating manipulative technology
- Existence of a spiritual order, discoverable and explorable, is assumed
- Creative work and self-realization ethics (a meaningful "central project")
- An ecological ethic of concern for the whole
- A teleological view of life and evolution, the future partly shaped by human choice

He suggests that this transformation is more profound than the Copernican (scientific) or Industrial Revolution.

Simmonds utilizes the concept of limited rationality: people will make the minimum adjustments necessary in a changing situation in terms of their perception of what the situation appears to be. The directions of such changes can be estimated in at least one way, by inquiring what would happen if their current objectives became the means to some further objectives. Thus consumption is an end-in-itself in the "Consumer Society" which requires no explanation, but why do we consume? Most of us do so in the hope of gaining a rewarding or useful experience for ourselves or for others, now or in the future. Thus the successor to the consumer society is, potentially, the "Experiencing Society." But such a transition will only come about if the internal pressures and external events reach the level of causing our perceptions of the world to begin to change. [19]

One major area ripe for change is that of information technology. As Gordon Thompson has pointed out,[20] we are still at the intensive point in the interaction of information technology and our socioeconomic system. We use it to reduce costs, to improve service, to release labor, but generally in terms of past, or industrial, society. But its real contribution to our economy may be, as Masuda argues, in its potential *extensive* use, in wealth-creative, labor-absorbing, new enterprises.[21] The key step may well be the development of a simple, ideographic language to make this technology as freely and "convivially" available to the ordinary person as citizen-band radio and hobby computers. Only then can we unleash the kind of explosion which followed the adoption of the phonetic alphabet by the Greeks and the interactive effects of the printed book and new

[18]W. Harman, op. cit.

[19]W. H. C. Simmonds, "Anticipating Changes in Society's Dominant Ideas," *Amer. Sociol. Assoc. Meeting,* Chicago, September 1977.

[20]G. Thompson, "Turning the World Upside Down," *Telecommunications Policy,* Vol. 1, No. 2, March 1977, pp. 153-157.

[21]Y. Masuda, "The Conceptual Framework of Information Economics," *IEEE Transactions on Communications,* Vol. Com-23, No. 10, 1975.

ISBN 0-201-04096-4

perspectives during the Renaissance. People may not even have to spend half their waking hours in front of the commercial television tube, given an ideographic language which spans the borders and walls that separate human beings today.[22]

Changes in Paradigms

The pieces in this book have stressed changes needed in the form of futures research.

The paradigms of modern science and technology — reductionism, objectivity (observed systems), quantification, deductive logic, analysis, cause and effect models, optimization, fail-safe design — are still deeply and firmly entrenched. There is a very large community of believers developing methodologies and quantitative models, intellectual drones who carve out researchable pieces, generate models with gusto, feed data into willing computer accomplices, pore over the tons of output data spewed out, convert them into more tons of reports, each replete with recommendations for more of the same.

But there is a growing rumble of criticism, a realization that this may reflect an imbalance undesirable in dealing with futures problems. Thus Simmonds (Part I) points out that futures problems are in many respects the opposite or inverse of conventional problems in the natural sciences and engineering. Linstone (Part II) and Teige et al. (Part V) present the dichotomy of characteristics in which the currently dominant pattern is contrasted with a "new" one whose key words are holism, observing systems, qualitative analysis, inductive logic, synthesis, maintenance or increase of options, safe-fail design.

The thrust is toward a *balance* between the two sets of attributes, not a replacement of one set by the other.

Several contributors have presented concepts appropriate to this changing perception of futures research. Sahal's self-referential systems, Vickers' cultural revolution, Von Foerster's recursive management, Sachs' active adaptation, Churchman's multiple *Weltanschauungen* (total system and self), Jones' and McLean's multiple models are indicative of a new look. Other concepts relevant in this context (and mentioned in the book) are Allison's three models,[23] Churchman's five inquiring systems,[24] Maruyama's higher level cybernetics,[23] Jantsch's higher level models,[23] and Simmonds' behavioral approach.[25] Alongside these concepts we should place qualitative mathematics.

The concepts are really "new" only in the framework of the dominant science-technology paradigms. We may not have seen them before only because we were

---

[22]Ideographic and pictographic languages were abandoned because they could not easily handle concepts. Electronic technology now allows us to reverse the process and develop languages for both halves of the brain.

[23]Part IV, Introduction.

[24]Part I, H. A. Linstone, "Confessions of a Forecaster."

[25]Part I, W. H. C. Simmonds, "The Nature of Futures Problems."

ISBN 0-201-04096-4

not looking for them and did not need them in the prevailing mode of problem-solving.

It is significant that ethics enters the discussion repeatedly. Churchman sees the discounting problem as an ethical one: Who is more important to me — my grandchildren or I? What would a future generation ask us to do if they were here to ask us?

Holling and Von Foerster both consider the possible foreclosure of future options by current decisions as a vital ethical issue. Churchman, Von Foerster, and Loveridge elevate the importance of the individual. The individual must enter the system, stipulate his purpose, and take responsibility for his decisions. Ethics becomes a theory of active management. Skolimowski focuses on the link between "right" knowledge and "right" action with reference to technology assessment. Churchman views the concept of complexity itself in ethical terms, i.e., is it valuable or undesirable?

In Conclusion

There can be no conclusion because there is no beginning and there is no end. If we are discovering the limits to thought implicit in long accepted paradigms and are beginning to see further by thinking in new modes, so be it. If we have been frightened by the apparent complexity of the problems of today and tomorrow, perhaps we will find that complexity is actually easier to deal with than we expect. What we can say is that a moment of real change is at hand — in both form and substance. Futures research must and can move in new directions. The contributions in this volume suggest that such changes form the cutting edge for the next twenty-five years, providing the incremental advance in capability to match the onward march of our perceived challenge.

ISBN 0-201-04096-4

Index